Spanish Speakers in the USA

MM Textbooks

Advisory Board:

Professor Colin Baker, *University of Wales, Bangor, UK*

Professor Viv Edwards, *University of Reading, Reading, UK*

Professor Ofelia García, *Columbia University, New York, USA*

Dr Aneta Pavlenko, *Temple University, Philadelphia, USA*

Professor David Singleton, *Trinity College, Dublin, Ireland*

Professor Terrence G. Wiley, *Arizona State University, Tempe, USA*

MM Textbooks bring the subjects covered in our successful range of academic monographs to a student audience. The books in this series explore education and all aspects of language learning and use, as well as other topics of interest to students of these subjects. Written by experts in the field, the books are supervised by a team of world-leading scholars and evaluated by instructors before publication. Each text is student-focused, with suggestions for further reading and study questions leading to a deeper understanding of the subject.

Full details of all the books in this series and of all our other publications can be found on http://www.multilingual-matters.com, or by writing to Multilingual Matters, St Nicholas House, 31-34 High Street, Bristol BS1 2AW, UK.

MM Textbooks

Spanish Speakers in the USA

Janet M. Fuller

MULTILINGUAL MATTERS
Bristol • Buffalo • Toronto

Library of Congress Cataloging in Publication Data
A catalog record for this book is available from the Library of Congress.
Fuller, Janet M.
Spanish Speakers in the USA/Janet M. Fuller.
MM Textbooks: 9
Includes bibliographical references and index.
1. Spanish language--United States. 2. Bilingualism--United States. 3. Languages in contact--United States. 4. Spanish language--Acquistion. 5. English language--Acquisition. 6. Hispanic Americans--Languages.
PC4826.S68 2013
305.7'61073–dc232012036461

British Library Cataloguing in Publication Data
A catalogue entry for this book is available from the British Library.

ISBN-13: 978-1-84769-878-0 (hbk)
ISBN-13: 978-1-84769-877-3 (pbk)

Multilingual Matters
UK: St Nicholas House, 31-34 High Street, Bristol BS1 2AW, UK.
USA: UTP, 2250 Military Road, Tonawanda, NY 14150, USA.
Canada: UTP, 5201 Dufferin Street, North York, Ontario M3H 5T8, Canada.

The policy of Multilingual Matters/Channel View Publications is to use papers that are natural, renewable and recyclable products, made from wood grown in sustainable forests. In the manufacturing process of our books, and to further support our policy, preference is given to printers that have FSC and PEFC Chain of Custody certification. The FSC and/or PEFC logos will appear on those books where full certification has been granted to the printer concerned.

Typeset by The Charlesworth Group.
Printed and bound in Great Britain by the MPG Books Group.

Contents

Acknowledgements

To begin at the beginning of this project, I first taught a course titled 'Spanish in the USA' in the spring of 2008, and taught it again in the spring of 2010. The students in those courses have been a lasting inspiration for me. I am in touch with some of the members of these classes, others I have not seen since, but they remain part of what was for me a transforming experience. At the time I first taught this course, I had long struggled to learn Spanish well enough that I would feel comfortable claiming to speak the language. I had spent two years doing research with Mexican American children in a bilingual program, and my son had entered a Spanish-English dual language program the previous fall. My interest in and commitment to Spanish, both personally and professionally, was in many ways already firmly in place. But what I did not expect was that it would explode in the way it did, and that I owe to my students.

I owe special thanks to the following students who read and offered comments and corrections on this manuscript in earlier stages: Genaro Escarzaga, Carlee Coplea and Aimee Hosemann. I am additionally grateful to Aimee for her excellent work on the glossary, and to Roberto Barrios for helpful discussions about the title. I am further in debt to Mike Hall, who helped me in many ways, including but not limited to editing services.

I could also not have begun to write this book without the experiences in the various bilingual classrooms in southern Illinois where I visited, volunteered and did research. I have much gratitude for the teachers, the students, and their families. My children, Arlette and Nicholas, have also provided me with a multitude of insights about Spanish in the US and its relationship to 'race', ethnicity and identity.

Spanish as a language remains for me at once intimately familiar and painfully distant. Through writing this book I have come to understand that my involvement with Spanish and its speakers has made me more wholly part of the US than I ever thought I would want to be. Many thanks to all of the speakers of Spanish, and scholars of Spanish in the US, who have contributed to my education.

Introduction

The topic of Spanish speakers in the US is inevitably an interdisciplinary one and covers a broad range of issues in language and society. This text is designed to offer an introduction to a different topic in each chapter, while also providing readers with an opportunity to delve more deeply into particular issues or disciplines. But more importantly, the aim of this text is to introduce readers to a variety of ways of looking at Spanish, its speakers, the communities in which it is spoken, the attitudes that surround it, and the ways in which it shapes and is shaped by US society. It is only through this prism of perspectives that we can appreciate the many themes which surround Spanish speakers in the US.

First, some matters of terminology and presentation:

Although this book does not focus on issues of gender, this is an aspect of social organization and language use which cannot be ignored. In the interest of modeling gender inclusive language, I therefore am adopting the use of 'Latin@', 'Chican@' and 'Mestiz@' instead of the usual use of the male form to supposedly include all speakers.

Although I use the term Latin@ with some frequency in this text, I also recognize that it is inherently problematic. I prefer it to 'Hispanic', which is a term which was coined by the government to refer to a group they felt was distinct from the mainstream. Latin@ is at least a word used within Latin America to refer to the people of these countries, and transplanted to the US it has been adapted to mean US residents with origins from these countries. However, like 'Hispanic', it throws together people of very different backgrounds and origins and legitimizes this kind of homogenization. Many of the speakers I will refer to here would probably not use the term Latin@ to refer to themselves. Nonetheless, there are contexts in which I wish to make comments about a heterogeneous group of people, and will use this term. In some cases I will also use 'Spanish speakers in the US', but since not all Latin@s speak Spanish, and not all Spanish speakers are Latin@, these terms are not interchangeable but focus on linguistic or (pan-) ethnic groups.

On a more practical note, key terms are in bold the first time they are used, and are defined in the glossary at the end of the book. Each chapter also ends with questions for discussion or research, and further readings or resources relevant for that topic of study.

Part 1 of this text deals with issues in the study of **language ideologies** and **identities**; it is comprised of four chapters. Chapter 1 is 'Language Ideologies and Language Policies'. Ideologies about Spanish and its speakers in the US are relevant for the material covered in all of the following chapters. The main ideology dealt with here is **normative monolingualism**, which has two parts. The first part is the idea that monolingualism is the natural state of a nation and speakers of other languages should assimilate to the dominant language and corresponding culture. Second, if speakers do speak two languages, they should keep their languages strictly separate. This means, above all, no **bilingual discourse**.

This ideology is apparent in political agendas such as the **English Only** movement (also called English First or US English), which seek legislation to declare English the official language of the US, or of an individual state or city (Baron, 1990). Normative monolingualism can also be seen in the choices made by schools about how to serve their English learner populations, and in signs, t-shirts and other facets of popular culture which espouse the value of English as the sole language of the United States.

The ideology of normative English monolingualism in the US has important implications for Spanish. Although Spanish is an important world language for business and education, it is not valued as such within the US. Instead, it is often seen as the language of (illegal) immigrants, and there is an **iconic** relationship between the perception of the speakers and the language: the people are seen as simple, uneducated rural folk, and their language is 'easy' and unsophisticated.

Chapter 2, 'Language and Identity', addresses the social identities of Spanish speakers and how they are constructed through language use. How choices to speak Spanish, English or a mixture of the two are made and interpreted is influenced by our ideologies about English and Spanish and speakers of those languages.

I discuss identity as a process, not a trait of an individual. Everyone has multiple identities, and these identities are not fixed but are constructed through ongoing social behavior. The focus in this text is **linguistic behavior**, especially (but not only) **language choice**. What does the choice to speak Spanish say about the social identity of the speaker? As we will see, there are many answers to this question, and they are dependent on the social context of the speech event. Speaking Spanish does not always mean the speaker is claiming a particular ethnic identity, and speaking English is not necessarily a rejection of Latin@ identity. Instead, language choice may construct a number of different aspects of social identity, or be a means of negotiating a relationship or striking a pose within an interaction.

In this context, we will discuss bilingual discourse, often called 'Spanglish'. What is Spanglish? How is it different from Spanish? Who speaks it, and what does it mean when they do? There is no one answer to this last question; this will be discussed in terms of its meaning within Latin@ communities and by outsiders. The concept of **translanguaging** will be introduced, which focuses on discourse as an activity, not an entity.

Chapter 3, '"Race", Ethnicity and Spanish Speakers in the US', begins with a focus on how racial and ethnic aspects of identity intertwine with linguistic proficiency and membership in heritage Spanish language communities. I begin with a general introduction to how the concepts of **'race'** and **ethnicity** are dealt with in the social sciences – beginning with why 'race' is written in quotation marks in this text. Empirical evidence of physical differences does not support the idea that human beings can be divided into distinct 'races'; instead, **phenotypic** features are on a continuum. The use of quotation marks is meant to indicate that race is not a biological reality, but a **socially constructed** system of categorization.

Nonetheless, the concept of 'race' is prevalent in US society, and is made salient by its use in the elicitation of **demographic information** (e.g. in the census and on other forms). This information often has quite serious social consequences in terms of opportunities and treatment of individuals. The US is usually described as a country with a **binary race system**, and this is reflected in the use of the terms 'non-White' or 'people of color', which set up racial belonging in terms of the default of Whiteness. However, such systems of social organization may change, and certainly differ across cultures. In the US, the binary system is slowly changing, but is still deeply embedded in social categories and societal practices.

For Latin@s in the US, racial categorization is never unproblematic and is intrinsically intertwined with **ethnicity** (Alcoff, 2000). Ethnicity is generally linked to the idea of common origin, but **ethnic group** membership boundaries are, like racial ones, socially constructed and are often intertwined with, or confused with, national origin, 'race' or linguistic group. This chapter will discuss what the terms 'race' and ethnicity mean in popular culture as well as in academic writing, particularly in Latin@ Studies.

Another way in which ideologies about Spanish and the identities of Spanish speakers are constructed is through the media. Chapter 4, 'Media Representations of Spanish and Spanish Speakers in US English Language TV and Film: Production and Reproduction of Ideologies', looks at themes in the portrayal of Latin@s on the big and small screen. The stereotypes of limited English proficiency, gang violence, 'Latin lovers', illegal immigration and extended, patriarchal families are shown to be standard aspects of representations of US Spanish speakers. The use of accented English is pervasive in the depiction of Latin@s, as is the pattern of the older generation speaking Spanish and the younger generation answering in English. Such language behaviors are primarily shown as part of being a poor, uneducated immigrant; Spanish is thus constructed as an encumbrance to the American dream.

This all changes when the target audience is under 10, however. In contrast to the films made for adult audiences, television programs aimed at young audiences have a vastly different portrayal of Latin@s. Although the stereotype of the co-habiting extended family is retained, the similarities stop there: the families are all middle class, there are no gangs, and there is no asymmetrical bilingual discourse. In the productions aimed at children, bilingualism is portrayed as a resource and a positive individual trait, not a societal problem. While this portrayal is a positive one, it is also one which is limited, as language is not linked to identity and ideologies are ignored.

Part 2 of this text looks more closely at language practices. In Chapter 5, 'Spanish Language Maintenance and Shift in the US', we start off with a discussion of the possible outcomes of Spanish speakers being in an English dominant country: learning English, not learning English, continuing to speak Spanish, or not. The degradation of Spanish discussed in Chapter 1 is a contributing factor in whether Spanish continues to be spoken within communities and over generations. In addition to status factors (i.e. the social value of Spanish), influences on **language maintenance** also include institutional and **demographic factors**. Ultimately, language maintenance is intertwined with ideologies and identities: if there is no ideological support for positive social identities of speakers of Spanish, the language will not continue to be spoken. One observation about the research done on this topic is that by and large it adheres to the second tenet of normative monolingualism, that languages should be kept strictly separate. Although it is clear from the discussion in Chapter 2 that bilingual discourse is common, it is not addressed as part of the landscape of bilingual communities.

This chapter concludes with a look at several examples of bilingual communities and what the picture of maintenance/shift is within them. In addition to presenting data from studies of communities, which are linked to different nations of origin and in different locales across the US, we will also examine the influence of rural and urban settings, the 'racial' make-up of the populations, and social class issues.

Chapter 6 is titled 'Linguistic Consequences of Spanish-English Bilingualism in the US: Spanglish and Chican@ English'. This chapter first looks at how the Spanish language itself undergoes change in the US. The full range of **language contact phenomena**, including lexical borrowing, semantic shifts, loan translations, structural changes and bilingual discourse, are outlined for Spanish in the US. These developments must also be seen from a broader perspective, however; all of these transfer features occur widely in the speech of bilinguals all around the world, and often become adopted into standard **varieties**.

Despite the naturalness and inevitability of these aspects of language mixing, such linguistic behavior is often stigmatized, and this is often the case for Spanish in the US. Contact varieties of Spanish are often referred to as 'Spanglish', which is often used as a pejorative term. In these first sections, I build on the earlier discussion of attitudes about Spanglish to examine structural aspects of Spanish varieties in the US.

The last section of this chapter looks at the influence of Spanish on English, what is sometimes called 'Chican@ English'. Chican@ English differs from 'learner English' in that it is spoken by people who have acquired English as children and, in some cases, speak it as their dominant or only language. I will address how and why **ethnic dialects** of English develop in language contact situations and the features of Chican@ English.

The final chapter, 'Latin@ Education in the US', begins with an overview of different types of programs which serve Latin@ students in general and Latin@s who are English learners in particular. Some of the relevant questions addressed include: what populations of students do different types of program serve? What does research show are the most effective programs for English language learners, and why?

The focus will then shift to address what the language ideologies behind program design and curricula are, and how hegemonic and alternative ideologies are manifest in educational settings. A common metaphor used by proponents of bilingual education is **language as a resource**; maintaining Spanish while learning English is thus presented as a means to achieve upward mobility. This perspective, while focusing on one positive impact of language maintenance, ignores the significance of language as a means of construction of identity. The importance of the use of Spanish in education, for many Latin@s, goes beyond the issue of academic success. How such factors can become part of educational planning is discussed in light of both research and practices in schooling.

While the primary goal of this text is to help students understand the complex social and linguistic issues which influence Spanish speakers in the US, additional goals are (1) to foster the ability for readers to be critical consumers of popular culture and (2) to encourage you to be proponents of institutional policies and social practices which do not discriminate or rely on stereotypes. While issues specific to Spanish in the US are important in and of themselves, they also serve as valuable examples of pervasive social and linguistic patterns which are repeated across languages and cultures. So as you go through these chapters, the challenge is to both appreciate Spanish in the US as a unique and fascinating sociolinguistic phenomenon, and to relate this discussion to other languages and cultures.

Happy reading!

Part 1
Ideologies and Identities

1
Language Ideologies and Language Policies

Objectives: To understand the concept of language ideology and to examine how language ideologies are produced and reproduced through popular culture and public policies in the US.

I begin this chapter with a general discussion of the concept of **language ideology** and then present the theoretical framework which will be used to discuss language ideologies in this text. The next section deals with specific ideologies in the US: **normative monolingualism** (the idea that speaking only one language is the norm and that bilinguals should behave like monolingual speakers in each of their languages) and the low social value of Spanish. Then, a particular way of speaking – what has been called **Mock Spanish** – will be discussed as a representation of these ideologies, and contrasted in the next section with ideologies about the status of English. The last section of this chapter presents a brief overview of language policies and planning in the US that have grown up out of these dominant ideologies, including legislation on bilingual education, language in the workplace and services in languages other than English.

Language ideology defined

Language ideology is defined by Errington (2000) as ideas about language structure and use relative to social contexts. The concept of **hegemony** is an important one here. Much work on language ideologies is concerned with **hegemonic discourses** and their consequences. The basic concept is a simple one: the state of hegemony means that one entity (usually one social group) is dominant over another and this dominance is thought of as 'just the way it is'. With language ideologies, we are concerned with the dominance of certain ideas about language over others. The example we will use here (which will be developed throughout this chapter) is the hegemony of English (and English speakers) in the US, in particular with regard to dominance over Spanish (and Spanish speakers).

Hegemonic ideologies achieve their dominance through wide acceptance. Both the socially dominant and dominated groups in a society believe that these ideologies are natural and universal (Woolard, 1998). This means that the hegemonic ideology that mastery of English is more important than mastery of Spanish is accepted as true by not only most **Anglophones** but also by many **heritage speakers** of Spanish. This leads to lack of pride or even shame about speaking Spanish, and may also lead to parents not passing on their **heritage language** to their children because they believe it will hinder their ability to learn English and 'get ahead' in US society. (As will be discussed in Chapters 5 and 7, this is a pervasive but false assumption; research has shown that the loss of Spanish is actually detrimental to academic achievement and overall upward mobility.)

Although there are hegemonic language ideologies within any given society, there are also always competing ideologies. Along with an ideology of the dominance of English in the US there is a pluralist ideology which includes belief in the positive aspects of multilingualism. For example, UNESCO has proclaimed that February 21 is International

Mother Language Day (see http://www.un.org/en/events/motherlanguageday) with the intent of promoting awareness and appreciation of language diversity; and eHow.com has a page which begins its pitch with:

> There is nothing like being bilingual. If you speak only one language, you may not know what you are missing out on. Being bilingual opens up different pathways of thinking, of expression and of being. Bilingualism allows communication in unusual circumstances and with people who would normally be incommunicable due to a wall of misunderstanding. (eHow, n.d.)

This advertisement for bilingualism portrays some common ideas about language. Language is portrayed as part of a person's identity ('expression of being') and linked to culture ('different pathways of thinking'); languages are also social resources ('allows communication...'). While these ideas about language are given a positive spin in this advertisement, it is easy to see how these same ideas might be twisted into something negative. In US society, monolinguals are envisioned as the ideal citizens (see the discussion of Theodore Roosevelt below). Bilingualism is not viewed as part of this ideal. Also, links to cultures which are not English-speaking can easily be seen as a deficit, instead of an asset, because this is seen as a lack of culture unity. Spanish is frequently depicted as the language of poor immigrants, gang members, etc. (see Chapter 4 for continued discussion of representations of Latin@s in the media). And while the **language as a resource** perspective can be a positive perspective on bilingualism, it can only overcome the negative perception of bilingualism if the particular language is seen as being useful – but what's the use of other languages if everyone speaks English, the way they should? Within the normative monolingualism ideology, none of these defenses of multilingualism carry much weight.

So, all ideologies are not equal and hegemonic ideologies are clearly more powerful. Many scholars of language ideologies (Gal, 1998; Kroskrity, 2004; Silverstein, 1996) demonstrate that even if an alternative ideology overtly challenges the hegemonic ideology, reference to the dominant ideology contributes to its hegemony. As we have seen, this is the case with the hegemony of English; it is difficult to discuss the value of other languages or linguistic pluralism without recognizing that the perceived mainstream norm is monolingualism in English.

Research on hegemonic ideologies addresses how they are part of the **production and reproduction of social inequality**. The phrase 'production and reproduction' is often used in discussions of ideologies to convey the idea that linguistic and social practices do not merely reflect social norms but also perpetuate and shape them. To give a simple example, a t-shirt depicting a stylized Uncle Sam with the caption 'I want you to speak English or get out!' not only reflects the idea that English is the only appropriate language in the US, but encourages the symbolic association between speaking English and being an American. It represents the views of the wearer as part of already existing social norms and simultaneously seeks to influence the behavior and views of others.

We talk about this in terms of 'social inequality' as a way of recognizing that there are always dominant and dominated groups. The members of these groups do not have equal opportunities because they are thought of as being different and considered deficient in some way(s). In terms of language ideologies, this means that non-'native' speakers of English often do not have the same opportunities in education, employment, housing, etc. as 'native' speakers of English (especially speakers of what are considered standard varieties of English). For example, the belief that second language speakers of English are difficult to understand may lead to individuals who speak English non-'natively' not being hired for a job or promoted, even if there is no evidence that their English is not comprehensible. Acting on such beliefs is the perpetuation of inequality.

Work on language ideologies and social inequality relies on Bourdieu's discussion of symbolic power and symbolic domination (Bourdieu, 1991). Symbolic value is achieved within what Bourdieu terms a 'linguistic community', traditionally defined as a 'group of people who use the same system of linguistic signs, the minimum of communication which is the precondition for economic production and even for symbolic domination' (Bourdieu, 1991: 45). Bourdieu stresses that the domination of one variety rests on the complicity of speakers of other varieties; as discussed above, this is often the case even when minority language speakers are negatively impacted by the dominance of the majority language.

The domination of an official language – or of a de facto national language in the case of English in the US – has its source in political authority, but the relationship between language and authority is circular. Once endorsed by educators, politicians and the media the national/official language may lend authority to those who speak it and those who are considered experts in it (e.g. educators, authors of dictionaries, national language societies). For example, (standard) English in the US has gained authority due to the practice of using it as the language of education and government, which in turn means that speaking (standard) English grants individuals authority they would not have in another language. Because (standard) English is used by people with power, it is then considered a powerful way of speaking, and so the cycle continues.

The following sections will discuss specific language ideologies found in the US. Evidence for language ideologies can be found in many venues; here, I will discuss how ideologies are apparent in public texts of different types. However, it is important to note that hegemonic ideologies are often not stated explicitly, as they are naturalized to an extent that they are taken for granted (Kroskrity, 1998). The concept of naturalization implies that an idea is not recognized as a cultural value but is seen as an inevitable truth or something inherent to the human experience. The dominance of English in the US has been naturalized; such products as the bumper sticker in Figure 1.1 ('Welcome to America: NOW SPEAK ENGLISH!') illustrate how this dominance is often viewed as something which needs no explanation. Yet despite naturalization, it is possible to find evidence of hegemonic and counter-hegemonic ideologies in the discussions and comments made in public forums such as blogs, chat rooms, social networking sites, etc. Before moving on to these public displays of ideology, however, I will next outline a theoretical framework for analyzing ideologies.

Figure 1.1 Bumper sticker

A framework for studying language ideologies

A framework for looking at language ideologies has been presented in research by Gal and Irvine (1995). This approach consists of the application of three concepts to ideological systems: iconicity, recursiveness and erasure.

Iconicity means that a language comes to be not only an **index** of a certain group, but an icon for the group; that is, it does not merely 'point to' the social group, but is assumed to be a representation of that group, sharing characteristics with it. Taking the case of Spanish in the US, we find that Spanish has become an icon for Latin@s, and there is a sense that the speakers and language share characteristics. The Spanish language is commonly viewed as 'easy' (Lipski, 2002: 1248), which fits with the common perception of its speakers as being simple rural folk. Spanish is seen as linguistically inferior to English; as will be discussed in more detail later in this chapter, use of **Mock Spanish** (e.g. 'no problemo', 'el cheapo') illustrate the attitude that Spanish is simply English with –o endings on nouns, and not a 'real' language (Barrett, 2006; Hill, 1995, 1998, 2005, 2008). It follows that speakers of Spanish are also inferior to English speakers – hence the common depiction of Mexicans (the prototypical Latin@) as stupid, lazy, sexually promiscuous and dirty (there's a fine example of this attitude in a discussion titled 'Mexicans are stupid' on potatoe.com, n.d.).

Finally, Spanish does not belong in the US, where English is regarded as the only legitimate language, and its speakers are equally unwanted and are not seen as legitimate Americans. All of these stereotypical attitudes reflect an iconic relationship between Spanish in the US and Latin@s.

Recursiveness means that a certain type of relationship (between social groups or languages) repeats itself on different levels in society. In this case, the relationship is one of hierarchy and dominance. Recursiveness in US language ideology can be found in the pervasive idea that certain ways of speaking are superior to others, and there is one 'right' way to speak a language. There is a hierarchy of languages, English being superior to Spanish (and other foreign languages), and there is also a hierarchy of dialects of American English – varieties associated with the educated middle class, or those varieties sometimes referred to as 'White' ways of speaking, are perceived as being at the top, and ethnic dialects (such as **African American Vernacular English (AAVE)** or **Chican@ English**) and **non-standard** dialects associated with poor, rural and uneducated people are at the bottom. This is also applied to other languages such as Spanish; US varieties are deemed inferior to standard Latin American varieties and Castilian Spanish (see Anzaldúa, 1999: 80 for a discussion of this for Chican@ Spanish, and Toribio, 2006 for a similar discussion of Dominican Spanish).

So the perspective of the existence of one 'correct' way of speaking and multiple inferior ways of speaking is seen on both the level of language (e.g. English over Spanish) as well as on the level of dialect (e.g. standard English over Chican@ English, standard Spanish over Chican@ Spanish). We also see recursiveness in the application of this hierarchy to the social groups connected to these particular language varieties; the speakers of particular high-ranked languages (i.e. speakers of standard English) have a higher social rank than those who speak stigmatized languages (e.g. speakers of Chican@ English or Spanish). Of course, social groups are not judged only in terms of the languages they speak. There are also other issues – most prominently **'race'** and **ethnicity**, to be discussed in Chapter 3 – which are intertwined with minority language and dialect groups. As we will see, the principle of recursiveness of relationships between groups is maintained regardless of how these groups are defined.

There is also recursiveness in popular ideas about the nature of language. Linguistic varieties (and especially prestigious ones) are usually perceived as being uniform or homogeneous; in reality, all 'languages' consist of many different varieties, usually called 'dialects' (Lippi-Green, 1997). In the context of discourse on bilingualism, English is presented as a uniform entity which is contrasted with Spanish, Chinese, Polish, Hmong, etc., which are all also seen as homogeneous. The parallel conceptualization is that the speakers of these languages also form homogeneous groups. All English speakers are superior, all Spanish speakers are poor, all Chinese speakers are industrious, and so forth. One piece of evidence of this view of language and language group as **monolithic** is the common reference to any Spanish speaker as 'Mexican'. This usage indicates a lack of understanding of differences between nationality and language (an idea which will be re-visited shortly) but also a lack of awareness about the variation within the category of Spanish speakers (i.e. not everyone who speaks Spanish is from Mexico). This is the recursive theme; both languages and the groups of people who speak them are framed as homogeneous entities, as if there were no different ways of speaking Spanish (or English), and a myriad of different national, cultural, ethnic, etc. ways of being a US Latin@.

Finally, **erasure** is the phenomenon of ignoring or rendering invisible any practices which would contradict the hegemonic ideology. The ideology of normative monolingualism in the US dictates that having one sole language within a national territory is the natural and 'right' way for a country to operate, and that multilingualism is a feature of poor immigrant communities which are separate from 'mainstream' America. In order for this ideology to stand, several sociolinguistic realities must undergo erasure. Middle class multilinguals, the success of bilingual education programs, and the existence of many multilingual nations must be ignored or refuted – or, at the minimum, portrayed as exceptions to the rule. In addition, selective erasure of many aspects of the linguistic history of the US must also take place, in which the multilingual nature of early settlements and maintenance of immigrant languages other than English are forgotten – along with the fact that English itself was a poor immigrant language when it arrived in what is now the US. In Figure 1.2, we see a bumper sticker which challenges the erasure of this history by playing on the slogan of the bumper sticker in Figure 1.1. Like most challenges to hegemonic ideologies, it necessarily establishes the hegemonic ideology as widespread while at the same time seeking to discredit it.

There is also erasure involved in beliefs about language learning. Although most of us know, on some level, that it takes time to learn a second language, this commonsense understanding of the process of language learning undergoes erasure to support ideologies of hostility toward languages other than English. In order to oppose services in minority languages in the US, one must assume a binary, static view of language competence which has little to do with the reality of most people's experiences. By binary I mean that people are viewed as either speakers of a language or not (see Pomerantz, 2002: 287), although obviously a continuum of abilities better reflects the nature of language acquisition. By static, what is meant is that the state of speaking a language or not is viewed as permanent. This breeds hostility toward services provided in foreign languages, such as voting materials or educational opportunities. Instead of being viewed as services for people transitioning to bilingualism, they are seen as a service enabling people who are in the fixed position of not speaking English. More details of Latin@s and English language learning will be presented in Chapter 5, so, for now, it suffices to say that the claim that immigrants from Latin America do not learn English is inaccurate. However, the reality of English acquisition by Latin@s must be erased in order to maintain the negative views of Spanish speakers which accompany normative monolingualism. Policies brought about by this perspective on language learning will be discussed in the section below on **language policies**, planning and practices.

Figure 1.2   *Bumper sticker*

Normative monolingualism

The ideology of normative monolingualism as I conceive of it has two parts: first, mono-lingualism is presented as the ideal state for social and political entities, such as nation states; this ideal is naturalized and does not usually require justification (see Fishman, 1985: 446ff). The second part of normative monolingualism is that if an individual is bilingual, the two languages must be kept strictly separate. This means, above all else, no **codeswitching** or **bilingual discourse**. Let's look at both of these aspects of normative monolingualism in more detail.

English only

The first part of the ideology of normative monolingualism in the US revolves around the underlying ideas of monolingualism as the norm, **linguistic diversity** as an impediment to unity, and language as an important symbol of national character. The idea of monolin-gualism as the norm relies on the erasure of the fact of multilingualism in the US. There were many languages spoken on this land before English speakers arrived to claim it, and many of them continue to be spoken. Also, many other immigrant languages, in addition to English, have been and are spoken in the US. In part of the southwestern US, Spanish was spoken before it became US territory, and before English speakers arrived there; in other parts of the country other immigrant languages (e.g. German, French) were the dominant local and regional languages before English became the de facto national language. Thus the area now designated as the US has always contained speakers of a multitude of languages.

And, perhaps even more significantly, this multilingual nature of the US population has not been documented as the cause of social divides, although this is a popular argument (Schmidt, 2007: 201). The idea of linguistic diversity as an impediment to unity ignores the reality that multilingualism does not mean there cannot be a **lingua franca** that can allow people to communicate effectively. Further, there is evidence that when issues of national unity arose, such as during the Revolutionary War, lines were not drawn based on linguistic boundaries. Many speakers of languages other than English (most notably German speakers) successfully joined forces with the Anglophone rebels. Further, the idea that multilingualism divides a nation disregards other, equally (if not more) important aspects of demographics that can divide or unite populations – 'race'/ethnicity, religion, social class, gender, age, sexual orientation, etc.

Language as a symbol for national character is also a key part of the ideology of norma-tive monolingualism. In the US, not just English but English monolingualism is an icon of American belonging. Theodore Roosevelt played on this sentiment in the early 1900s when he wrote: 'we have room for but one language here, and that is the English lan-guage...' (Roosevelt, 1919: 1). It is important to note the other parallels he draws: there is room for but one flag, the American flag, and room for but one sole loyalty, the loyalty to the American people. Language is unambiguously made into a symbol of belonging, and speaking English – and only English – is portrayed as the choice to be American. Here we see iconicity, as English monolingualism is a transparent representation of American identity. The alternative, Roosevelt suggests, is a 'polyglot boarding house' (Roosevelt, 1919: 2) – implying that multilingualism brings with it a certain déclassé working class transience that can only be avoided by assimilation to English monolingualism.

Although the sentiment Roosevelt voiced has never disappeared, it was given new life in the early 1980s with what is often called the English Only Movement. A series of bills proposing English as the official language of the US were proposed in Congress and on some occasions passed in either the House or the Senate, but never both. Legislation has also been sought at the state level, with individual states creating policies naming English as their official language (Crawford, 2007). What this means in terms of language practices varies widely – Illinois, for example, has a statute declaring English the official language of the state, but also has quite progressive bilingual education laws. As a symbolic statement, however, declaring English the official language is a clear reinforce-ment of normative monolingualism. Some analyses of the English Only Movement point out that the fear of foreign languages, and Spanish in particular, is puzzling in light of statistics which show that only 3% of Latin@s do not speak English, and that second and third generation immigrants are usually dominant in English and often do not learn Spanish at all (Mar-Molino, 2000; Ricento, 2009; Schmidt, 2007). In short, there is no need to shore up the power of English with language policy; the ideology which motivates such policies involves erasure of the fact that linguistic assimilation is already occurring.

In addition to policies that reflect normative monolingualism, it is also possible to find public discourse that is indicative of language ideologies, and a number of these phenomena will be discussed in the following sections in more detail. Here, I would like to note that although we know there are competing ideologies, it is primarily the hegemonic ideology of normative monolingualism which is shown in signs and merchandise. I have seen bumper stickers that say 'Why the hell should I have to press "1" for English?' along with various merchandise such as the 'Welcome to America – Now Speak English' bumper sticker shown in Figure 1.1. Although the people who hold these sentiments may be a minority, they function as a majority in the display of their views. Although the bumper sticker shown in Figure 1.2 ('Welcome to America – Now Speak Cherokee') exists, the only one I have ever seen is the one on my own bumper, and I have never seen a bumper sticker sporting a motto such as 'My child is learning two languages at Roosevelt Elementary School!' Public displays of opinion support the idea that we should stigmatize and reject languages other than English, but only rarely that we should embrace multilingualism.

The ideology of normative monolingualism is also played out in educational settings. Anti-bilingual education rhetoric frames English as the only language which leads to people being successful in school. Although there is no real reason why being bilingual could not be part of a person's success in school, hegemonic language ideologies do not allow for heritage languages to be valued alongside English in the educational context. One reason for this is that in the US, bilingualism is usually assumed to be the result of **immigration**, and **immigrant bilingualism** is not prestigious because it is linked to working class status. Although of course not all immigrants are poor and uneducated, this is the stereotype, especially for Spanish-speaking immigrants. The received wisdom is that speaking a language other than English hinders academic achievement. The reasons for this are usually vaguely articulated, as shown in this quote from a website debating an English Immersion Measure for schools in Oregon:

> For the first 200 years of our republic people have come from all over the world and immigrated to America. They spoke every language on earth. With the exception of few isolated exceptions there were no ELL, ESL or dual language programs, just English immersion. Because immigrants were forced to learn English they became better citizens, more productive people and better educated. (answerbag, 2009)

As will be discussed in Chapter 7, the type of instruction referred to here should correctly be called 'submersion', which has been shown to be ineffective in raising English proficiency and in leading to academic achievement for minority language students. The claim that immigrants became better educated because they were forced to learn English is not supported here, and there is a great deal of room for arguments that, historically, the opposite was true (see Montero-Sieburth & LaCelle-Peterson, 1991). Further, there is much evidence from recent research that shifting to English does not necessarily mean academic success (see Meador, 2005; Valenzuela, 1999).

In sum, the ideology that English monolingualism in the US is natural, promotes unity, and is the best way to educate all children is not supported by a look at the social history of the US or pedagogical studies of immigrant children. These refutations must undergo erasure in order to allow reproduction of the normative monolingualism ideology.

Monoglossic language ideologies

The second part of the ideology of normative monolingualism dictates that languages should be kept strictly separate. García (2008, 2009a, 2011a) discusses this in terms of **monoglossic language ideology**. Within this ideological system, languages are valued only as distinct, pure entities; if they are mixed, they lose value and are not taken seriously. The reality of linguistic practices that involve two or more languages thus must be ignored or stigmatized. For Spanish, this means that it may be recognized as a global language and valued for that reason but the local varieties of Spanish and the ways they are used in everyday speech (i.e. often alternated and intertwined with English) are not valued.

The idea that languages are clearly delineated entities, with the norm being monolingual discourse, has been pervasive in common understandings of language, even among scholars in the fields of sociolinguistics and linguistic anthropology, until fairly recently. This viewpoint ignores what is argued to be the naturalness of bilingual discourse (e.g. Ardilla, 2005; Bhatt, 2008; Fuller, 2009; García, 2011a; Lipski, 2007a; Morales, 2002; Stavans, 2000) and what is more generally called **heteroglossia** (Bailey, 2007; Baktin, 1981; García, 2009b). The concept of heteroglossia rests on the understanding that all ways of speaking include multiple voices; our conceptualization of languages as distinct, bounded, uniform entities is a product of the social and political histories of different ways of speaking, not a linguistic reality. Not only is bilingual discourse common, but viewing a language as a single entity is ignoring the multitude of registers, styles, genres and dialects that make up all languages.

The pervasiveness of heteroglossic language practices must undergo erasure in order to maintain the ideology of normative monolingualism. I suggest that part of the discomfort, and thus stigmatization, of multilingual discourse is related to iconicity. If a language is an icon for a social category, then multilingual discourse means that the speakers are from multiple social categories. This blurring of boundaries and potential ambiguity of category membership is problematic in a society where these categories are part of the everyday ways in which we define our population. Language which cannot be clearly labeled as 'English' or 'Spanish' means that the speaker cannot be clearly labeled, either. This challenge to **essentialist** social categories is thus uncomfortable, and this discomfort leads to erasure or stigmatization.

Ideologies about the value of Spanish

While the previous section discussed how multilingual language practices are stigmatized, it is important to recognize that even when a standard variety of Spanish is spoken, with no mixing in of elements of English, it is also not a valued way of speaking. Schmidt (2002: 154–5) discusses the rhetoric and counter-rhetoric in the English Only debate. One salient aspect of the rhetoric of English Only proponents is the depiction of assimilation as egalitarian: if English is the official language, the privileges of being an English speaker are available to all (Schmidt, 2007: 202). Pluralists claim that this position denies that US social structure is in fact inegalitarian and that the mastering of English does not ensure access to privileges for people of color. Thus the English Only position discriminates against speakers of languages other than English, and they are thus doubly discriminated against if they are not White.

Schmidt references writing on 'new racism' to explain this phenomenon in which 'race' becomes coded as culture (see also Urciuoli, 2009 on this topic). In particular, he focuses on Spanish speakers. Speaking Spanish is seen as part of a culture which marginalizes its members; it is an index of the underclass. Although in reality there is a positive relationship between being bilingual and being upwardly mobile (Linton, 2003), a common belief is that continuing to speak Spanish condemns Latin@s to an impoverished existence (that polyglot boarding house Roosevelt refers to with such disdain). Because speaking a heritage language is seen as a choice, not part of a life experience, speakers of Spanish are thus seen as choosing life in the barrio and constructing their own barriers to socio-economic mobility. As will be discussed below, this attitude about the language one speaks being a free choice (and why would anyone choose Spanish over English?) also finds its way into policy decisions (Del Valle, 2009).

While English Only discourse implicitly contains the ideology that Spanish is inferior to English, there is a great deal of public discourse which explicitly states this as well. The ideologies surrounding Spanish in the US, as discussed by Schmidt (2002), revolve largely around Spanish as a minority immigrant language, spoken by the underclass. Spanish might be valuable to English speakers because this underclass represents an increasing market; Anglophones who can also speak Spanish may have employment opportunities in education and social services as well as in business realms. But there is little recognition of Spanish as a global language, or a powerful language for business transactions. There is erasure of Spanish within any communities or social groups, other than in immigrant ghettos, in the US.

These attitudes inevitably influence how Spanish is used in public arenas. For the most part, we see Spanish relegated to the role of a subordinate language; it is used for translations of information that is deemed essential for people who cannot understand English, or to appeal to a Spanish-speaking market. Thus we often see bilingual signs such as the one shown in Figure 1.3; Lowe's home improvement store (among other establishments) has all its signs in both English and Spanish; and telephone helplines often have an option of assistance in Spanish. All of these uses of Spanish are in keeping with the second half of the normative monolingualism ideology: if you do speak two languages, keep them strictly separate. Translation is an acceptable way of using two languages; bilingual discourse is not. Part of this unacceptability runs deeper than

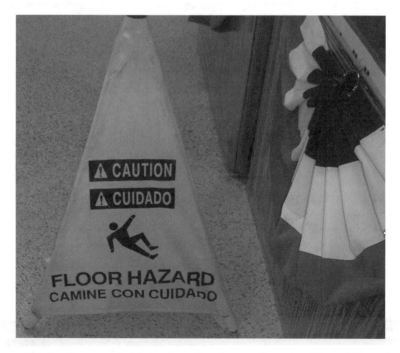

Figure 1.3 *This 'caution – cuidado' sign is as American as the red, white and blue 4th of July decoration next to it*

prescriptive norms about language and rests in the iconic relationship between language and speakers, as mentioned above: if the language is hybrid, then the speakers are too, and hybridity is disruptive to essentialist, naturalized ideas about social order being maintained through neat categorizations of people.

However, attitudes toward Spanish in the US show much more than feelings of superiority by English speakers over Spanish speakers. There is a fear and hostility toward Spanish speakers which can only be described as irrational (see Schmidt, 2007 for a discussion of why people are threatened by Spanish, despite the clear dominance of English). For instance, this is illustrated by the writings on the webpage *My Biggest Complaint* about having to press one for English on automated telephone services (*My Biggest Complaint*, n.d.). The initial complaint is given in example (1):

(1)   I live in the USA. I do not understand why I have to press 1 for English for many business calls I make. English is the language of the USA. I resent others thinking their language is number 1.
        When my father came to the US he had to learn English to survive. I believe that any foreigner who comes to the US should learn to speak our tongue, no questions asked. (*My Biggest Complaint*, n.d.)

Although the posting date of this original comment is not listed, the first comment was posted on June 18, 2007, so we can assume that the original posting was at some point shortly before that. As of August 1, 2012, the interest in this topic continued and included 187 comments, including 79 supporting the sentiments of the original post, 77 which were critical of it, and 31 which were on tangential subjects. (Lest you think the supporters of this complaint are merely a small group of people, let me point out that there is also a Facebook page devoted to this topic, which on August 1, 2012 had 8,112 people who 'liked' it (see Facebook, n.d.).) Some of the comments which built on the ideas of the original posting on mybiggestcomplaint.com include the following (all following quotes were copied verbatim from the website):

(2)   So, gang, what can we do to put an end to this Press One for English nonsense? I'm willing to participate in anything that makes sense and has a Chinaman's chance of actually working. Any ideas?
        (I've done some preliminary arithmetic and determined that, if left unabated, because of immigration – both legal and illegal – and of internal birthrates, that in a decade or so Spanish will become the majority language here, hence becoming the de facto 'official' language of the USA.) (*Ralph Rogers* on February 23, 2008 at 6:34 pm)

(3)   OK..
        The way it is... Since the time of Ellis Island To come to Ameica was.. To Prove who you were..Your intent of being here??.. To get a job or start a business, Every-one was documented and informed that the above would be watched... They would talk English Here..To Become an American Citizen... And if found that they wiere sick or nothing could be documented you GOT SENT BACK TO THAT COUNTRY ..You Came From!!!..DUH

Get That Illegals No Green Cards... No Amnesty ...You Had To Be Dcoumented And Become An American Citizen!!! And Learn English !!!
No More Crap From You Damn Illegals GOT THAT YET!!! This Land Is NOT YOURS!! DON'T LIKE IT!!! GO BACK TO MEKKICO TIA-JUANA Your all a bunch of freeloading banchees (bringing you damn illnesses into our America!!).. That think you can come here and live like a bunch of SLOBS!!! And Get It All For Free!! 'NOT ON MY SHIFT'!!! NO More Push 1 For English (Talk English)!!!! Or GO AWAAAAAAAAY !!! (*Laura Reed* on June 3, 2008 at 12:32 pm)

(4) WE ARE ENABLING OTHER LANGUAGE SPEAKING PERSONS!!! AND ALLOWING THEM... TO MAKE US CONFORM TO APPEASE THEM!!! 'NOT ON MY SHIFT'!! LEARN ENGLISH !!!! DANG IT!! (*Laura* on February 1, 2009 at 1:47 pm)

(5) All phone messages should sound like this. Hello this is *&%*&. and thank you for calling *&*&##. Press 1 for English, press 2 if you can't understand this message and either go back to the country you came from or get in line to become a citizen and learn the language. (*BIGBROTHER* on July 23, 2010 at 7:30 am)

The claims here represent discourses which are echoed in many venues. The main ideas include: English is (deservedly!) the one and only language of the US; earlier immigrants learned English so why don't these Spanish speakers; and if we 'coddle' Spanish speakers by allowing them to communicate in their heritage language (because they don't want to learn English) they will take over the country. Although I am tempted to simply reply in the words of one of the other posters to the list (see example 6), I will respond to each of these points in turn.

(6) After reading this, I think the #1 language of the US might be 'dumb@ss' (*Timinator* on July 8, 2008 at 8:52 am)

First, as discussed by some of the posters in this thread, English may be the de facto national language of the United States, but the US does not have an official language. A casual glance at the history of the US makes it clear that multilingualism, not monolingualism, has been the norm. Again we see naturalization at work; first the one-to-one relationship between nationality and language is naturalized, and then the hegemony of English makes it appear as if it is somehow the 'natural' language choice in this country, when actually it has always been one choice of many.

There are also problems with the second claim, which holds that earlier immigrants – and today's non-Spanish-speaking immigrants, another claim made in this thread – all learn English, it's just the 'wetbacks' who can't be bothered. It is absolutely untrue that earlier immigrants assimilated linguistically (or otherwise) any faster than today's immigrants (Bigler, 1996). In fact, in some areas of Wisconsin which were densely populated with German speakers, failing to learn English quickly or well did not prevent their full participation in society or even their upward mobility (Wilkerson & Salmons, 2008). However, in some cases the lack of educational opportunities for children who did not speak English at home and job opportunities for those who did not master English were quite limited (e.g. see Montero-Sieburth & LaCelle-Peterson, 1991).

This brings us to another attitude portrayed in the mybiggestcomplaint.com postings: immigrants don't WANT to learn English. Although I am no more privy to the inner desires of Spanish speaking immigrants than anyone else who is not one, I find it highly doubtful that a high percentage of immigrants living in the US don't WANT to learn English. In my experience with children in bilingual education programs, both the children and their parents recognize the importance of learning English. This motivation has many aspects, including a desire to integrate into the larger society, but also a clear material motivation. As the US economy moves to being more based on the production of services than goods, today, more than ever, those who cannot speak English well are disadvantaged.

But the desire to learn English does not always translate into learning English quickly or well. Anyone who has tried to learn a foreign or second language can attest that it is a long and difficult process. So slow progress in learning English should not be interpreted as lack of interest in or value of the English language, nor should it cause the learner to be categorized forever as a non-English speaker.

What is overlooked in the discourse about immigrants and language learning is that the current Latin@ immigrants are different than earlier waves of immigrants in two ways. First, there are more of them, and they keep coming; this gives the impression, especially to those eager to assign negative attributes to them, that as a group they are not learning English. In reality, research carried out by the Pew Center shows that 35% of first generation Hispanic immigrants speak English well or pretty well, and 91% and 97% of the second and third generations, respectively (Hakimzadeh & Cohn, 2007). And many of the 65% of the first generation who do not speak English well or pretty well do speak enough English to communicate basic information. So not every Spanish speaker who comes to the United States learns English, but then, neither did every German or Polish speaker in earlier times. So it's simply not true that Latin@s don't learn English like earlier immigrants; it's that there is not a wave of immigration but a constant flow, so there are always new immigrants who have limited English skills. This is different from earlier patterns of immigration.

The second difference between Latin@ immigrants and earlier immigrants, especially those from Europe, is that the European immigrants were more easily integrated into a two-way racial system as 'White', while many Latin@ immigrants are seen as 'Brown', 'Black', 'Non-White', 'People of Color', etc. As will be discussed in Chapter 3, such categories are socially constructed and are based on ideologies about the inherent value of certain groups of people as much as on phenotypic characteristics. For instance, Asian immigrants, who are stereotyped as intelligent and hardworking, are much more easily given status as 'honorary Whites' than Latin@s, who are stereotyped as lazy and stupid. Yes, that is harsh, but unfortunately not an exaggeration, as attested by the following post on our favorite thread on mybiggestcomplaint.com:

(7)   will you people quit picking on the mexicans its obvious they are too lazy & stupid to learn anything but how to get a free ride much less our English *(Troy* on October 27, 2009 at 2:08 pm)

All of this sets up Spanish as a language which is open to ridicule, and there we are not disappointed. In the next section, what has been called Mock Spanish will be discussed as one way of further depicting Spanish speakers as 'Other'.

Mock Spanish

What has been called Mock Spanish involves a conscious effort to say things that sound like Spanish but with no real attempt to actually speak Spanish (Barrett, 2006; Hill, 1995, 1998, 2005, 2008). Santiago (2008: 91–2) gives a light-hearted perspective on this with his Top Ten Tips for Speaking Spanglish Like a Gringo. Included in the list are tips such as 'Add Spanish articles to English words, being careful to screw up gender and number agreement' and 'When all else fails, throw in an '¡Ay Caramba!'. A darker side of Speaking Spanglish Like a Gringo is hinted at in the following tips, however: 'Always maintain the following attitude: "What do you expect? I'm a gringo"'; and 'Remember what they told you in Spanish class about how the double "l" (el) sound is pronounced like a "y" in English? Well, forget that and just pronounce it like a law-abiding American citizen'. So even this account, which is intended to be humorous and written for a popular audience, cannot help but show resentment about the attitude of English speakers about speaking Spanish.

Hill (1995, 1998, 2005, 2008) discusses how Mock Spanish not only devalues Spanish, but also constructs Whiteness as **normative**. Barrett (2006) similarly shows how Mock Spanish can be used as a marker of Anglo identity; he also argues that Anglo appropriation of Spanish reproduces the context of racial inequality. As further articulated by Zentella, although Mock Spanish is a very conscious use of language mixing, it is seen as simply 'multicultural "with-it-ness"' (Zentella, 2003: 53) when used by members of the White Anglophone majority. Yet actual bilingualism and use of Spanish-English bilingual discourse by people who speak both languages fluently is seen as in need of correction and control (Hill, 1995, 1998, 2008; Zentella, 2003).

The data used to discuss Mock Spanish by Hill include signs (e.g. '¡Adios, Cucaracha!' as the slogan for a bug exterminator company), greeting cards ('Fleas Navidad' as the text in a Christmas card), and popular expressions such as 'no problemo' or 'hasta la vista'. She argues that while such usages directly construct the speaker/author as jovial, indirectly they construct Spanish speakers as inferior. As Hill (2005: 113) writes: 'Mock Spanish keys an easygoing, humorous, yet cosmopolitan persona and positioning. Mock Spanish also reproduces racist stereotypes of Spanish speakers.' The racist meanings are indirect because it makes no sense to overtly deny them. For example, if one were to make the statement 'Mexicans are lazy', it could be prefaced with 'I'm not a racist, but...' as it is an overt stereotype. But it makes no sense to say 'I'm not a racist, but "no problemo"' (Hill, 1999: 683–4). Thus, Mock Spanish is what Hill calls 'covert racist discourse'; it does not overtly assign negative attributes to a certain group of people, but rather implies them.

For instance, Hill (2005) discusses how use of the word 'mañana' is used to reinforce the stereotype of Latin@s (and particularly Mexicans) as lazy, putting off until tomorrow what they should do today, and the use of 'comprende?' builds on the stereotype of Spanish speakers being ignorant and unable to understand English.

My own discussions with students about Hill's work have often revealed discomfort with the idea that use of token Spanish utterances by non-Latin@s is necessarily racist. Upon reading Hill's work, one feels defensive and perhaps a bit guilty, remembering saying '¿Qué pasa?' as a greeting or using 'amigo' as a term of affection. Are these necessarily 'racist' comments? This is not a question that should be answered easily or lightly. We all must acknowledge having stereotypes and prejudices, even if we think of them as positive stereotypes. For example, the use of 'amigo' as a sign of affection may stem from the stereotype of Mexicans as warm and friendly people – especially if one would be unlikely to use 'Freund' (German) or 'ami' (French) in the same way. This is nonetheless a cultural stereotype, and ultimately saying 'Mexicans are all so friendly' is no more empowering to those included in the stereotyped group than saying 'Mexicans are lazy'.
It pays to be aware of the potential pitfalls of assuming that all members of a group share certain characteristics. Also, of course, we sometimes make generalizations in the other direction; if you have a Latina friend who is constantly late, do you assume that it is because she is 'running on Latin time' (i.e. that she is a representative of her nation in all that she does), or that her lateness is a personal characteristic? Such associations depersonalize and dehumanize both groups and individuals. Language choice is one way in which cultural stereotypes are referenced, so it is worthwhile for all of us to think about our language use in terms of avoiding the reproduction of discrimination.

That said, I think it is important to note the obvious: not all uses of Spanish by non-fluent Spanish speakers necessarily indicate a stance of racism. Speaker intent matters – but let's not forget the saying 'The road to hell is paved with good intentions'. However, there is never a one-to-one correspondence between language choice and social meaning; the choice to use a particular language does not always construct a particular identity. Instead, meanings of language choices depend on the particular context in which they are uttered. So, if I greet a friend with, '¿Qué pasa?', maybe I am just trying to establish myself as a Spanish speaker, however feebly that phrase can do so. If I try to move a group of people along by calling out 'Let's Go! ¡Vámonos!', perhaps I am relying on a switch in code for emphasis, not creating a stance linked to Spanish (or perhaps I have just been watching too much *Dora the Explorer*).

I do not want to suggest, however, that it is SOLELY a matter of intent; obliviousness to potential racism in one's speech does not make it less racist, and lack of intent to harm does not make you harmless. How we choose to say things carries meaning, and that meaning is socially embedded and not simply a matter of speaker intent. Failure to recognize the social significance of code choice can perpetuate stereotypes whether we are conscious of them or not.

So while there may be uses of Spanish phrases by semi-speakers of Spanish that are not mocking in nature, there are also clear cases of racism in the use of Mock Spanish.

Barrett (2006) gives a depressing account of how this works in his data from a Mexican restaurant in Austin, Texas. There was a clear divide between the brown-skinned Spanish-speaking kitchen staff and the White Anglophone servers and managers, and this divide was intensified through the use of Mock Spanish by some of the Anglo employees. Many of the examples show not just a lack of attempt to actually speak Spanish, but a clearly belittling attitude about the Spanish language (e.g. the use of 'ice-o' for 'ice'). Even worse, Mock Spanish often served to IMPEDE communication; in many cases, an attempt to speak English slowly and clearly might have cleared up any misunderstanding, but the use of Mock Spanish increased confusion. Inevitably the Spanish speakers were blamed for the miscommunication, and they were often portrayed as unwilling as well as unable to understand. In this case, the burden of comprehension lay completely on the hearer, even when the speaker produced purposely incomprehensible **input**.

Examples of Mock Spanish can also be found in a children's book called *Skippyjon Jones* (Schachner, 2003) and its sequels, primarily *Skippyjon Jones in the Dog House* (Schachner, 2005). This book series stars a Siamese cat (Skippyjon) who does not act like a proper Siamese cat. His mother sends him to his room to 'do some serious thinking...about just what it means to be a cat' (Schachner, 2003: 4). But Skippyjon doesn't want to be a Siamese cat, he wants to be a Chihuahua, so he puts a black mask over his eyes (Zorro style, the first hint of things to come) and goes into his closet, which leads him (in his imagination) to Mexico. Once there, he meets a band of Chihuahuas called the Chimichangos and manages to rescue them from a 'bandito' (a giant bumblebee) who has been stealing their beans. In *Skippyjon Jones in the Dog House*, Skippyjon is again sent to his room to 'think Siamese' (Schachner, 2005: 4), and he again ventures into his fantasy Mexico and encounters his Chihuahua friends.

Although there is some use of real Spanish words in the text (e.g. *Yo quiero frijoles* 'I love beans', *Buenas noches* 'Good night', *mis amigos* 'my friends'), most of what appears is definitively Mock Spanish: Skippyjon calls himself 'El Skippito' and makes exclamations like 'holy guacamole' and 'holy jalapeño', and the text features rhymes created by adding –o or –ito to the ends of English words in time-tested Mock Spanish style – indeed-o, eato, birdito, snap-ito. Every cliché about Mexican culture is included in the storyline: fiestas, siestas, castanets, burritos, banditos and piñatas. There are also a couple of examples of a Spanish accent, a phenomenon which increases in frequency in *Skippyjon Jones in the Dog House*. In every case, a Spanish accent is affected through the use of an 'ee' to represent the use of [i] instead of [I] in English words such as 'is' and 'big'.

(8)   Then, using his very best Spanish accent, he said, 'My ears are too beeg for my head. My head ees too beeg for my body. I am not a Siamese cat...I AM A CHIHUAHUA!' (Schactner, 2003)

(9)   'It ees I, El Skippito Friskito...' (Schachner, 2005)

The language play in this book is a realistic depiction of how Anglophones incorporate Spanish elements into their English – making rhymes through adding final –o's and –ito's, tossing in simple Spanish words understood by everyone such as *gracias* and *vamos*, and using faux translations from English to Spanish (e.g. 'la casa perrito' for 'the little doghouse'). This is authentic Mock Spanish, with all of the social meanings discussed by Hill, Barrett and Zentella, and it is being sold to small children as something that is playful, with special thanks and much love in the dedication to the *muchachas hispanas* ('Hispanic girls') who helped the author learn Spanish. I somehow doubt that these children used expressions such as 'holy frijoles' (which, reminiscent as it is of exclamations from 1970s Batman and Robin, seems more like something an adult of my generation would come up with) or 'yes, indeed-o'. This is not a serious attempt to use Spanish; instead, Spanish is made to appear easy – just add an 'o' to English words! – and not a real language. Just as described by Hill, these usages, which on the surface show a willingness to accommodate a Spanish-speaking interlocutor, on a more substantive level indicate a rejection of Spanish as a real language. This positions Spanish speakers as inferior, no matter how cute it is when a Siamese cat puts on a black mask and rides a pogo stick and pretends to be a Chihuahua.

Another problem Mock Spanish creates is that it is often conflated with Spanish and 'Spanglish'. Even Barrett (2006), whose article is a critical analysis of the practice of using Mock Spanish, is somewhat guilty of this. The title of his article, 'Language ideology and racial inequality: Competing functions of Spanish in an Anglo-owned Mexican restaurant', implies that Mock Spanish is a form of Spanish, a representation which underlies the whole problem with Mock Spanish. Mock Spanish is NOT Spanish; it is simply adding pseudo-Spanish endings or articles to English words. While there may be some overlap between Mock Spanish and Spanglish in terms of structure, the faux Hispanicization of English words is clearly Mock Spanish, as we saw in examples such as 'indeed-o' from *Skippyjon Jones* (Schachner, 2003: 9) or 'ice-o' (Barrett, 2006: 182). Such usages are not potentially Spanglish, and neither are phrases which make jokes based on the pronunciation of Spanish words ('Fleas Navidad' in a Christmas card discussed in Hill (1995), or 'holy frijoles' uttered by Skippyjon (Schachner, 2003)). These examples are not attempts to speak Spanish but efforts to mock it. As Hill (1998) discusses, while this directly indexes a jovial identity for the speaker, it indirectly indexes the normativity of White (or at least Anglophone) identity. Thus in both linguistic and social terms, these uses cannot be discussed as if they are Spanglish, and they are certainly not Spanish.

The existence of Mock Spanish in US society is a sign of the devaluation of Spanish. Because of iconic relations between language and speakers, its use stigmatizes Latin@s. This stigmatization is not only damaging for individuals but leads to systematic and societal discrimination. In the final section of this chapter, policy decisions relevant to bilingualism and Spanish language use in the United States, the direct result of the negative attitudes attested to by Mock Spanish, will be outlined. But first, what about ideologies about English?

The status of English

The US has no official language; while English is the de facto national language, there is no legislation, and has never been, that declares English the official language of the United States. An oft-cited myth is that at one time there was a run-off between German and English for status as the official language of the US, and that English won by one vote; this is an urban legend (see Barron, 1996) akin to stories of alligators coming up out of the toilets in New York City and the tourist who comes home with a dog from Mexico and discovers it's actually a rat. While there were some votes in colonial America concerning language, no language has ever been voted as the official languages of the United States. This is not common knowledge, and is a topic that is touched on in the afore-mentioned posts about 'press 1 for English'. The following excerpts show how even when told they are wrong, some people still cling to the position that English is the official languages of the United States.

(10) If enough Americans refuse to deal with companies that force us to do ANYTHING in order to speak the official language of the USA, we might get somewhere on this. BOYCOTT fascist corporations! (*Alex* on February 18, 2008 at 2:17 pm)

(11) I would like to agree with the fact that it is very irritating at times; however, I do have to play devil's advocate and say that if you really want to get technical there is NO official language in the United States. Yes, English is the language spoken by the majority, but for those who are using the argument that English is the offical [sic] language, I hate to tell you that you are mistaken. It helps to do some research before you start throwing false statements out. (*Melissa* on November 3, 2008 at 1:35 pm)

(12) I would like to start off by saying Melissa, you are an idiot. English IS the official language of the United States. So do not tell others to research your lies, it kind of contradicts your point. (*Dbo* on November 3, 2008 at 4:41 pm)

(13) If I remember right the official language of airline pilots talking to inflight services (controllers, air ports etc.) is english and is a requirement sounds pretty official to me.
(*Dennis M. So Cal.* on February 20, 2009 at 6:09 am)

As can be seen here, the idea that English is not the official language is often rejected, because its naturalized hegemony has never been questioned for many people. Also, what the consequence is of a country having an official language is never addressed; there is no reason that a country with an official language cannot also endorse the use of other languages.

The following sections will give a brief thematic history of language policy in the US to give a general impression of the shifting attitudes about bilingualism and some explanation about where events in social history have brought us to up to this point. Then we will return to the present to examine some specific issues in the language ideologies and policy disputes of today.

Language policies, planning and practices

Having discussed some of the language ideologies at work in US society, we now turn to a historical account of political events and social practices which have both displayed and helped to shape those ideologies. The general term **language policy** is used to describe the more general linguistic, political and social goals which underlie these events and practices; specific attempts to shape language practices are usually referred to as **language planning**.

There are various types of language planning, all of which have occurred in the history of the US. The first type of planning is **status planning**; this involves changing the functions a language fulfills in a particular society and the rights of those who use it. Proposed legislation which declares English the official language is an attempt to do this kind of language planning.

Corpus planning is the development of language variety, usually in terms of standardization. The United States does not have official institutions that determine acceptable English, so this type of planning is done through less direct methods of education and mass media. The teaching of prescriptive grammar in schools and, perhaps more importantly, the discrimination in academic realms against non-standard and non-'native' varieties does not ensure that people speak in certain ways deemed standard, but does influence their attitudes about varieties of English. That is, prescriptive approaches to the study of language encourage students to develop prejudices against those who do not speak standard varieties.

Prestige planning seeks to create a higher social standing for a particular linguistic variety; this type of planning may lead to status planning. For instance, it would be possible to do prestige planning to raise the value of Spanish, and then status planning to declare the US a bilingual nation. Prestige planning is generally not necessary for English in the US, as it enjoys a high level of prestige, but there are grassroots movements to change the prestige of other languages and to encourage the use of them in education – most notably Chinese (Mandarin and Cantonese) and Spanish.

This leads us to the final type of planning, **acquisition planning**, in which efforts are made to have certain populations learn particular languages. Most common are programs to teach English to non-English speakers, but there are growing efforts to offer two-way immersion programs in which English instruction for minority language speakers is combined with teaching Anglophone children the languages of their peers. (See Center for Applied Linguistics (CAL), 2012 for a list of two-way immersion programs in the US.) While foreign language teaching is also part of acquisition planning, in the US it generally has modest goals and does not lead to widespread use of foreign languages.

Language policy in the US

The use of language to gain power relies primarily on the close association between language and social identity, especially national identity. The following section outlines language policy decisions in the US and the underlying ideologies which drive them. There is relatively little written about language ideology in the pre-colonial era or earliest centuries of European settlement, so the main focus of this discussion will be on events and policies during the 1900s and early 2000s.

Despite the long history of linguistic diversity, language rights have never been, and continue not to be, protected in the US. While the constitution and subsequent anti-discrimination policies provide legal means to ensure equal opportunity according to race, color, creed, religion, national origin, disability, sexual orientation, age and gender, it is fine to discriminate against people if you don't like the way they talk. We are not allowed to deny people the right to employment, housing or benefits based on their membership of a particular group (racial, religious or otherwise), but it's considered legitimate for a lay person with no linguistic training to decide that an individual's linguistic competence disqualifies them from employment. In some cases, perhaps all cases, language is a stand-in for the 'real' criteria, which are race, color, creed, religion, national origin, disability, sexual orientation, age, gender, social class or some other association we have with a particular way of speaking (for more discussion of this see Baugh, 2003, and HUD's (2012) advertisement). Our discrimination policies allow scenarios where an employer can't say 'I don't want to hire you because you are Black', but she can say 'I don't want to hire you because I don't think you speak English properly', even if what this really means is 'I don't want to hire you because you sound Black'. There is no easy recourse for showing that 'proper' English is not well-defined and subjectively determined. Similarly, an employer can't say 'I don't hire Latinos', but can say 'I only hire native speakers of English'. There is no way to prove that this criterion is not objective and may just mean 'I don't want to hire people who don't speak like me'.

This allowance of discrimination based on language variety and proficiency is based on the beliefs that there is one acceptable way of speaking and that evaluation of language ability is a straightforward, objective matter. From a linguist's point of view, neither of these views is valid. First, linguistically, all language varieties are created equal. Certain ways of speaking are not linguistically superior to others, and non-standard dialects are not a sign of being lazy or stupid or uneducated. Standard dialects are considered standard because people in power speak them, and they take on the power of their speakers. They are not linguistically more correct than any other dialect.

Second, the 'acceptability' of a person's language use is not something that can be judged objectively. One person's 'unintelligible' is another's 'charming accent' and what some may consider 'cool' may be 'unprofessional' to others. **Matched guise research** has taught us that certain language varieties are thought to sound 'more intelligent' or 'more competent', but this also varies with the listener (Lambert, 2003; Lambert et al., 1966). In short, language, like race, color, creed, and so on, is something about which people hold prejudices – but unlike race, color and creed, it continues to be an area of our society in which we are allowed to act freely and openly on these prejudices.

The policy consequences of these prejudices have been many. One particularly shameful episode in the history of the hegemony of English in the US involved the so-called **Indian Schools**. In 1819, Congress passed the Civilization Act (!!) which allocated money to operate 'mission schools', which were schools for Native American children in which they received instruction in English. The 'Five Civilized Tribes' – the Cherokee, Creek, Choctaw, Chickasaw and Seminole – were allowed to control their own education until 1898 (García, 2009a: 161). Later, the mission of Native language extermination was escalated and the US government built boarding schools for Native American children, who were removed from their parental homes and forced to attend schools where they were forbidden to speak their first languages (García, 2009a: 162).

Unsurprisingly, African languages spoken by slaves fared even worse. The common practice in bringing slaves to the Americas was to mix slaves with different language backgrounds so that they could not communicate with each other in their native tongues (García, 2009a: 162). Many Creolists believe that this social situation gave rise to an English Creole which was the precursor of AAVE (i.e. the variety sometimes colloquially referred to as Ebonics).

European languages were, on the whole, more widely tolerated. German is especially well-known for its strong presence in the early states and colonies, especially Pennsylvania, and as a language used in churches, schools and many areas of government into the 20th century. Hostility towards Germany following the world wars is frequently believed to be the cause of the downward shift in the use of German in the US, although recent research has shown that the language shift was already underway and that the shift to English was not significantly affected by public sentiment (Wilkerson & Salmons, 2008). But it is certainly the case that attitudes towards foreign languages at this time were largely negative; foreign language study was not emphasized in high school curricula and was rare in the lower grades (Ricento, 2009: 116).

Negative attitudes about foreign languages were of course coupled with a focus on English and this is reflected in the 1950 Amendment to the Nationality Act which required English literacy for naturalization as a US citizen. However, this focus on English Only, although clearly a continuing theme in US language ideologies, was challenged in the later 20th century by some ideologies of **pluralism** and corresponding legislation. The Bilingual Education Act (Title VII of the Elementary and Secondary Education Act) was passed in 1968. Although this Act was vague and did little to specify how bilingual education should be put into practice, it was symbolically important in its support for bilingual education for minority children.

In 1975, the Voting Rights Act (originally passed in 1965) was amended to provide non-English language voting notices, forms, ballots and so on, in areas with high populations of speakers of languages other than English. According to Ricento (2009: 117), this amendment '...recognized language as a proxy for "race" or national origin, the categories enumerated in the original (1965) Voting Rights Act' (Ricento, 2009: 117) and worked against the prevention of speakers of languages other than English from voting.

Schmidt (2009: 135) writes of this period, 'By the mid-1970s, then, the foundation for a national shift toward support for linguistic pluralism in the US seemed to be taking shape.' He goes on to cite as evidence the presence of bilingual education programs, the recognition of the legitimacy and value of languages other than English, and what he aptly calls 'economically driven linguistic diversification', as well as multilingual media and a 'pragmatic stance' by local governments about the linguistic diversity in their communities.

So what happened? Somehow assimilation regained hegemonic status and in 1982 an amendment to the constitution was proposed to make English, and only English, the official language of the United States. This amendment did not pass but marked the beginning of a series of attempts to pass bills restricting the use of languages other than English; since that date, over 50 federal bills aimed at making English the official language of the United States have been proposed. None of these bills have passed in both the House and the Senate and some have not passed in either body. So the tide (or worm?) has not turned completely but there is a constant barrage of proposals to make English the official language of the United States of America (see US English, 2012a for more information).

Because of failure at the federal level, more recent effort has been focused on state legislation, and with considerably more success. Many states now have official language policies. At the time of writing, the group US English reports that 29 states have passed legislation declaring English the official language (see US English, 2012b). However, we also see counter-hegemonic ideologies in the English-Plus movement. As described by the Center for Applied Linguistics, '**English Plus** is based on the belief that all US residents should have the opportunity to become proficient in English PLUS one or more other languages' (CAL, 1997). English-Plus resolutions have been passed in New Mexico, Washington, Oregon and Rhode Island. Counties and municipalities with English Plus endorsements include Atlanta, GA; Cleveland, OH; Dallas and San Antonio, TX; Globe, Hayden, Miami, Pima, South Tucson, Superior and Tucson, AZ; Adams County, Boulder County, and Pueblo, CO; and Washington, DC (CAL, 1992).

What exactly the effect is of these official language policies varies considerably. There are three areas of potential influence that I will address in the next pages: bilingual education, workplace practices and policies, and the general issue of providing services in languages other than English.

Bilingual education

Chapter 7 will provide a more thorough discussion of bilingual education, so the focus here is merely legislation which has directly addressed this issue. As mentioned above, the Bilingual Education Act was passed in 1968, and some bilingual programs began to receive federal support to serve minority language speaking children. However, in keeping with the general attitudes regarding bilingualism in the 1980s, such programs were increasingly seen as 'coddling' minority language students (the correct path apparently being to submerge them in English and let them sink or swim). A major blow to bilingual education was struck in 1998, when Proposition 227 was passed in California, mandating English Only schooling. This was followed by Proposition 203 in Arizona in 2000, with the same effect. In 2002, the No Child Left Behind Act renamed the Bilingual Education Act the 'English Language Acquisition Act' (Schmidt, 2009: 136), and the official focus of education in the United States became high standardized test scores; bilingual education was not recognized as an effective means to that end.

However, even as states and municipalities began making laws declaring English the official language, some local school districts began to recognize that **two-way immersion programs** were the best means to serve their student populations. These programs offer bilingual education for both minority language and majority language students; together they learn both languages. Although such programs still represent only a fraction of the opportunities in the US, their numbers have increased exponentially in the last decades (Baker, 2001).

Workplace practices and policies

In 1980, as a result of Garcia v. Gloor, the Equal Employment Opportunity Commission (EEOC) created guidelines to aid businesses in the application of Title VII legislation. According to the guidelines, language is 'often an essential national origin characteristic' and English Only rules are discriminatory if applied at all times, particularly to language used during breaks. However, employers may have an English Only rule if they can show business justification for it. It is important to note that the EEOC cannot create binding laws, but merely offers guidelines, so the reality is that there is a steady stream of court cases on this issue. The defense of languages other than English in the workplace invariably revolves around the idea that people should not be discriminated against for their national origin, and preventing them from using their languages is often a form of such discrimination. Those in favor of policies restricting languages other than English in the workplace invariably include the justification that it is deemed 'inappropriate' because of the surrounding English speakers. Those who do not speak the minority language feel threatened by it, and if they are the managers, they feel they have the right to understand what employees are saying (in some cases, even when the conversation takes place during a break).

Part of the ideology underlying workplace policies, and court decisions supporting firing workers for speaking languages other than English, has to do with an understanding of language proficiency as being an either/or proposition. If employees are described as 'bilingual', then it follows, within this view, that they could speak English in every situation, if only they were willing (see Del Valle, 2009 for a discussion of this). In reality, of course, even fluent bilinguals usually prefer one language over another in certain situations or to discuss certain topics, and many people who may be hired for their ability to (for example) talk to Spanish-speaking customers may be dominant in Spanish and thus have difficulty expressing certain things in English. However, in two subsequent court cases, Garcia v. Spun Steak and EEOC v. Beauty Enterprises, Inc, the ruling was that an English Only policy in the workplace does not injure bilinguals, as they are capable of speaking English and thus can comply with the policy without inconvenience (Del Valle, 2009).

Along with ignoring possible issues of proficiency, this ruling illustrates the claim made above that linguistic discrimination is fully legal in the US. In the Garcia v. Spun Steak case, the court dismissed the idea that being allowed to speak Spanish was part of the right of cultural expression (Del Valle, 2009: 976). Again, this is tied to the idea that speakers can freely choose the language they speak based on instrumental goals, and ignores the possibility that the use of a language may be about culture and identity (Ricento, 2009).

Services in languages other than English

The basic theme in the discourses and policies regarding providing services in languages other than English is equal opportunity for all versus assimilationist nationalism, both of which are (perhaps ironically) ideals based on patriotic sentiments about the United States. On the one hand, the rhetoric goes, we believe in equal opportunity and that means providing services for those who do not (yet) speak English. The assimilationist counter-argument is that this is America and everyone SHOULD speak English and we are only doing people a favor by insisting that they learn it (Schmidt, 2007, 2009); see the above excerpts of the thread on *Why do I have to press 1 for English?* if you have forgotten how this is expressed. The particular services being provided are almost irrelevant; the arguments remain essentially the same. I will give three examples regarding voting forms, driver's license tests and service in a restaurant.

Iowa has long had a law declaring English as the Official Language of the state, but recently application of this law became an issue because voting forms in languages other than English (Spanish, Laotian, Bosnian and Vietnamese) were posted on the secretary of state's webpage. In 2008 a lawsuit was filed by US Representative Steve King, an Iowa Republican, and Polk County District Judge Douglas Staskal ruled that the forms must be removed from the website. Discussion about the ruling was reported in the Des Moines Register:

King issued a statement praising Staskal's decision. 'English is our official language. The English language unites us as a state and as a nation. ... I believe that, and I am thankful that our official English law has been upheld.'

The ruling will have a chilling effect on voter registration for those whose first language isn't English, said Des Moines immigration attorney Lori Chesser.

'It definitely is creating a barrier for them to voting,' Chesser said. 'I don't know how big of an effect that will be, but I think that will fall predominantly on people with less financial means.'

The ruling could be taken as a sign against Spanish-speakers' inclusion in every facet of government, said Jorge Espejel, the Mexican consul in Omaha. (Petroski & Duara, 2008)

The legal issue here relates back to discrimination against people of particular national origins but ideologically the issue is about access: do we, as a nation, want to provide access to participation in our government by people who do not (yet) master English? Part of the problem in this debate has to do with ideas about language in general which I have discussed above; language proficiency is seen as a static, binary phenomenon. The view is that either someone masters English or they do not, and if they do not that is a negative personal characteristic which will not change. There is little understanding about the idea of providing services which function as transitional help for individuals learning English, which is ironic given that this is the misguided idea behind many bilingual programs (see Chapter 7 for a discussion of the lack of effectiveness of transitional bilingual education programs). Mainstream ideas about language seem to view only children as developing linguistic competence in a foreign language – adults either have it or they don't.

Offering driver's license tests in languages other than English is another service which is sometimes controversial, for very similar reasons. In April 2010 an Alabama gubernatorial candidate, Tim James, claimed that if elected he would see to it that driver's license tests would only be offered in English. 'This is Alabama. We speak English. If you want to live here, learn it' he is reported as saying in an editorial in the New York Times (*New York Times*, 2010). As with the voter forms, driver's license tests in languages other than English are framed as catering to the whims of immigrants who 'refuse' to learn English. As a campaign issue, it focuses on **xenophobia** as a voting motivation.

A similar rhetoric around a different service can be found in the press about Geno's Steaks in Philadelphia, an establishment that infamously posted a sign saying 'This Is America: When ordering "speak English"'. The sign/policy of the restaurant got national press and caused controversy. The owner, Joseph Vento, cited the common rationale for such bigotry: his grandparents came from Sicily and they learned English, why can't today's immigrants? Again, the static, binary conception of language proficiency is paramount. This ideology involves a great deal of erasure; the reality and consequences of earlier immigrants and their language proficiencies are whitewashed to an almost meaningless claim. How quickly did they learn English? How well? What restrictions did their limited English place on their lives, and what options did they have for language learning and employment? There is little doubt that the grandchildren of today's immigrants who are struggling to order a cheesesteak will also look back and say, 'MY grandparents learned English when they came to America'. The process of language learning is often, usually even, over-simplified in retrospect. More importantly here, however, the hegemony of English remains intact.

Discussion questions and activities

1. What do you think is the social value of Spanish in the US? That is, is it prestigious to speak Spanish and, if so, in what contexts/which varieties/by whom?

2. Do you think it is reasonable to expect people to speak English at all times in the workplace so that their supervisors and colleagues can understand them? Why or why not?

3. It has been argued (see Arizona Daily Wildcat, 2000) that Mock Spanish is simply the results of the blending of cultures; like language mixing of other sorts, it is natural and inoffensive. What do you think of this position?

4. In 2006 a ringtone named 'Migra' was released by Cingular Wireless that features the sounds of sirens and then a man with a southern accent saying 'I repeat-o, put the oranges down and step away from the telephone-o. I'm deporting you back home-o.' After being condemned from various quarters, it was found to have been produced by Mexican American comic Paul Saucido as a work of satire. If we accept Saucido's contention (see report of an interview with him below) how do we make a distinction between Mock Spanish and 'Mock Mock Spanish'? See the following websites for discussion of this:

   http://itre.cis.upenn.edu/~myl/languagelog/archives/003137.html
   http://www.gearlog.com/2006/05/cingular_la_migra_ringtone_tho.php
   http://vivirlatino.com/2006/05/12/cingular-pulls-la-migra-ringtone.php

5. Go to http://www.cal.org/yol/newyolquiz.html to take a short quiz about language policy in the US.

6. Given that English proficiency is necessary for naturalization in the US, what do you think should be included in an English proficiency test – should it focus on oral proficiency, literacy, knowledge of English (or American) literature, accent-free production...?

Recommended reading

Cepeda, M.E. (2000) *Much loco* for Ricky Martin or the politics of chronology, crossover, and language within the Latino(a) music boom. *Popular Music and Society* 24 (3), 55–71.

García, O. (1993) From Goya portraits to Goya beans: Elite traditions and popular streams in US Spanish language policy. *Southwest Journal of Linguistics* 12 (1–2), 69–86.

Patrick, P. (2005) Linguistic human rights: A sociolinguistic introduction. Online at: http://privatewww.essex.ac.uk/~patrickp/lhr/lhrengonlywork.htm .

Rodriguez, C. (2006) Language diversity in the workplace. *Northwestern University Law Review* 100, 6 –35. NYU Law School, Public Law Research Paper No. 06-35.

2

Language and Identity

Objectives: To introduce students to the process of social identity construction through language and discourse, with a particular focus on Latin@ identities. Who speaks Spanish, why, with whom? All of those questions won't be answered, but you will learn why it's important to ask them.

Social constructionist approaches to identity

The term **identity** is used in contemporary social theory not to talk about one's sense of self as predetermined and static but as something which is fluid, varied and multiple, and determined by social behavior. We call identity 'socially constructed' because identity is not something that exists outside of our construction of it. You may be thinking, wait, but aren't certain aspects of identity – ethnicity and gender, for example – predetermined? Well, yes and no. As we'll discuss in more detail in the next chapter on 'race' and ethnicity, certainly we have physical characteristics which cause us to see ourselves, and be seen by others, in particular social categories – 'White' or 'female', for instance. However, there are many different ways to be female or male, what we call different femininities or masculinities. And 'race' and ethnicity are even more fluid, with the boundaries between categories and the criteria for inclusion in a particular group varying over time, space, culture and even across different interactions.

So the main idea in this chapter is that our identities are not fixed or assigned to us, but something we construct ourselves. Of course we have certain limitations on our identities – how we look, for example, or, as is the focus here, the way we speak. But we also have multiple resources, including language, which can be used in the construction of all of the facets of our identities. As García (2010: 524) writes, 'people do not use language based on their identity, but instead, perform identity using language'.

This chapter will introduce the sociolinguistic and linguistic anthropological literature on how identity is socially constructed through language (Kroskrity, 2000; Mendoza-Denton, 2002). It's important to note that the term 'identity' is used in a myriad of ways in scholarly literature. In many cases, 'identity' is presented as something that can be correlated with other features, such as language use, academic achievement or social network. In such studies, 'identity' is thus viewed as a fixed entity which a person 'has', and this static factor influences what s/he does – for example, if you have a 'Latin@ identity' this correlates with speaking Spanish, and having lots of friends who speak Spanish. In studies such as Potowski (2007), 'identity' is not something which emerges in the discourse, which is how I use the term, but a more static characteristic; in some studies, (e.g. Phinney *et al.*, 1997) identity is portrayed as something that can be ascertained through a questionnaire, thus also a static and quantifiable characteristic of a speaker. This is common in social science research, even in this age where studies which focus on 'identity' as socially constructed have become the dominant paradigm. However, in this text 'identity' is not seen as an attribute of a speaker but something a speaker constructs through social behavior.

Language is not the only type of social behavior that contributes to the construction of identity; how we dress, our body language, the type of food we eat and the music we listen to, along with endless other social activities, all contribute to our social identities. But how we talk and what we say are key ingredients in the construction of identity, and here we will explore the linguistic aspects of identity construction in US Latin@ communities. First, however, I need to present a few more central ideas about the concept of identity: the multiple levels of identity, the multiplicity of identities, the variability of identity and finally, a **non-essentialist** perspective on identity (Bucholtz & Hall, 2004, 2005, 2008).

Social identities are on many levels

Although what is mentioned above are mostly **macro-level demographic categories** of 'race' and ethnicity (Black, White, Latin@) or sex classes (male v. female), our identities are not just about these labels and categories. For example, regardless of the racial or ethnic identity an individual would like to construct, there are times when other aspects of self are equally, if not more, important. At a meeting with my colleagues, I may be first and foremost concerned with my identity as an anthropologist. At a party, I may be constructing myself as a wine connoisseur. When talking to my children's teachers, my identity as a mother may be paramount. These levels of identity are often connected to aspects of identity such as 'race', ethnicity or social class. For instance, my positioning of myself as an anthropologist may be intertwined with a performance of being a member of the educated middle class; in speaking to teachers in my son's Spanish-English bilingual program, my identity as a non-Latina may also be made relevant, or my status as a second language speaker of Spanish. In some interactions membership in such macro-level social categories is of little importance; in others, such as in a discussion about race relations, it may be very important. In most cases, the identities we construct involve all of these levels of identity.

Social identities are multiple

Because we have all of these different aspects of identity, we usually talk about our identities in the plural. No one is just one thing, e.g. a woman; there are also other aspects of identity that are relevant in different interactions (e.g. identity as a manager of a chain of department stores, a lesbian, an avid gardener, an immigrant from Guatemala). In many cases, there are multiple, and sometimes even seemingly conflicting, aspects of our identity that we wish to construct simultaneously. The most difficult conflict is when a person has more than one allegiance in what is perceived as one category – for instance, ethnicity or nationality. This has been discussed as **dual identity** (Attinasi, 1979; Zentella, 1982); for example, a speaker may construct an identity that is both 'Dominican' and 'American'. However, there has also been a more recent trend to look at identities in terms of **hybridity**, a concept which rests on the idea that different languages are combined to create new, hybrid ways of speaking. In this body of literature, there is often a correlation between hybrid codes and hybrid identities (e.g. Bhatt, 2008; Jaffe, 2000; Schutte, 2000; Spitulnik, 1999; Swigart, 1994). Instead of viewing a speaker as going back and forth between two identities, we see speakers as creating a new identity which is a combination of two established categories, e.g. Dominican American. In some cases it is also described as a 'both/and' existence (Moreman, 2008), with shifting identification dependent on context (Anzaldúa, 1999).

A criticism of this perspective, however, is that it assumes that before hybridization the languages and cultures were somehow 'pure'. In some ways this merely imposes the **monoglossic ideology** on the past instead of the present (see Makoni & Pennycook, 2007: 25) and contains an essentialist view of identity categories. However, this approach to the study of US Latin@ language recognizes that bilinguals themselves often perceive their way of speaking and their identities as the mixture of two distinct languages and cultures (Sanchez, 2007). I will work to reconcile these positions below in the section on non-essentialist perspectives on identity. For now, it is important to recognize that everyone, regardless of ethnic or linguistic background, has multiple identities.

Social identities are continually shifting

In addition to simultaneously being multiple, the focus of our identities shifts depending on the social context. In addition to shifts in our identity construction based on the different roles we play in different situations (e.g. professional v. personal facets of identity), we may also shift the way in which we construct our identities to create different types of alignment with other **interlocutors**. A famous (albeit fictitious) example of this can be found in a joke about an interaction in the mythical Wild West between the Lone Ranger (a White guy) and Tonto, his Native American sidekick, shown in (1).

(1)   The old joke goes that the Lone Ranger and Tonto are watching a horde of Indian braves bear down on them in full battle fury. 'Looks like we're in trouble, Tonto,' says the Lone Ranger to his pal. 'What you mean "we," White man?' Tonto responds. (Adventus blogspot, 2006)

Here Tonto, usually portrayed as unswervingly loyal to the Lone Ranger, shifts his alignment with respect to the attacking hordes from opponent to that of a fellow Indian, and his alignment vis-à-vis the Lone Ranger from faithful sidekick to ethnic Other. (I can't help but mention the obvious – part of the reason this is funny, if it is funny, is that in the context of the Lone Ranger radio and TV show, it was the Lone Ranger's acceptance of Tonto which was usually seen as contributing to a heightened status for Tonto, a lowly Redskin; here the tables are turned and it is his very stigmatized Indian identity which may save him.)

While this example is from a joke about characters from a radio and television show, and not an example of a real life interaction, I think we can extrapolate from this to see how such shifts in alignments might work in our own lives. For instance, you may ignore your little brother while at school, instead aligning yourself with your friends, but seek out an alliance with him at home when lobbying your parents for pizza for dinner. You may speak Spanish in a public context to distinguish yourself from the Anglophone mainstream, but English at home to align yourself with your generational peers, in opposition to your parents and their generation of Spanish speakers. Social alignments are not fixed, and we use language to create stances vis-à-vis other speakers. So identities are not static; we need to keep viewing identity as something that we DO, not something we ARE, and our behavior is not always the same. We change how we act and how we talk based on who we are with, our mood, where we are, what we are doing, and so forth.

What I'll be addressing in the next section of this chapter is how language choice – in particular, the use of Spanish or English, or particular varieties of Spanish or English – contributes to the construction if identity. First, however, there is one critical piece of theoretical background about identity I need to cover: **essentialism**.

Towards a non-essentialist perspective on identity

So far, I've been talking about identities as if they are pre-existing categories – as if a person has the identity of a Latin@ or an African American, as a man or a woman, as a doctor or a butcher. It's easy to fall into talking about these categories as if they exist somewhere 'out there' in our culture, and we fit ourselves into them. However, scholars of social constructionism object to this essentialist approach to identity. The main thinking is that we construct our identities in an individual and ongoing fashion; we do not merely place ourselves into pre-existing categories, but create identities and new categories that we may or may not be able to name. Further, named categories are not really internally homogeneous; although we have a sense of what it means to be, for example, 'Chican@', there are in reality many, many different ways of being Chican@ – saliently for the focus of this volume, a Chican@ identity may or may not be constructed through speaking Spanish or Chican@ English.

But, of course, pre-existing categories do exist in our minds and in our cultures, as do our stereotypes about the people we place in those categories. We have labels for groups of people and we are constantly assessing others in terms of how they fit into the different rubrics we have in our heads. The point is that although these categories exist in tangible ways – for instance, in census questions – and that they may exist in our heads and in our language use through named categories, they do not reflect the reality of social identities as we construct them. They may influence how we construct our own identities, but identity categories are not the same thing as identities. First of all, as discussed above, we are more than just the member of a particular category – no one is simply their nationality, ethnic group, gender or occupation. Further, not only do we need multiple levels to talk about our identities, but the social groupings that exist in public discourse do not necessarily match the social identities of particular individuals. For example, we don't have a pre-existing social category for the daughter of a Puerto Rican and a Saudi Arabian who was raised in Chicago. We can't always adequately categorize the social class membership of someone whose parents were a physician and a prison guard and is currently attending junior college. Individuals construct their own identities, and identities are not simply a list of demographics (e.g. White, middle class, middle-aged female). Further, some social categories – socio-economic class categories being the best examples of this – are very difficult to define; what makes a person middle class, or working class, or upper class? Is it how much money they earn, how much education they have, where they live, the way they dress. . .or maybe how they talk? The criteria for membership in a socio-economic class are often murky, and we often judge people's social class by their behavior – which is a clear indicator that socio-economic class identity is socially constructed, not a fixed, objectively determined category.

Additionally, we may not claim all aspects of identity that could be assigned to us. For instance, although others may assign you to the category of middle class, you may identify much more with your working class roots; or while strangers may assume you are White, you may identify as a person of color, and so forth. This is another indication that these categories themselves are socially constructed, and not fixed and permanent.

So we need to get away from thinking of identities as the same as demographic categories. The catch is, of course, that we make use of these pre-existing labels when we construct our identities. We are aware of named social categories, and we construct our identities in relation to them; we may try to fit with the ideals about how an X type of person acts, or we may challenge or resist them. For instance, although I was raised in the Upper Midwestern United States, I will often use the plural form of you, 'ya'll' (something I became accustomed to while living in South Carolina). At times, this is an act of resistance at being pigeonholed as being from Minnesota (where I grew up but have not lived for almost 30 years), although it may also be an attempt to show solidarity with friends from the American South. So while the categories of 'Yankee' and 'South-erner' exist in my mind, and I position myself in relation to them, my construction of myself does not place me easily in either of those social groups.

The way to view these named social categories, however, is not as if they are somehow 'out there', free-floating and autonomous things, some sort of 'culture' that exists separately from people. Instead, these categories, along with identities, are **constituted** through discourse. That is, we do not just construct identities, we also construct identity categories. Both are fluid.

There is an interesting example of how the category of 'Latin@' is being constituted in a series of online columns from *Latina* magazine which names famous people that are assumed to be Latin@ but aren't ('15 stars you thought were Latino – but aren't!', June 13, 2011) and also famous people who are not thought to be Latin@, but are ('¡No me digas! 15 MORE stars you never knew were Latino', July 7, 2011). Although the columns them-selves treat the category of 'Latin@' as something fixed, with concrete criteria, the online discussion clearly indicates that this category is still under construction. The discussion addresses issues such as whether people from Spain are Latin@ (while *Latina* magazine says yes, most of the readers say no), and if it is possible to be Black AND Latin@. *Latina* magazine places these two categories in opposition, as can be seen in example (2), while most readers point out that there are many Dominicans, Puerto Ricans, etc., who would fall into both categories.

(2)　**Reggie Jackson** (born **Reginald Martinez Jackson**) is the legendary New York Yankee who everyone thought was Black, but who is actually Latino. ('¡No me digas! 15 MORE stars you never knew were Latino', July 7, 2011)

Also addressed are issues of mixed ancestry, cultural upbringing (one actor is accused by a reader of being raised by a White momma, and thus not being authentically Latin@), and if the term 'Latin', as a way of describing people, includes those from all countries which speak the languages derived from the Latin language (e.g. Spain, Portugal, Italy). The point of this discussion is not whether *Latina* magazine is 'right' in how it defines being Latin@, but that this category is something which is negotiated. The writers and publisher for *Latina*, as well as the readers, are all involved in the construction of this social category.

So yes, we have named social categories, and the ideas about what it means to be X or Y or Z are important in identity construction. However, those social categories are not identities themselves, but ideologies about identities. They include criteria for inclusion based on ideologies of what is important – as is apparent from the discussion of the *Latina* magazine columns above and, as will be discussed in more detail in the next chapter, the category of 'Latin@' being defined by some according to blood or appearance, by some based on nationality and geography (with conflicting ideas about what countries count), and by still others based on language and culture. And how these individuals construct themselves may be important in how they are perceived. For instance, speaking Spanish may outweigh being blonde and fair because it is a common **index** of Latin@ identity.

If all of this gives you the feeling that the sand is shifting beneath your feet, then good, you are still with me! This is complicated material. In the rest of this chapter, I'll be discussing research on Latin@ language and identity construction in the US, and providing more concrete examples which will hopefully make you feel as if you are on firmer ground.

Identity construction through language use

Identity is seen as not the source but the outcome of linguistic practice (Bucholtz & Hall, 2005); that is, we don't speak a certain way because of our identity, we have particular identities because we speak in certain ways. As discussed above, the term 'identity' is used to discuss the speakers' identification with social categories of all types – not just enduring social categories such as 'race' but also situational roles such as 'class clown'. Further, part of identification is positioning oneself with respect to other people, particularly as similar or different from the people you are addressing or talking about.

When I talk about language use, this is meant to encompass everything about how we speak – what varieties we use, what kind of accent we have, what words we choose to use, if we interrupt or listen silently or say 'right on' while others are talking, and so on and so forth (see Fought, 2006: 21–23; Kroskrity, 2000: 111). That said, my main focus is on the first item on that list – the varieties we use, with special attention to Spanish and English.

One thing to be clear on when talking about language choice and identity is that there is no one-to-one correspondence between a particular variety and a particular identity (Blackledge & Pavlenko, 2001, 2002). There are, of course, common associations. So if someone speaks Spanish, many people are going to assume this means that they 'have' (or 'are doing') a Latin@ identity – especially if they 'look Latin@', that is, have an appearance which corresponds to the hearer's ideas about the phenotype of Latin@s (such ideas will be discussed more in the next chapter). But in reality, speaking Spanish may have a lot of additional social meanings, depending on the speaker's experiences with the language. It may convey intimacy, especially among family members, if it was the language the speaker grew up speaking in the home. It may be a language used to convey defiance, if it was discouraged or even disallowed in the school context. On the other hand, English might be the language used for defiance in the home, if the speakers' parents want them to speak Spanish. For some people, speaking Spanish may have social class connotations; for emigrants from Latin America who also speak indigenous languages, it may be the language of middle class standing or aspirations; for people in the US it may carry associations of a working class existence. Some may find the use of Spanish part of a masculine identity in an ethnic community; others may associate speaking Spanish with women's roles in a traditional Latin@ home. None of these associations are more accurate than others; they are all attitudes which could grow out of someone's personal experience with Spanish and its speakers. It is possible for one individual to have all of these social meanings for Spanish, and more. So, our starting place is an assumption that the sociopragmatic meanings of certain ways of speaking are not fixed; these meanings are produced and reproduced through discourse.

For example, in one group of four fourth graders that I studied in my research in a Spanish-English bilingual classroom (Fuller, 2007, 2010), the two girls in this cohort were more proficient in **colloquial** English than the two boys. This is not indicative of some overall pattern in Latin@ communities, or in this particular Mexican American community, or even in this classroom. It just so happened that of these four fourth graders, the two girls had been in the US longer than their male counterparts, and they were more oriented toward English and US popular culture than the boys. Because these four children spent a lot of time together in the bilingual classroom, the girls' relative proficiency in English became socially significant: I suggest that English became associated with being a girl (Fuller, 2010). The boys, who because of less exposure to English were already more inclined to speak Spanish in their social interactions, were motivated even more to do so because speaking English, in their experience within this cohort, was something that girls did. However during English instruction, the boys readily used English because in that context it helped to construct their identities as good students and knowledgeable people, which was part of constructing their masculine identities. So, speaking English was avoided because it made them sound like the girls – except in contexts where it made them sound more like boys. Clear and simple? No, never. But these 10-year-old children had already mastered the concept of shifting meanings of language choices; they did it every day. (And you do too, even if you don't know it yet.)

Identities in bilingual discourse: Translanguaging

This section will focus on the concept of 'translanguaging' (García, 2011a, 2011b; Li Wei, 2011), with a mention of some parallel terms: 'crossing' (Rampton, 1995), 'languaging' (Jørgensen, 2003, 2008) and 'metrolingualism' (Otsuji & Pennycook, 2010). These concepts are not all identical, but all describe a way of resisting monoglossic ideologies through the use of multiple languages, dialects, registers, styles, and so on, of speaking. That is, these authors focus on the idea that all speakers use linguistic resources from various sources – not just a single standard language – to express themselves. Further, these varieties are not in a one-to-one relationship with particular identity categories. For Latin@s, this means that they make use of both Spanish and English. Further, they use different varieties of Spanish and English, and perhaps other languages, which are not necessarily ways of indexing their belonging to clear social categories such as 'Mexican' or 'American', but also other aspects of their social identities, roles and relationships.

The study of the use of two or more languages in a single conversation has often been called **codeswitching**, and there is a large body of literature about how code choice can be used to construct identity. These studies deal with languages as separate and distinct entities. However, there has been a recent shift in focus in the study of multilinguals to look at how speakers challenge the ideology of normative monolingualism. This research is interdisciplinary, and incorporates perspectives and foci from the social sciences and education (Canagarajah, 2011).

Work by Rampton (1995, 1999) addresses the issue of **crossing**, looking at how children in multilingual and multicultural neighborhoods in London make creative use of varieties not normally associated with the ethnic group to which they are assigned. This term thus emphasizes that speakers cross, or perhaps re-negotiate, the boundaries between languages and between the social groups associated with them.

Jørgensen (2003, 2008) discusses polylingual **languaging** in the speech of Turkish heritage children in Denmark, who combine various varieties of Turkish, Danish, Swedish, German and English (the latter three being languages they do not speak fluently, but can produce some phrases in) to position themselves vis-à-vis the other children in their schools. This work focuses on how speakers, and especially youths, employ all of the linguistic resources at their disposal; thus monolinguals are also 'languagers' (Jørgensen, 2003: 146), just with a different type of repertoire. Otsuji and Pennycook (2010: 246) introduce the term **metrolingualism**, saying it:

describes the ways in which people of different and mixed background use, play with and negotiate identities through language; it does not assume connections between language, culture, ethnicity, nationality or geography, but rather seeks to explore how such relations are produced, resisted, defied or rearranged; its focus is not on language systems but on languages as emergent from contexts of interaction.

The term **translanguaging**, which is the term which will be adopted in this text, similarly challenges the idea of distinct languages with distinct functions and instead describes language use in which the boundaries between languages are permeable (Creese & Blackledge, 2010; García, 2009c). Like metrolingualism, it abandons the one-to-one correlations between language and ethnic identity in favor of a 'more fluid positioning of identity' (García, 2010: 522). Much of the literature on this topic has to do with multilingual education (e.g. Creese & Blackledge, 2010; García, 2011a, 2011b).

In sum, the concept of translanguaging is concerned with the following four interrelated themes. First, heteroglossia is recognized. The goal is to move beyond the concept of multilingualism, which assumes multiple, but still distinctly separate, languages, to focus on complexity instead of plurality. The different forms of language involved include different ways of speaking that may be part of one language, two languages, or many languages (Bailey, 2007).

Second, translanguaging as a concept seeks to get away from essentialist categories; it goes beyond the idea of hybridity, which can become as fixed a category as the original categories (Otsuji & Pennycook, 2010), to focus on fluidity and variability of language and its relationship to identity.

Third, the concept of translanguaging brings to the forefront the idea that the particular languages (as well as the general concept of languages as distinct systems) are social constructions based on ideologies about language. Boundaries between languages are sociohistorical constructions, meaning that they develop through the political and social events that give particular languages meaning, and they change over time (Bailey, 2007). An example of this that might help make it clearer is that 'Serbo-Croatian' used to be what we called a language spoken in Yugoslavia; now, with political and social change, 'Serbian' and 'Croatian' are considered separate languages. So while speakers do not necessarily use languages in ways which adhere to social boundaries, the social context in which languages are named and deemed standard or non-standard is part of the heteroglossic nature of translanguaging.

Fourth, translanguaging is often seen as creating a transnational and multilingual space; so along with challenging the idea that certain languages 'belong' to certain groups of people, it also challenges the idea that certain languages 'belong' in certain spaces.

> ...it creates a social space for the multilingual language user by bringing together different dimensions of their personal history, experience and environment, their attitude, belief and ideology, their cognitive and physical capacity into one coordinated and meaningful performance, and making it into a lived experience. (Wei, 2011: 1223)

In (3) to (6) below, I provide some examples of bilingual discourse from my own research on Spanish-English bilingual pre-teens. In Chapter 5, we will return to similar examples to discuss structural aspects of bilingual discourse. In (3) and (4), both English and Spanish elements are used within a single utterance by an individual. In (5), one speaker switches from Spanish to English as she goes from one sentence to the next. In (6), the first speaker uses Spanish, the second speaker uses English. In the remainder of this chapter, I will address how such translanguaging among Latin@s constructs social identity.

(3) /¡dejala! ¡dejala! por que luego te metes en problems./
     ['Leave it leave it because then you get in trouble']
(4) xxx es que kickó maestra!
     ['what happened was that he kicked me teacher!']
(5) *Por qué no se enseña que queremos (saber)?* (.) Open that!
         'Why don't they teach us what we want (to know)?'
(6) JMF: *No puedo leer (.) porque es (.) demasiado pequeño.*
          'I can't read because it's too small.'
     D: O/kay, I'll read./

Language choice and identity among Latin@s in the US

To summarize the above, a social constructionist approach to the study of bilingual discourse and identity stresses the fluid and multiple nature of identities and languages. Different varieties can construct a number of different identities, and different levels of identity may be simultaneously constructed through language use. Speakers are assumed to construct their identities by orienting themselves towards their interlocutors as well as towards societal norms.

Further, the terminology of 'identity construction' is indicative of a less essentialist and more fluid concept of the identities or roles of speakers. That is, speakers are not merely indexing a pre-existent identity category, but constructing something new and unique.

One of the common findings in studies on bilingual discourse is that a particular language does not have one constant social meaning; social meanings are locally constructed (see examples in Cashman, 2005 and Fuller, 2010). However, particular languages do, of course, have salient associations, and these associations often have to do with national or ethnic background. In the United States, it is not uncommon to hear all Spanish speakers referred to as 'Mexicans', and the Spanish language called 'Mexican'. This is a crass example of overgeneralization of the association between language and nationality, and usually associated with negative depictions of the so-called Mexicans. Note these definitions from Urban Dictionary:

(7)   Mexican
The Language that Mexicans speak. Not related to spanish.
'That Mexican was speaking Mexican to me. He asked me if I wanted to buy any orangi-noes or mangones.' (Urban Dictionary, 2012a)
(8)   mexican
Any person of ibero-american heritage who speaks spanish in america.
dude 1: 'That cleaning lady is a fucking mexican!'
dude 2: 'No, she's from puerto rico.'
dude 1: 'Exactly!' (Urban Dictionary, 2012b)

Lest the reader assume I am condemning all Urban Dictionary contributors, I hasten to add that most of the posts under 'Mexican' made reference to the fact that all Spanish speakers are not Mexican, and that 'Mexican' is not the name of a language. So my point is not that all, or even most, contributors to Urban Dictionary have offensive and ignorant attitudes – my point is that these attitudes are prevalent enough that people feel they are entitled to state them in public.

Such associations of the Spanish language with national or ethnic identity are not solely assigned by outsiders; these associations are also made evident by some Spanish speakers. In some cases, being able to speak Spanish is presented as a sign of **authenticity**; that is, Spanish language proficiency makes someone authentically Mexican, Puerto Rican, etc. Shenk (2007) gives an example of this in discourse among Mexican American college students; when one mispronounces the word *jueves* 'Thursday', a friend corrects her and jokes, 'I'm revoking your Mexican privileges.' (Shenk, 2007: 211). And although there are many other criteria invoked for claiming Mexican (or any other national) identity – where one was born, one's ancestry, for instance – language is frequently viewed as an important ethnic or national identity marker. Many studies report that children, grandchildren, and so on, of emigrants from Spanish-speaking countries report feeling self-conscious if they lack Spanish competence, and language shift is often seen as a loss of ethnic identity (see Chapter 5 for more on language maintenance and shift).

The attitude that the lack of Spanish language skills means the lack of authentic Chican@ identity is reported by Bejarano (2005) in her work on youth culture on the Mexico/Arizona border. Of course, Spanish is not the only language which marks group membership; English is also a salient marker of belonging, indexing a Chican@ identity as opposed to a Mexican@ one. Yet the distinction between Chican@ and Mexican@ is not clear-cut, and can certainly not be determined by language proficiency; people who have Mexican citizenship may have come to the US at a young age and speak English natively, and people born in the US may be dominant in Spanish. So here we see quite clearly that there is no one-to-one correspondence between language and ethnic identity; ethnicity may be shared but orientation towards US culture – and especially the English language – may be used to further differentiate between members of what may be seen as the same ethnic group. National belonging, along with other aspects of identity, is also something that is constructed, by people themselves but also by others' ideas of what it means to be authentically 'American', 'Mexican', etc.

The tension between relative newcomers to the US and those who have lived in the US for all or most of their lives is a common theme in studies of immigrant language use. In Bailey's work on Dominican Americans, he reports an example from a conversation between two teenage girls in which one speaker says to another 'You're a bootleg, I forgot'. As Bailey explains, '"bootleg Dominicans" are those individuals who are Dominican by parentage but who lack the traits of true, authentic Dominicans' (Bailey, 2001: 212–213). So these speakers imply that it detracts from one's authenticity as a Dominican to not have experience living in the Dominican Republic. However, being too closely associated with the Dominican Republic is also a bad thing. In an example involving the same two teenage girls, one of the girls complains about a boy she is dating 'And he's like – I don't know, he talk, he's like a hick, he talks so much Spanish!' (Bailey, 2001: 210). In this case, speaking Spanish is seen as part of the construction of a Dominican identity that is undesirable; more orientation to the US, as signaled by speaking English, is preferable. The boy is also described as undesirable because he is jealous and possessive; although it is not explicitly stated that this is also linked to his Dominican identity, the implication is strong that this is a trait more common with Dominican than American-oriented men/boys. Speaking 'too much' Spanish therefore indexes a particular type of Dominican male. It is important to note that this girl herself uses Spanish in conversations with her friends; thus it is not that speaking Spanish is categorically bad. Quite the contrary, being able to speak Spanish is an important part of being Dominican American, an identity that these speakers often emphasize. But this identity is one which requires a careful balance of knowledge of Dominican language and culture and integration into US society.

This discussion leads us back to the idea of hybridity. I have stated above that everyone has multiple aspects to their identity which are sometimes conflicting and must be balanced; in this sense, we all have hybrid identities. But there are some hybrids that are more difficult to maintain than others. For example, belonging, in one way or another, to two national groupings is something that is seen as a deviation from the norm. The balancing act done by the Dominican Americans in Bailey's study is in some ways not unique; what makes it more salient is that it is about nationality. Many people do a similar balancing act around their gender identity, trying to be feminine but not too girly, masculine without being too macho. The difference is that this is a more universal experience; many people in the US never have to give any thought to being 'too American' or 'not American enough' for their friends or families. However, people with immigrant backgrounds must contend with this on a daily basis. Not only may they have friends who have different orientations to the US or the ancestral homeland, there are often generational differences, and they need to act differently than they might around their friends in order to show their parents that they are authentically part of the ethnic group.

Racial categorization also plays a role in identification as a speaker of a minority language. Speaking Spanish in the US is often considered an index of non-White identity, as the generalization is that people from Latin America are 'Brown'. This raises issues for Latin@s who are classified as 'White' or 'Black' in terms of how they are pigeonholed by others, and how they construct their own identities (in part as a response to this pigeonholing). For instance, looking at Bailey's and Toribio's (Bailey, 2000, 2001, 2002; Toribio, 2003, 2006) work on Dominican Americans, we see multiple examples of how the use of English and Spanish helps to construct racial identities. In one example from Bailey's work, a speaker uses the term 'bro' to address Wilson, a fellow Dominican American; based on Bailey's ethnographic research and interviews with these interlocutors, he interprets this term as associated with AAVE and part of the complex negotiation of ethnic and 'racial' identity (Bailey, 2000: 565). But across interactions, Wilson's identity as 'Spanish' (a term commonly used by Dominican Americans to describe themselves) is sometimes seen in contrast with being 'Black' and sometimes incorporates 'Blackness' (see Bailey, 2001, 2002). Generally, some (Black) Dominicans in both Bailey's and Toribio's studies will speak Spanish to construct an identity that is distinct from African Americans, but there are also instances in which Black Dominicans will use their appearance to pretend to be something other than Dominican. For instance, in one example Wilson and his friend Eduardo are joking around and tell Bailey that Wilson is from Haiti (Bailey, 2000: 566).

Similarly, Toribio (2003) examines the issue of 'race' and language loyalty among Dominican Americans in a study looking at one Black Dominican American family and one White Dominican American family. She found that for the Black Dominican Americans, Spanish was key in differentiating themselves from African Americans; for the White Dominican Americans, who were more readily integrated into a mainstream society which values Whiteness, Spanish was more of an impediment to integration than a positive aspect of identification.

Urciuoli discusses this 'racialization of language difference' (1996: 35) as also involving social class; often non-White and Spanish-speaking identities are assigned a working class value. For the Puerto Rican bilinguals she interviewed, there was a sense that class mobility required linguistic conformity, which meant speaking monolingual English (not using Spanish, and not translanguaging). However, it was difficult to balance the construction of this upwardly mobile English speaker with a Puerto Rican identity; conforming to mainstream ways of speaking had the positive potential of aiding the climb up the social class ladder, but also ran the risk of being viewed as 'acting White', a denial of ethnic and 'racial' identity (Urciuoli, 1996: 173).

In the next chapter, we will delve deeper into the concepts of 'race' and ethnicity and their relationship to the language of Latin@s in the US. The theme of language as a means of constructing Latin@ identity will also be re-visited in Chapter 4, on media representations of Spanish speakers, and in Chapter 8, on Latin@ education in the US.

Discussion questions and activities

1. Are there aspects of your own identity that you could describe as 'hybrid'? Are you sometimes assigned an identity that you don't want to claim? Write a short essay about the multiple layers and variation in your own identity, discussing particular situations in which you claim particular identities.

2. Do you speak different ways in different situations? Give an example, framing this description within a social constructionist approach to the study of language and identity.

3. How is language choice a part of the construction of social identity in the following excerpt?
   Setting and interlocutors:
   JMF is the researcher, who is reading a story with the children about three children, ages 11, eight and three, who were left alone to fend for themselves. In line one of this excerpt, JMF asks the children's age in order to contextualize this aspect of the story (see her attempt to return to this in line 23), unwittingly opening up the opportunity for an age dispute. R, M, D and A are all fourth graders.

   1 JMF: How old are you guys.
   2 R, M, D: I'm nine. I'm nine, I'm nine.
   3 D: I'm almost ten.
   4 R: I'm nine.
   5 M: He's eight.
   6 D: He's eight.{pointing at A} He =
   7 A: = {protesting} 9.
   8 M: ¡A que sí! !A / que sí /!
      'Uh-huh! Uh-huh!'
   9 A: {protesting}/ <u>nine</u> /
   10 M: Tienes ocho.
      ' [You]'re eight.'
   11 R: <u>nine</u>!
   12 D: He's eight.
   13 M: Ocho
      'Eight.'
   14 A: ¡Dije nueve!
      'I said nine!'
   15 D: He's eight, *ocho*, he's eight.
      'eight,'
   16 A: Unh-unh, I'm nine!
   17 M: ¡A que no! Tienes ocho.
      'Unh-unhh! You're eight.'
   18 JMF: Uhm, so who in this classroom is eleven years old?
   19 R: Eleven?
   20 D: Some of them {pointing to the fifth grade group}
   21 JMF: So maybe, if the fifth / graders are eleven /
   22 M: / I'm <u>9</u>. /
   23 JMF: So say, J- was x J- was in charge /of / an eighth grader [sic] and a 3 /year old/
   24 M: /He's seven / (1.5)   /he's seven./

Discussion questions and activities (continued)

25 D: I'm almost ten.

26 M: Uh-huh, he's seven {meaning A-}

27 R: I'm nine. He's nine. All, all of us are nine.

28 M: ¡A que no! !Tú no! {directed at A}
   'Unh-unhh! No, you're not.'

29 R & D: ¡A que sí!
   'Uh-huh!'

30 M: ¡A que no!
   'Unh-unhh!'

31 D: ¡A /que siii!/
   'Uh-huh!'

32 R: /El nació en / el mismo año que / yo. /
   'He was born in the same year I was.'

33 JMF: /Okay/, wait (2) the next page.

Does it change your analysis of the conversation at all if you know that:

a. All of these children have Spanish as their first language?

b. A and M are boys while R and D are girls?

c. The researcher JMF is English dominant and the children usually address her in English?

d. A and M are rivals, and R and A are cousins?

Recommended reading

Aldave, C. (2010) Chad Ochocinco, Black Mexicans & Afro-Latino Identity. *Heavy Mentalist*. Online document: http://www.heavymentalist.com/2010/07/chad-ochocinco-black-mexicans-afro-latino-identity/

Carris, L.M. (2011) 'La voz gringa': Latino stylization of linguistic (in)authenticity as social critique. *Discourse & Society* 22 (4), 474–490.

Lopez-Rosas, M. (2011) La Casa hosts talk on Latino identity. *Yale Daily News*, March 23. Online document: http://www.yaledailynews.com/news/2011/mar/23/la-casa-hosts-talk-on-latino-identity/

Mahootian, S. (2005) Linguistic change and social meaning: Codeswitching in the media. *International Journal of Bilingualism* 9 (3/4), 361–375.

Mendoza-Denton, N. (2008) *Homegirls: Language and Cultural Practice among Latina Youth Gangs*. Oxford: Blackwell Publishing.

3
'Race', Ethnicity and Spanish Speakers in the US

Objectives: To introduce the concepts of 'race' and ethnicity as culturally constructed categories, and explain how these concepts are related to the study of Spanish speakers in the US.

This chapter is structured as follows. The first section addresses the concept of 'race' and the second shows how this concept has been applied in studies of Latin@ groups. In the third section, the related concept of ethnicity is defined and discussed, followed by an introduction to how both of these concepts – along with nationality – are related to the study of language and social identity. Throughout this chapter, we discuss how scholarly work on these subjects and popular ideas about them are related.

'Race' as a social construct

Most people tend to think of 'race' as a biologically determined way of categorizing people which is neither debatable nor changeable. This is certainly the way 'race' is talked about and dealt with in US society; for instance, we have to assign ourselves to a particular 'race' when we fill out forms and we are expected to always assign ourselves to the same category.

So what does it mean when social scientists say that 'race' is 'socially constructed'? First, I want to make it clear what this does NOT mean – it doesn't mean that biological differences do not exist or that only racists notice these differences. The basic idea about the social construction of 'race' is that how we deal with physical differences (not the physical differences themselves) is culturally determined. The concept of 'race' is not just about dividing people into categories without reason; those categories are used to explain the behavior of their members (Wade, 2008: 178). Which physical traits are considered important for categorizing people and how many racial categories we have are things that are cultural; they vary across societies and also over time. Further, what the relationships are assumed to be between people who have different physical characteristics and what social traits are associated with the particular **phenotypes** are all things that vary historically and from one society to the next. Thus the use of the quotation marks around the term 'race' is an indication that this is not an objective biologically determined category but a social one (Chancer & Watkins, 2006: 49).

Physical anthropologists who study skeletal remains talk about 'race' in terms of **human variation**. This means that people vary physically along numerous continua; some often- mentioned features of living people that can be viewed in this way involve skin color, hair color and texture, and eye color. However, it should be noted that there is more variation WITHIN racial categories than BETWEEN them. According to the American Anthropological Association's Statement on 'Race':

> Evidence from the analysis of genetics (e.g. DNA) indicates that most physical variation, about 94%, lies *within* so-called racial groups. Conventional geographic 'racial' groupings differ from one another only in about 6% of their genes. This means that there is greater variation within 'racial' groups than between them. In neighboring populations there is much overlapping of genes and their phenotypic (physical) expressions. Throughout history whenever different groups have come into contact, they have interbred. The continued sharing of genetic materials has maintained all of humankind as a single species. (American Anthropological Association, 1998: italics in original)

Human variation is often mapped on to social categories. Forensic anthropologists (as we know from watching TV) are asked to assign **demographic information** to human remains with the most common ones being sex, age and 'race'. The general process of categorizing human remains involves comparison of the skeleton with standards developed from other skeletal collections (Nafte, 2000: 83ff.). While none of these features can be ascertained reliably with a single glance (despite what is shown on the TV series *Bones*), at least with sex and age there are relatively stable social categories to which we can assign the remains. Most adult skeletons can be put in the category of male or female with an analysis which focuses primarily on the pelvis and the skull (Nafte, 2000: 87–92). Growth and wear of the bones and teeth can give us some idea of the age of a person at the time of death.

However, with racial categorization there is a different problem: we do not have stable systems of racial categorization across either space or time. Within physical anthropology, a standard three-race model was used for some time (Mongoloid [Asian], Caucasoid [White] and Negroid [Black]), but this was expanded in the 1990s to include Australoid [Melanesian/Australian], American Indian and Polynesian (Nafte, 2000: 111). Regardless of the classification scheme, there are several problems with classification. First, the unknown material is compared to known samples, but these samples are based on geographical region, with the idea being that people of a particular region belonged to a certain 'race'. But the skeletons from the samples may or may not have been people who would fit into contemporary racial categories in a particular society. Further, the use of these categories relies on the assumptions that particular physical traits are 'inherited in a consistent pattern and can be generalized into well-defined geographic categories', which are problematic assumptions (Nafte, 2000: 111). I'm sure you know people who look nothing like their biological parents or their biological siblings, for instance. And although we have stereotypes about what it means to look 'Asian' or 'Scandinavian', a visit to Asia or Scandinavia reveals that there is a lot of variation in the appearance of the people who live there and much of it has nothing to do with recent immigration patterns.

Nonetheless forensic anthropologists are asked to provide information on the racial categorization of the remains they work with and so they comply. To do this they look at **craniofacial traits**, which involve the face, cranium and mandible (Nafte, 2000: 111–113), as well as looking at the length of long bones like the femur or tibia bones in the leg (Nafte, 2000: 114). Again, the size and shape of these bones are compared to standards developed from looking at known populations and the similarities can be assessed to see how particular skeletal remains fit into the categories thus established.

While the TV show *Bones*, which features a forensic anthropologist, is quite unrealistic in many regards, in several episodes it does address an aspect of categorization of skeletal remains which is a bit more true to life: in some cases, skeletons have characteristics of more than one racial category, or traits which are not clearly in one category or the other. So part of the problem with saying that 'race' is based on biological differences is that those differences are along a continuum and not in discrete groups. Even if we manage to establish categories based on statistical differences, there are many people who have physical characteristics of more than one racial category.

Although this discussion of forensic anthropology is clearly very simplified, hopefully it has made one thing clear: the biological differences between 'races' are difficult to establish. This doesn't mean that some people don't have phenotypic features which we associate with particular racial categories and it doesn't mean that we should pretend we don't notice these physical differences. But it does mean that perhaps those differences are not as absolute or as linearly inherited as we are often led to believe by popular discourse about 'race'.

How the continuum of human variation is divided up is cultural and how people who do not fit neatly into one category are viewed is also culturally specific. In the United States, most people – like President Obama – who have one White parent and one Black parent are categorized as 'Black'. This is based on the historical context of contact between people of African descent and people of European descent in the United States. The colloquial phrase 'the one drop rule' makes reference to the idea that anyone with any trace of sub-Saharan ancestry is not accepted as 'White' (see BlackHistory.com, 2008). This is indicative of the cultural perspective on Whiteness in the US. Whiteness is something which is 'pure' while Blackness is something which is maintained even when diluted. This is because of the cultural value of Whiteness over Blackness; it has nothing to do with biology.

But let's back up even farther; not only are the distinctions between racial categories cultural but the importance of this type of physical characteristic is also entirely based on societal norms. Historically we see two patterns of behavior that contrast with how we conceive of racial/ethnic categories in the US. First, in many cultures such differences were not important in social organization (I'll discuss this in more detail below). Second, there are countless examples of how people and groups adapted and changed their ethnic identities; that is, they changed from being perceived as belonging to group X to being considered a member of group Y. This mutability of people and fluidity of identification was more the norm than the rule and is still often the case (although rarely acknowledged). I'll come back to this point later in the chapter when I discuss the concept of ethnicity.

There is no objective reason that phenotypic differences need to be integral to social organization and they were not in all earlier societies. 'Race' as an organizing principle in society became widespread as late as the 1700s. There are many other aspects of human identity that are usually deemed much more important. Some of them, such as occupation, are based on choices made by individuals. Others are related to biology; for instance kinship is an important way in which people identify in most societies. And even in US society, in which 'race' is seen as an integral part of a person's identity, kinship trumps 'race' in terms of importance in social connection for most of us. Many families contain people of what are considered to be different 'races' for a myriad of reasons, adoption and biological parents of difference 'races' being two of the more obvious and common reasons. So while 'racial' differences have been **naturalized** to seem as if they are facts and not cultural constructions, at the same time we can see that they need not be the most important way of categorizing people.

In the Greco-Roman tradition there was no systematic structuring of inequalities or social relationships which relied on skin color or other phenotypic characteristics as a means of determining a person's social worth. Herodotus, a 5th century B.C. Greek historian, is often cited on this topic (see Smedly, 1999: 693) as saying that although he noted physical differences of some social groups, characteristics such as dark skin and 'wooly hair' were not unique to any group. Physical differences such as skin color were attributed to different living environments – 'the sunny south generating blackness, the north "glacial whiteness"' (Hornblower & Spawforth, 1996: 1293). More importantly, these characteristics were not used to determine the social status of groups of people in Greek and Roman societies. Although slavery did exist, people were enslaved for political reasons (i.e. their communities were conquered) not because of their membership in a particular 'racial' group. While Greco-Roman culture was profoundly ethnocentric and idealized their own culture and people far above all others, the inferiority of others was not based on physical traits but cultural customs and practices (Hornblower & Spawforth, 1996: 1293).

Given this historical background, we can see that our focus on a set of biological differences as important to a person's social identity is not a given. While many, probably even most, contemporary societies have adopted this practice, 'race' was not a universal **social construct** in earlier times.

There are also many different systems of racial categorization. The US is often described as a culture in which there is a racial binary – if you are not White, you are Black – although this appears to be changing (Waterston, 2006). However this binary system is by no means the only way, or even the most common way, to divide up the continuum of skin colors and other associated physical traits. To give just one example, in South Africa there is a notoriously tripartite system of White, Black and Colored; while people who tracked their ancestors back to India were the most common members of the 'Colored' category, there were others who did not meet the criteria for White or Black who were also in this group. How the different systems of racial categorization from Latin America impact US Latin@s, and how Latin@s impact the system of racial categorization in the US, will be the topic of the next section.

'Race' in Latin@ studies

This section provides a very quick discussion of systems of 'race' in Latin America, and then moves on to address 'race' and Latin@ status in the US in slightly more depth. In both contexts, we will see that 'race' is intertwined with socio-economic class: the higher a person's social class, the more Whiteness is attributed to them.

Racial categorization systems in Latin America tend not to be binary. This difference to the binary US system is in part due to the history of Latin America; Portuguese and Spanish colonialists, Africans (often brought to the '**New World**' as slaves), and the indigenous populations were mixed and created *mestiz@s* who were considered socially distinct from parents who were generally considered to belong to one particular 'racial' category. Post-colonial immigration of people from Asia and the Middle East also contributed to the mixing of people of purportedly difference 'races' (Wade, 2008: 179). It should be noted however, that in many ways this history is not so vastly different from that of what is now the US: Europeans colonized an area that was already inhabited by indigenous people, brought Africans into the society (for the most part against their will), and sexual contact led to offspring of 'mixed race'. Yet how this 'mixture' was viewed has created differences between the US and Latin America.

One important distinction between the US and Latin America in ideas about 'racial mixing' was how children of parents assigned to different 'races' were classified. In Latin America, we can generally say that they were assigned to the new category of *mestiz@* (although keep in mind here, and in all of this discussion, that Latin America is not homogeneous; this is painting the picture with very broad strokes). Instead of a binary system, which ignored many deviations, in Latin America there were more racial categories. How many categories and what they were called and what social behaviors were associated with them varied, and vary greatly across and within Latin American countries. For instance in some areas on the southern Pacific coast of Mexico, the category of *moreno* (used to describe what in the US we might call 'Black') is a significant category for local social organization (Lewis, 2000). In other places, such as Michoacán, there are few people with sub-Saharan African ancestors and this category is far less relevant than identification with indigenous or non-indigenous ancestry (Farr, 2006).

In Farr's work on Mexican emigrants living in Chicago we see another example of how 'race' is socially constructed. While all of the people in Farr's study acknowledged some indigenous ancestry, many of them nonetheless categorized themselves as non-indigenous, a status which carried higher social status in their perspectives. The identification as 'non-indigenous' had little to do with their appearance: some were fair-skinned and had blue or green eyes; others had darker skin and brown eyes. The word they used to describe themselves was *ranchero*, which literally means 'rancher'. However this term signified more than occupation – use of the term *ranchero* was their way of distinguishing themselves from others they might call *mestiz@*, a term they did not use to refer to themselves despite their acknowledgment of mixed (i.e. European and indigenous) ancestry.

North of the Rio Grande, the manner of classifying children born of parents from what were considered different 'races' has been quite different. In the US, children were generally placed in the category of the parent in the subordinate social status; for example, children born of one White and one Black parent were considered Black, as Whites had higher social status. This practice of categorization continues today; people who have any 'Black' phenotypic features are categorized as 'Black' or 'African American' even if they also have 'White' phenotypic features.

Further differences between the Latin American systems and the US system came through the fact that *mestiz@s* in Latin American became the majority group in many countries by the late 18th century (Wade, 2008: 179). Of course this occurred in part because mestiz@ existed as a social category; it is impossible to say if the majority of US Americans now or at any point in history have 'mixed race' ancestry because until recently a category of 'mixed race' was not acknowledged. (I will return to this topic in a discussion about census categories in the next section.) So the difference between Latin America and the United States is not necessarily that there really were more offspring produced from coupling across 'racial' lines in Latin America but that such identities were less stigmatized and were legitimated with a term to describe them: *mestiz@*.
In the US, sexual relations with someone of a different 'race' was illegal in some states until relatively recently (1967), which is about as far as you can go to make something socially illegitimate. But more importantly, the lack of 'mixed' as a category in the census (until the 2000 census) or other records of national population makes it impossible to ascertain who might have fallen into this category and what percentage of the population they comprised.

And speaking of census numbers, we take for granted that we will be categorized according to 'race' in the US. Racialization in this country is institutionalized, as we are asked for racial identification in forms we fill out starting with preschools ('race' is no longer recorded on birth certificates although the 'race' of the mother and father is included (see Centers for Disease Control and Prevention, 2003)). This constant racial categorization is not as prevalent in Latin America (Alcoff, 2008: 24).

Another difference in the attitudes toward 'mixed' ancestry in Latin America and the US actually highlights a similarity in ideologies about 'race' – that there is a similar valuation of Whiteness above Black or Brownness. In research on Latin American racial categories, scholars frequently make references to how high socio-economic status influences racial categorization (e.g. Hernandez, 2002; Wade, 2008). Hernandez states:

> In Latin American settings, social status informs formal racial classification, as illustrated by the common belief that persons of prominence should not be 'insult-ed' by referencing their visible African ancestry. Additionally, it is generally pre-sumed that because no person of prominence could be Black, these persons should be designated distinctly. (Hernandez, 2002: 7)

The different systems of racial categorization in Latin America and the US, despite some underlying similarities in ideology, can clearly create dissonance for emigrants from Latin America. People who view themselves as, for example, *rancheros* in Mexico are lumped together with *mestiz@s* by White Americans. Many Latin@s simply do not fit into the conventional categories for 'race' that have been dominant in the history of the US (Alcoff, 2000: 24). However, as mentioned above, systems of racial categorization are not fixed but can change over time. Latin@s in the US are part of the changing ideologies about 'race' and ethnicity; this topic will be addressed in the next two sections.

Ethnicity

What is ethnicity? How is it different from 'race'? I am concerned here with both how academics discuss ethnicity and popular uses of the term – the goal of this section is to see how these two different perspectives on the concept of ethnicity are intertwined.

It is important to note that the term 'ethnicity' was not used by scholars until the mid-20th century (Zelinsky, 2001: 44–47) and its use in social science research generally preceded its presence in everyday speech. The rise of this word is rooted in what Zelinsky aptly calls 'attitudes toward the Other': a word was needed to describe people who were different from the majority and old words depicting racial or national groups did not capture this essence of Otherness. The word 'ethnicity' then is a word which arose not as recognition that we all have some sort of heritage that transcends racial or national categories, but that certain people – others, not us! – are in some way different and distinct, are 'ethnic'. This usage, as will be discussed below, is firmly part of the popular use of the word today.

Like 'race', social scientists consider ethnicity a socially constructed category. Like 'race', phenotype may play a role in how people are assigned to ethnic groups. Like 'race', self-identification and presentation are important aspects of how ethnic group membership is defined (Fought, 2006). Like 'race', most people consider ethnicity to have something to do with descent (Barth, 1969; Cohen, 1978). But it is also considered to be more than this – members of an ethnic group are thought to share cultural traits, such as religion, language, and particular practices such as eating certain foods or listening to certain types of music. The American Heritage New Dictionary of Cultural Literacy (2005) defines ethnicity as 'Identity with or membership in a particular racial, national, or cultural group and observance of that group's customs, beliefs, and language.'

Zelinsky (2001: 2) cites a number of definitions that focus on shared traditions which set one ethnic group apart from other groups. He also raises a number of other issues that are often fuzzy in the definition of an ethnic group – how large must a collection of people be to claim status as an ethnic group? What about locality – must the group be linked to a particular place of origin? And must an 'ethnic group' be a minority group? Don't people in the majority group have ethnicity, too?

The use of the term ethnicity in the United States developed as a way of creating boundaries within the category of 'White' people (Omi & Winant, 1994) and was usually based on national origin. This perspective of ethnicity as something White people have is

more or less the opposite of what I perceive to be the contemporary popular use of the word in American English. Usually 'ethnic' means 'not mainstream' and 'mainstream' has been defined as White. Although 'ethnic' foods may include foods associated with groups generally considered to be White (Italian or Jews, for instance), 'ethnic hair care products' are usually for Blacks. 'Ethnic clothing' is usually East Indian, African, Native American or Latin American; generally European clothing would not be considered 'ethnic' although traditional folk clothing – Lederhosen for instance – would be. 'Ethnic food' in the supermarket is usually Italian, Asian or Mexican cuisine. However I will note that this use seems to be fading in popular culture; while my local grocery stores have sections for 'Asian', 'Hispanic', 'International' and 'Mexican' foods, the sign labeling frozen pasta and taquitos as 'Ethnic' has been taken down and none of the drugstores
I visited have a section labeled 'Ethnic Hair Care' for relaxers and pomades marketed to Black women, although just a few years ago this was common. Perhaps this is a sign of a heightened sense of awareness that everyone has some sort of ethnicity? This change in meaning over time is something that is typical of socially constructed social categories.

The World English Dictionary (2009) cites the following definition for 'ethnic':

> ***adj*** 1. relating to or characteristic of a human group having racial, religious, linguistic, and certain other traits in common
> 2. relating to the classification of mankind into groups, esp on the basis of racial characteristics
> 3. denoting or deriving from the cultural traditions of a group of people: *the ethnic dances of Slovakia*
> 4. characteristic of another culture: *the ethnic look* ; *ethnic food*

What emerges from this picture is the idea that ethnicity is a means of categorizing people that involves descent but also cultural practices, and there is a strong tendency for assignment of ethnic group membership in the US to mean that the individuals being depicted are not part of the White mainstream. Although they may be White (e.g. Polish American, Irish American), the longer a (White) group is in the US, the less 'ethnic' they become.

So what is the difference between 'race' and ethnicity? Are there different types of ethnicities within different 'races', or different 'races' within particular ethnic groups? Confusingly enough, BOTH of these relationships sometimes appear to be the case. Let's take, as one example of categories of 'race' and ethnicity, the US census. In Figures 3.1 and 3.2, you can see a sample of the questions from the 2010 US Census on ethnicity and race. Question 5 (Figure 3.1) deals with what has been called by the government 'Hispanic identity', now referred to with the terms 'Spanish/Hispanic/Latino'; in this case, this is the only ethnicity it is possible to claim. You can either claim not to be Spanish/ Hispanic/Latin@ or to be of a particular type of Spanish/Hispanic/Latin@ ethnicity: Mexican, Puerto Rican, Cuban, or something else you can write in.

The 'race' question, Question 6 (see Figure 3.2), is independent of ethnicity – you can claim 'Mexican, Mexican American, Chicano' origin in Question 5 and then one of 14 racial categories or 'some other race' in Question 6. (Starting in the 2000 census,

5. Is this person of Hispanic, Latino, or Spanish origin?

☐ **No,** not of Hispanic, Latino, or Spanish origin

☐ Yes, Mexican, Mexican Am., Chicano

☐ Yes, Puerto Rican

☐ Yes, Cuban

☐ Yes, another Hispanic, Latino, or Spanish origin — *Print origin, for example, Argentinean, Colombian, Dominican, Nicaraguan, Salvadoran, Spaniard, and so on.* ⟋

Figure 3.1 *The ethnicity question from the US census*

respondents were instructed that they could check multiple boxes for race, so, for instance, the rancheros discussed by Farr might check 'White' and 'American Indian' and write in 'Purépecha' or 'Tarascan' or just 'White'.)

One way of interpreting the relationship between racial and ethnic categories based on the questions of the US census would be that there are many different possibilities for racial categorizations within the ethnic group 'Spanish/Hispanic/Latin@'. Thus ethnicity

6. What is this person's race? *Mark* ☒ *one or more boxes.*

☐ White

☐ Black, African Am., or Negro

☐ American Indian or Alaska Native — *Print name of enrolled or principal tribe.* ⟋

☐ Asian Indian	☐ Japanese	☐ Native Hawaiian
☐ Chinese	☐ Korean	☐ Guamanian or Chamorro
☐ Filipino	☐ Vietnamese	☐ Samoan
☐ Other Asian — *Print race, for example, Hmong, Laotian, Thai, Pakistani, Cambodian, and so on.* ⟋		☐ Other Pacific Islander — *Print race, for example, Fijian, Tongan, and so on.* ⟋

☐ Some other race — *Print race.* ⟋

Figure 3.2 *The race question from the US census*

is the superordinate classification and 'race' is a subordinate category. This only seems to be the case for this one ethnic group, however, as in the US census, Hispanic is the only ethnicity possible.

There are also other perspectives on the relationship between 'race' and ethnicity. Work by Bailey (2000, 2001, 2002) on Dominican Americans brings some of these different perspectives to light. The participants in his research were often identified by others and themselves as 'Black' but were not 'African American'; in other words, 'Black' is a higher-level classification, and within that group there may be different sub-categories – African American and Dominican American being two distinct groups. However this perspective on the relationship between 'race' and ethnicity is confounded by the frequent occurrence in Bailey's data of re-categorization of Dominican Americans based on linguistic proficiency. Comments such as 'she thought I was Black until she heard me speak Spanish' indicate that Blackness is somehow negated by Spanish language competence; so Black is not a biological category but a cultural one, and we see that the distinction between 'race' and ethnicity becomes blurred. This blurring occurs both in the understanding of race and ethnicity in popular culture and in scholarly work on this topic. For instance, in studies by social scientists or scholars in the field of education, it is common to look at the groups of White, Black/African American, and Hispanic, as if these were three distinct categories of the same type.

One of the problems with the ethnic category of Hispanic (or Latin@) is that it lumps together many people of many different backgrounds and experiences (Oboler, 1998). People who have emigrated in different eras, from different countries, and for different reasons are all put into the same demographic category because they are (supposedly) Spanish-speaking. In some cases members of a particular 'Hispanic' community may have more affinity with people from other linguistic groups who are similar in terms of social class, area of residence, or length of stay in the US. One theme which recurs in this book is the idea of the very heterogeneous nature of this category 'Latin@'. Although our focus is the common language, we will see that the variety of Spanish itself, as well as the use and experience with it in the United States, also varies considerably across Latin@ communities. Also, it is important to note that not all 'Hispanics' speak Spanish. Obviously many speak English as their sole or primarily language and Latin America is also multilingual. Many people from what are viewed as 'Spanish-speaking countries' would not necessarily categorize themselves as Spanish speakers; many speak indigenous languages either in addition to or instead of Spanish. Thus the category of 'Hispanic/ Latin@', although I describe it above as being a category which implies a common heritage language, falls short even on this overly broad criterion.

The last topic I would like to address in this section on ethnicity is a topic foreshadowed above: the change over time of perceptions of ethnicity (and 'race'). Waterston (2006), in her essay titled 'Are Latinos becoming 'White' folk?: And what that still says about race in America', discusses the interaction between the Black/White racial binary and social class markers in the US. Her discussion rests heavily on the idea that 'race' is socially constructed. Briefly, she argues that English-proficient Latin@s, especially those who are middle class, are more readily considered 'White' folks; she notes that historically, a number of other ethnic groups have undergone this 'Whitening process' – Jews, Slavs and Italians, to name just a few groups, were all initially not accepted as 'White' in the US but became incorporated into that category as they came to be seen as assimilated into mainstream culture. Language plays a key role in the perception of assimilation; speaking a variety of English which is not ethnically marked, and not speaking Spanish, contributes to the likelihood that Latin@s will be perceived as 'White' (see discussion of this by Roth-Gordon, 2011). Affluence helps too of course, in terms of others' perceptions as well as an individual's feeling of national belonging. Jensen *et al.*'s (2006) findings in a study of Dominican Americans also illustrate this intertwining of 'race', linguistic ability and assimilation. They found that Dominicans who had been in the US longer, had higher English ability, and lighter skin tone tended to have higher socio-economic status.

Similarly, Mendoza-Denton (2008) writes about how Latina gang members use English and Spanish to position themselves as Whiter *Norteñas* or darker, more Indian *Sureñas*.

Here we are reminded of the description of 'race' in Mexico referenced above: people of prominence cannot be presumed to be 'Black'. In the US, on the one hand, the media focuses obsessively on the ethnic backgrounds of people of prominence – Alberto Gonzales was the first Hispanic attorney general, Barack Obama the first Black president, Hiram L. Fong was the first Asian American to serve in the US senate, and so on. Every time a Black, Latin@ or Asian politician is elected the victory becomes about 'race' or ethnicity, a self-congratulatory theme of **diversity** and openness in American politics. But on the other hand, being considered 'White' is for many people a classification that means you are an acceptable citizen of the US. I am reminded of what my grandmother (a White American) said to me once about a friend of mine who had a White European father and an East Indian mother. He had just moved to South Carolina and, as a newcomer to the south myself, I wasn't sure how he would be racially categorized or what that might mean for him. When I expressed my concerns to my grandmother, she was aghast; he was smart and educated, how could anyone not think he was White?

'Race', ethnicity and the linguistic construction of identity

From the previous discussion of 'race' and ethnicity it becomes clear that in the minds of many people racial and ethnic identity is about 'who one really is', as if we all have a fixed and biologically determined self that we either acknowledge or try to hide. We have multiple words about people who do not fit our expectations for their racial category – 'Oreos' are Blacks who are White inside (i.e. 'act White'), 'Twinkies' are yellow (Asian) on the outside but White on the inside, and Rusty Barrett, a White American, recounts being called a 'burrito' (White on the outside, brown on the inside) by his colleagues when he worked at a restaurant because he spoke Spanish and associated with the Latin@ kitchen workers (Barrett, 2006: 178). These words indicate an attitude that says there is a prede-termined identity for us based on our racial/ethnic background, and to not live up to that destiny is simply being a wannabe.

This attitude is deeply problematic, as it ignores several important aspects of identity. First, any aspect of identity, including ethnic identity, is socially constructed; identity is not something we ARE, but something we DO. This was discussed at some length in Chapter 2. Second, our identities are forged, changed and developed by the people around us, along with other social influences – there is no biologically determined way of acting like a member of a particular ethnic group. Third, and perhaps most importantly, there is no one way of 'being Black' or 'being White' or 'being Latin@' or any other 'racial' or ethnic group; so not acting like a stereotypical Black or Latin@, etc., should not mean that one is 'acting White' or somehow disloyal to one's racial or ethnic group.

'Race', ethnicity and national identity

Ideologies which equate a particular nationality – here, we'll be talking about US American nationality – with a particular 'race' of people are called **ethnonational** ideologies. And although there are countries with ideologies and laws which are explicitly ethnonational, in the US this is more subtle. Once Blacks were given the right of citizenship and anyone born on US soil had a right to citizenship, clearly US nationality was not limited to the descendents of Anglo-Saxon settlers, despite this ideology often being found in the US (Monsivais, 2004). Popular culture seems to have embraced the idea that the US is a multiethnic nation. We assign certain months as the time to celebrate the heritage of different groups (Black History Month, National Hispanic Heritage Month, Native American Heritage Month, etc.), happily claim African Ameri-cans, Asian Americans and Hispanic Americans as part of our US Olympic teams, and at my university, every student is required to take a general education course which teaches them about 'multiculturalism', defined as diversity within the US population. Yet despite this apparent acceptance and even celebration of differences in cultural background and national origin and ethnolinguistic heritage, research shows that many Latin@s in the US do not identify as 'American' but instead with their country of origin or, in some cases, with their parents' or grandparents' country of origin – and one of the reasons cited was that to be an American, you need to be White (Monsivias, 2004: 117). There are parallel findings in a study by Golash-Boza (2006) from her analysis of the 1989 Latino National Political Survey and the 2002 National Survey of Latinos. She found that Latin@s who had experienced racial discrimination were more likely to identify as Latin@ (or Latin@ American) than simply American because they felt they were often treated as if they were not 'real' Americans.

However if we think back to the discussion of normative monolingualism in Chapter 1, it becomes apparent that this is not only about 'race'; it's also about language. In the US, speaking English, and only English, is something which makes you American. So if you speak Spanish, or even if you don't but identify with an ethnic group that is associated with speaking Spanish, within the hegemonic ideology this also makes you less authentically 'American'.

Language ideologies and Latin@ identities

We aren't born with our identities intact and having certain biological characteristics doesn't make us act certain ways. We learn how to act from the people around us. If we look at language this is quite obvious; we learn to speak like our families and other members of our communities because that's what we hear. If Spanish is spoken around us, we learn Spanish, whether we are Latin@ or not. If English is spoken around us, we learn English, regardless of what languages our ancestors spoke. The same is true of other cultural behaviors.

In addition to these behaviors themselves we also absorb the attitudes about certain behaviors and ideologies about ways of being. There is a strong sense that being monolingual in English is somehow the best way to be an American and we see this attitude represented over and over again in popular media and everyday interactions (see Chapters 1 and 4 for more discussion on this topic). Such ideologies inevitably influence the identities we choose to develop. If I am repeatedly given the perception that being a monolingual English speaker is advantageous, I am likely to want to be a monolingual English speaker. Even if people speak Spanish around me, I might start to answer them in English. Ideologies are one influence on our cultural behaviors, which is how we construct our identities. All options that are open to us in terms of identity are not equal; some look better than others. And while of course we do not always conform to mainstream expectations, those expectations shape us. For example, if you are aware of the push towards monolingualism, speaking Spanish can become a way of consciously rejecting mainstream values. So the very act of speaking Spanish changes; this is what we call the **socio-pragmatic meaning** of a variety.

In Chapter 2 we discussed the concept of 'translanguaging', the use of different ways of speaking to construct a social identity which rejects the idea of languages or identities as fixed, bounded entities. García (2010) also introduces the term **ethnifying**. By using this term as a verb, she calls attention to the idea that people use ethnic practices to signify who they want to be (García, 2010: 519). Paramount among these ethnic practices is language use. García points out that one sign of the close alignment of language and ethnicity is that the same terms are often used to refer to them – someone of French background speaks French, someone of German background speaks German. With Spanish we see this extended in various ways; as discussed in both Chapters 1 and 2, Mexicans are sometimes described as 'speaking Mexican' and Latin Americans are sometimes called 'Spanish' because of the language they speak. Although this designation is often applied by outsiders as a kind of denigration and lumping together of all groups, Dominican Americans (Bailey, 2001, 2002) and also some Mexican Americans in the southwest use this term to refer to themselves. Regardless of who uses it, it is indicative of a close association between ethnic identity and language. Thus one of the challenges for US Latin@s is the potential conflict between their construction of themselves as Latin@ through Spanish and the construction of themselves as American through (only) English.

This complex negotiation of identity and influences of ideology will be discussed further in this text in several ways. In the next chapter I will look at media representations of Latin@s and their languages, an analysis which primarily focuses on mainstream interpretations of *Latinidad*. In Chapter 5 I address Spanish language maintenance and shift, phenomena which revolve around identity issues. Chapter 6 addresses so-called **Spanglish** and **Chican@ English** and how these different linguistic structures are embedded in the social world. Finally, Chapter 7 will look at how all of these attitudes and ways of being influence educational practices for Latin@s in the US.

Discussion questions and activities

1. Go to http://www.understandinggrace.org/home.html. Click on 'lived experience' and then 'Who is White?' and take the survey. How do you make your decisions about if the people in certain countries are White or not White?

2. Go to http://www.understandinggrace.org/home.html. Click on 'lived experience' and 'sports quiz', and learn about some biological differences and a lot of myths about biological differences.

3. Go to a local drug store and/or supermarket and see if you see uses of the word 'ethnic' to describe food or beauty products. If so, what groups are these products associated with or marketed to? If not, what words are used to describe Italian, Mexican or Asian food, or hair care products for Black women, which have in the past been labeled 'ethnic'? What can your observations tell us about the changing definition of 'ethnicity' in US society?

4. Do you think that information about 'race and ethnicity' on forms we fill out is important, or should we simply ignore these categories? Why do we want this information, and what do we use it for? (If necessary, consult information about census results, or results of surveys about education, crime or birth rate.)

Recommended reading

Comas-Diaz, L. (2001) Hispanics, Latin@s, or Americanos: The evolution of identity. *Cultural Diversity and Ethnic Minority Psychology* 7 (2), 115–120.

Davila, A. (2008) *Latin@ Spin: Public Image and the Whitewashing of Race*. New York: New York University Press.

Santa Ana, O. (2004) 'Is there such a thing as Latino identity?' Online at: http://www.pbs.org/americanfamily/latino2.html.

Smedly, A. (1999) 'Race' and the construction of human identity. *American Anthropologist* 100 (3), 690–702.

Uricoli, B. (2003) Boundaries, language, and the self: Issues faced by Puerto Ricans and other Latin@/o college students. *The Journal of Latin American Anthropology* 8 (2), 152–173.

4

Media Representations of Spanish and Spanish Speakers in US English Language TV and Film: Production and Reproduction of Ideologies

Objectives: To discuss the relationship between language ideologies and media representations of Latin@s and their language use, and to encourage critical consumption of TV and film productions.

Chapter 1 addressed ideologies about Spanish and Spanish speakers, and Chapters 2 and 3 built on that to address how those ideologies are part of the construction of Latin@ identity and how the concepts of 'race' and ethnicity are intertwined into ideologies that are, on the surface, about language. This chapter looks at how all of these ideas manifest themselves in mainstream US movies and television programs about Latin@s.

The main questions to be addressed here are how Latin@s and their language are portrayed in these media and what ideologies are produced and reproduced through these portrayals. After a brief discussion about the number of representations of Latin@s in film and on TV, the next section looks at what stereotypical images of Latin@s have been presented to us by popular media. This is followed by a discussion of media portrayals of Latin@s in the new millennium; this discussion focuses on films and TV shows that depict Latin@ families or communities.

I also address how dominant language ideologies are reproduced in these media representations. Lippi-Green (1997: 79–103) has shown that the accents used for certain characters rely on social stereotypes about members of particular social and ethnic groups and are a means of discriminating against linguistic minorities. In this chapter, I show that there are a number of predictable stereotypes about Latin@s which appear over and over again in films, and give some historical perspective on how these stereotypes have developed over the last century.

In the final section, I address how Latin@s are portrayed in the growing number of children's shows which focus on Spanish speakers. Here we will see a disconnect between portrayals of Latin@s in media aimed at adults, and portrayals aimed at a child viewing audience.

An unrepresentative representation of Latin@s

Before I begin looking at HOW Latin@s are portrayed on the screen, I want to comment on HOW MUCH they are represented. There is a short and easy answer to this: Latin@s are underrepresented in poplar media. According to Mastro and Behm-Morawitz (2005: 110), Latin@s comprise 12.5% of the US population, but only 1% to 3% of the characters portrayed on prime time television. This is an improvement over the previous decade, when Latin@ characters were at about 1% (Mastro & Behm-Morawitz, 2005: 111; Rodriguez, 1997: 23). So although the situation has improved markedly in the last few decades (Beltrán, 2008), we are still not being given a picture of Latin@s as an integral part of US society when we watch TV. Lichter and Amundson (1997) trace the history of Latin@s in television, noting that an essentially all-White world was marred only by very stereotypical portrayals of Blacks as porters and Hispanics as bandits up until the 1960s, when the number, range and quality of ethnic minority characters slowly began to increase. During the late 1960s we see the first signs of what I call 'The Benetton commercial syndrome' in which the characters are a careful, self-conscious mix of ethnicities (and genders). *The Mod Squad* television show (1968–1973), with one White (man), one Black (man) and one (White) woman, was one of the pioneers in this model of representation. It was not until more recently – perhaps the 1990s – that Latin@s were routinely included in these attempts to show diversity.

Children's shows seem to be especially prone to using this quota system for representing diversity. For preschoolers, the characters in *Barney & Friends* (since 1992) always include children with identifiably different 'racial' or ethnic backgrounds. For pre-teens and adolescents, shows like *Lizzie McGuire* (2001–2004) kept up the diversity; this particular show starred a White American girl who was best friends with a Latina girl and a Jewish boy. In these programs, ethnic minorities are largely portrayed as not being different from the White characters on the show, aside from an occasional display of ethnic or religious group belonging to establish their authenticity. I'll come back later to the idea of normalizing minority characters, something that is often done when they are part of a diverse group in a program. This is generally not the case when the movie or TV program focuses on the Latin@ experience, which will be the focus of the discussion of contemporary media representations.

Stereotypical portrayals of Latin@s

Berg (2002) discusses six stereotypical Latin@ roles which he describes as part of the moviemaking storytelling convention (Berg, 2002: 68). These roles are *El Bandido, The Harlot, The Male Buffoon, The Female Clown, The Latin Lover* and *The Dark Lady*. All of these stock characters tended to be presented in contrast to the WASP male hero; I will briefly give some examples of each of these stereotypical roles.

El Bandido is the Mexican bandit, and this portrayal goes back to silent films such as *Broncho Billy and the Greaser* produced in 1914 (yes, that's right, the Latin@ character was actually referred to as a 'greaser' in the title). But this role continues in various permutations: the Latin American gangster/drug runner or, as I will discuss below, the Latin@ inner city gang member are the more contemporary versions of this same Latin@ villain (Berg, 2002: 68–9). Mexican bandits were the back-up bad guys in Westerns (following Indians, the staple bad guys); the heroes were rarely Latin@ (Chávez, 2003: 96). There are a few exceptions to this; the Cisco Kid (1950–1956), who is a Robin Hood-type hero, and the character of Mexican narcotics detective Miguel 'Mike' Vargas in *Touch of Evil*

(1958), who exposes the shady doings of a US American Sheriff. It should be noted that the Cisco Kid is played by a Spaniard, and Miguel Vargas by Charlton Heston (a White American) – as discussed below for the 'Latin Lover', Latin@ good guys are never mestiz@.

Other male stereotypical characters include the Male Buffoon and the Latin Lover. Berg (1990, 2002) cites Ricky Ricardo in *I Love Lucy* as the most famous Male Buffoon, although Lucy was arguably the one that everyone was laughing at, not Ricky. Other examples include Pancho in *The Cisco Kid* (1951–1956) and Sergeant Garcia in the 'Zorro' series (1957–1959) (Subervi-Vélez, 1994: 312). It is interesting to note that the buffoonish-ness of these characters is linked to language use in two of these examples – Ricky Ricardo for his emotional outbursts in Spanish, and Pancho for not being able to speak English well (Berg, 1990: 295).

The Latin Lover, on the other hand, provides the image of the erotic Latin@, often dangerous and violent but filled with sexual promise. This character can be traced back to Rudolph Valentino, who was an Italian immigrant who played various 'exotic' roles calling for a dark-haired and dark-eyed sex symbol, such as an Arabian sheik, an Indian rajah or a Spanish bullfighter. In more recent times, many Latin Lovers are Latin@ characters and/or actors; we see this in such roles as Zorro in *The Mask of Zorro* (1998) and *The Legend of Zorro* (2005), played by Antonio Banderas. Rodríguez (1997) notes that there were physical differences between the Latin Lover types and the 'bandidos', with '...the Latino villains being poorer and darker in coloration and the Latin lovers being upper class and conforming physically to European prototypes' (Rodríguez, 1997: 81).

The Harlot is a lusty, hot-tempered woman, a temptress and a nymphomaniac, while the Female Clown is a Latina who is portrayed as silly, usually in addition to being sexually promiscuous. Both of these characters have characteristics which make them undesirable to the WASP male hero, who they inevitably lust after. The classic example of the Harlot is the character Chihuahua (?!) in *My Darling Clementine* (1946), while Angelica in *Six Days, Seven Nights* (1998) nicely fits the stereotype of the Female Clown (Berg, 2002: 70–75).

In contrast, the Dark Lady is cool and classy; see for instance Dolores Del Río in *Flying Down to Rio* (1933) and *In Caliente* (1935) (Berg, 2002: 76). Again, this character's portrayal largely revolves around lust; the difference is that the Dark Lady inspires lust in others while the Harlot and the Female Clown display passions of their own. Rodríguez (1997: 80) conflates these three categories into two, what she calls 'señoritas' (wealthy and virtuous women) and 'spitfires' (poorer women portrayed as 'easy').

Berg also discusses what he calls 'the Chicano social problem film' (Berg, 2002: 111–12), which focuses on the ideology of assimilation. While Berg discusses *Bordertown* (2006) as the prototype of this genre, this theme resonates in most of the films for adults I will discuss in the section below and is seen in movies produced long before the turn of the 21st century.

Cultural stereotypes in the new millennium

Guzmán and Valdivia (2004: 208) describe the dominant discourses about Latin@s as 'ethnically homogenous, racially non-White, Spanish-dominant, socio-economically poor and most often of Mexican origin', but it seems that marketing professionals are working to change this stereotypical representation. Changing demographics in the United States have influenced media representations of Latin@s; film producers do not want to offend the potentially lucrative Latin@ market (Chávez, 2003: 96). This has resulted in more representation of Latin@s in the media and an avoidance of the stereotypes of the past – kind of.

Cortés (1997: 131) notes that Chicanas began to appear as 'real people' in the mid-1940s; in the 1970s, the ethnic stereotyping decreased and since then 'movies have littered the screen with Latinas who come off as little more than Spanish-surnamed Anglas' (Cortés, 1997: 134). The exception to this is what he calls 'urban violence films' which he claims is the main genre of film which depicts Latin@ experiences; a quick glance at what Netflix offers in the rubric of 'Latino dramas' would support this contention.

Berg (2002) suggests that this depiction of Latin@s as members of street gangs builds on the 'bandido' stereotype. The list of movies portraying Latino men as gang members is long and growing: *West Side Story* (1961), *American Me* (2002), *Blood in, Blood Out* (1993), *Boulevard Nights* (1972), *Colors* (1988), *Drive By* (2001), *Latin Kingz* (2003), *South Central* (1992), *The Street King* (2002), *Walk Proud* (1979), *Zoot Suit* (1981). The films *Down for Life* (2010), *Living the Life* (2000) and *Mi Vida Loca* (1994) extend this theme to females. Other films, such as *All Night Bodega* (2002), focus not just solely on gangs, but on a broader portrayal of Latin@ neighborhoods as dangerous, and escape from the barrio being the answer to the characters' problems.

This depiction is rooted in a kind of assimilation-gone-bad ideology, in which Latino men are portrayed as violent and uneducated and part of the worst of US society. It should be noted that this is a departure from earlier conceptions of Latin@s in the US as being mostly farmworkers living in rural areas. *The Milagro Beanfield Wars* (1998) is one depiction of this, although in this case the Latin@s are actual farmers and not illegal immigrants working as farmhands, which is the frequent stereotype. However, it is safe to say that in the new millennium film depictions of Latin@s overwhelmingly show them in urban settings. (One notable exception is *How the Garcia Girls Spent Their Summer* (2005), which is set in a sleepy border town in Arizona.)

There are, of course, other depictions of the difficulties of immigrant life, including the portrayal of noble attempts to transcend poverty through hard work and perhaps even a bit of talent or intellect (e.g. *Spanglish* (2004), *Real Women Have Curves* (2002), *Manito* (2003) and *Spin* (2007)). This theme reaches back several decades, including films from the late 1980s such as *Stand and Deliver* (1988) and *Salsa* (1988). There is also a gang-oriented sub-genre of these films, in which young men are gang members, go to prison, and try to reform their ways (*Clash* (2002), *Down for the Barrio* (1997), *East L.A. King* (2004)). The portrayal of Latin@s struggling to integrate into the middle class is one way of representing authentic *latinidad* (Sowards & Pineda, 2011: 137) but at the same time serves to reinforce the stereotype of the poor, uneducated Latin American immigrants, as these success stories are largely portrayed as exceptions to the rule.

The 'Latin Lover' and 'Dark Lady' stereotypes have also evolved to survive in films of the 21st century. The general theme here is the exotic sensuality of Latin@s, although it becomes a bit more varied and complicated as time goes on. As discussed by Guzmán and Valdivia (2004: 217), representations of Latinas continue to 'build on a tradition of exoticization, racialization and sexualization, – a tradition that serves to position Latinas as continual foreigners and a cultural threat.' In *Quinceañera* (2006) there is some critique offered of the Latin Lover role. One of the main characters, a young gay Latino, becomes involved in a ménage-a-trois with an Anglo couple and then continues an illicit relationship with one of the men without the knowledge of the other. This depiction is one which makes the Anglo men involved appear shallow and uncaring; they treat the young Latino man like a sex object and because he is poor and Latino he is not someone they take seriously. The Anglo men are clearly the bad guys as the plot develops. Another variation on the Latin Lover trope is found in *How the Garcia Girls Spent Their Summer*. The three generations of Garcia women are exoticized, but are also shown to be dealing with different, age-related issues in their relationships which transcend ethnic stereotypes. *Raising Victor Vargas* (2002) also provides a twist on the 'Latin Lover' theme by depicting both Victor and his girlfriend as suffering from, as much as enjoying, their positions as sexually desirable. Baez (2007) argues that the three movies she examines – *Selena* (1997), *Girlfight* (2000) and *Real Women Have Curves* (2002) – present more nuanced depictions of Latinas and challenge some of these stereotypes about gender and ethnicity. The use of the stereotypical exotic Latin@ is more common in films that are not depictions of Latin@ communities; in other words, the Latin Lover or Dark Lady are more likely to appear in all their glory in movies which are largely comprised of White characters and the Latin@ character is the uniquely dark and mysterious outsider.

One of the other developments in portrayals of Latin@s is that they have become more specific in terms of the countries of origins. Characters, and their communities, are increasingly portrayed as not just vaguely Latin@ but Mexican, Dominican, Puerto Rican, etc. For example, Victor in *Raising Victor Vargas* has a Dominican background, as do apparently the other Latin@s in the film; *Real Women Have Curves* is explicitly about a Mexican American family in East LA; and *West Side Story* was of course a portrayal of Puerto Rican barrios in New York City. While this aspect of the identity of the characters is sometimes given and even part of the plot line, it's also clear that viewers – or filmmakers – do not seem to be very aware of what differences there are between Latin@ groups. In many ways the more specific national origins for the characters seems to be a way of capitalizing on stereotypes about certain localities being Mexican, Puerto Rican, etc., and have very little to do with an authentic focus on a particular group. It sometimes takes a careful viewer to discern which Latin@ group is being portrayed and the stereotypes are largely the same regardless of whether the characters are explicitly

Chican@, Puerto Rican, Dominican or from some other Latin@ group. In all cases Latin@s are usually portrayed as being poor, living in neighborhoods plagued by gangs, and living in extended family households. There are traditional gender roles revolving around machismo for men and the 'Madonna and the whore' dichotomy for women. And perhaps most importantly, the success stories are inevitably about those who leave their ethnic neighborhoods behind.

Even when the film itself is a portrayal of a particular community or Latin@ group, publicity for the movies only inconsistently specifies the country of origin of the characters. This reveals that despite the intent of some filmmakers the majority culture is not all that interested in a more nuanced understanding of Latin@s. In fact in many cases the publicity blurb about the movie does not even say explicitly that the film depicts a Latin@ community. Although an alert viewer can figure it out while watching the movie, nowhere on Netflix, the internet movie database, or even Wikipedia, does it state that *Raising Victor Vargas* is about a Dominican American character. The setting is described as merely being 'Lower East Side'; while this may be code for 'Dominican and Puerto Rican' for some, the implication is more of a general poor immigrant neighborhood than a specifically Dominican one. A similar code is used to describe *American Me*, *East L.A. King* and *Colors* – all set in East LA. which is stereotypically Mexican American (although according to the 2000 census, 11% of LA's population was made up of Latin@s who were NOT Mexican American, while 34% were Mexican American (Garcia, 2003)). *Mi Vida Loca* is set in 'Echo Park' (for those in the know, this is in Los Angeles, again a hint that it deals with Mexican Americans) and *All Night Bodega*, according to Netflix, is set in 'Spanish Harlem', again code for Puerto Rican. While descriptions of *Real Women Have Curves* explicitly include the term 'Mexican-American' (Netflix), *Stand and Deliver* is described as dealing with 'mostly Hispanic' students (Netflix). All of these films are categorized as 'Latino dramas' but the descriptions of their plots do not otherwise explicitly thematize either a pan-Latin@ experience or one specific to an immigrant group. In other words, the marketing of these films seems to employ commodification of ethnicity without a great deal of effort to provide detail or accuracy, instead relying on stereotypes about the populations of certain urban neighborhoods.

In contrast to the depiction of gritty life on the streets is the somewhat sanitized portrayal of Latin@ life shown in the sitcoms *George Lopez* (2002–2007), *American Family* (2002–2004) and *Ugly Betty* (2006–2010). The extent to which these television shows focus on the Latin@ experience varies greatly. In *Ugly Betty* the focus of the show is Betty's personal and professional growth and development through her work in the fashion world. In *George Lopez* the goal seems to be a portrayal of the trials and tribulations of marriage, child-raising, dealing with one's parents and in-laws, and being a supervisor in an airplane parts factory. Ethnicity is part of what makes George Lopez's life what it is and it is also a constant source of jokes and stereotypes about the motivations of the characters. In *American Family*, similar to *George Lopez*, not all of the episodes focus on ethnic themes but there are constant reminders of the ethnicity of the characters through depictions of the Latin@ neighborhood, eating of tortillas, and the emblematic use of Spanish. There are also occasional comments which reference the Latin@ identity of the characters. For instance in the *American Family* pilot episode, the youngest son refers to a condominium complex as 'like a strange planet from Star Trek – planet Gringo'. All of these shows seem to be seeking a balance between presenting Latin@s as just like everyone else (i.e. **normalizing** US Latin@s) and presenting Latin@s as inherently different and outside the mainstream (i.e. **otherizing** or **exoticizing** US Latin@s).

One of the stereotypes we can see in films that also occur on TV include a mitigated version of the extended family. In *George Lopez*, George's mother does not live with them but apparently lives close by, as she carpools with George and is frequently at their house. *Ugly Betty* does not have the ubiquitous *abuela* in her household but there are three generations as she, her sister, and her sister's son live with her father. In *American Family* three generations live together in one household.

Gangs and urban violence seem far from the worlds of Betty or George, but do appear as part of the depiction of Mexican Americans more generally in the *George Lopez* show. While George does not have gang member affiliation, he does have a clearly working class background which he has managed to transcend by hard work to become the manager at the factory. (This is, of course, similar to the upwardly mobile trajectory of Betty and some of the adult children in *American Family*.) In other ways the association of Mexican Americans with gangs and street life is made clear; George is represented as being highly assimilated and an exception to the norm. In an episode in which his Cuban American in-laws come to visit, this is explicit. George's father-in-law accuses George of not passing down his Mexican traditions, so George arranges for the whole extended family to go to a Chican@ version of 'A Christmas Carol'. In this version, Señor Scrooge is a drug kingpin and Bob Cratchit is one of his street dealers. Drive-by shootings and pit bull attacks are part of the hardships of life in the barrio for the Cratchits. The point of this theater experience for George and his family is that while this may be 'authentically Mexican', it's not the reality for George and his family, who are assimilated into mainstream culture. After trying to fake some sort of 'ethnic' Christmas tradition, George finally tells his father-in-law: 'You know what our Mexican American tradition is? We open presents and spend time together as a family' (*George Lopez* season 1, episode 15). Now if that isn't a depiction of a red, white and blue-blooded US American family, I don't know what is.

The life in the streets is a bit closer in *American Family* as one of the adult sons, Esteban, has been in prison and is on parole. This is the reason for the extended family living situation – Esteban has a son, Pablito, whose mother is a drug addict and is not allowed contact with him and Esteban as a parolee also cannot have custody; thus Esteban and Pablito live with their parents/grandparents. The other siblings are models of upwardly mobile achievement – Nina is a lawyer, Vangie is a fashion designer, and Cisco is an aspiring filmmaker. But Esteban and his former girlfriend are a reminder to viewers of the constant temptation for Latin@s to run with gangs and do drugs.

So while assimilation is clearly part of the picture for George Lopez and his family, Betty, and most of the 'American Family', ethnicity is nonetheless portrayed in some of the same ways we see in films. There is specificity of national origin – George's family is from Mexico and his wife Angie's family is from Cuba. The tensions created by this difference are portrayed as largely being about social class as Angie's parents are physicians and well-off while George has had to work his way up from the factory floor (where his mother still works). While providing some nuance to the general portrayal of Latin@s by differentiating between the Cuban American and Mexican American experience, this contrast stresses the poverty associated with being Mexican American in much the same way as all of the movies discussed above.

Betty's family and the 'American Family' are of Mexican origin. In *Ugly Betty*, her father's difficulties connected to his undocumented status are part of the creation of Latin@ authenticity (Sowards & Pineda, 2011). In contrast, the patriarch of the *American Family* was born in the US. He explicitly identifies as an American, not a Mexican, and he grumbles about his daughter Nina's attempts to embrace her Mexican heritage. Of course her understanding of Mexican heritage is clichéd and sometimes ridiculous – as when they have Aztec dancers in body paint and feathers performing in the living room.

Finally, there is an element of the portrayal of Latin@s which appears in television programs but rarely makes its way into movies: jokes about Latin@s are funny! Or at least the audience of *George Lopez* seems to think so. For example, in the first episode of the first season, George and his wife Angie discover that their daughter has been forging notes to excuse herself from swimming instruction. Angie is very upset and wants to talk about the situation but George is starting his first day on his new job and is eager to leave for work. To brush the matter aside George says, 'Why does she need to know how to swim? We're already here' (a reference to Mexicans swimming their way across the Rio Grande, I assume). George also makes fun of the heavy accents of his Cuban American parents-in-law and his father-in-law's frequent mention of Castro. The resulting message is: being Latin@ is funny! You just need to have a sense of humor about it all. Because George is himself Latin@, he can make jokes about Latin@s and we are allowed to laugh – which provides the opportunity not just for comic relief but also the perpetuation of stereotypes.

Language use: Monolingual norms and deviant behavior

This section addresses representations of the language use of Latin@s in Hollywood films and on TV. As has been discussed in earlier chapters, certain ways of speaking index particular identities for speakers and this is also true for characters in fictional settings. I suggest that these representations are a reproduction of particular ideologies about Spanish speakers in the US.

One of the ideologies discussed in Chapter 3 is what I have called 'normative monolingualism', the ideology that monolingualism is, and should be, the norm for US society.

Petrucci (2008) discusses how the representations of languages other than English in American films reinforce the monolingual norm. Looking at 10 films involving supposed Spanish speakers produced between 2000 and 2004, he outlines three strategies used to 'signal Spanish' in the films. (Note that none of them is simply having the actors speak Spanish and providing subtitles for an Anglophone audience.) One strategy is to have Spanish audible in the background, not as part of the plot but as part of the setting. Another is to have the actors speak Spanish-accented English. Emblematic use of Spanish is also employed; endearments, profanity and easily recognizable **cognates** are produced in Spanish with the assumption that all of these linguistic elements are easily understood. Many people recognize things such as 'mi amor' or 'hijo de puta' even if they do not speak Spanish, and most can also make sense of such things as '¡Vive el Presidente!' (Petrucci, 2008: 411). But even if the semantic content of these phrases is not understood, this does not prevent the viewer from following the plot of the movie. Petrucci argues that although this seems to be done with artistic license and with pragmatic motivation – after all, the target audience is largely English-speaking – the consequence is the representation of the world as normatively Anglophone.

I would take this criticism a step further and argue that along with silencing languages other than English, such representations put Spanish speakers in a decidedly negative light. First, take the use of accented English. One of the problems with this representa-tion is that it conflates two different situations – people who speak English as a second language and have transfer from their first language and people who speak Chican@ English as their dominant language and may or may not speak Spanish (see the section on Chican@ English in Chapter 6 for a fuller description of this issue). Of course in many ways it doesn't matter that these two things are conflated because they are both indexical of belonging to a Latin@ community, and thus of poverty, lack of assimilation, traditional gender roles, and so forth. Such accents are used to distinguish characters along these lines. For example, although Betty from *Ugly Betty* speaks perfectly standard English, her sister Hilda has a marked accent. Hilda is not an unsympathetic character but she is less educated and less intelligent than Betty and we are given the impression that she is sexually promiscuous as well. Such linking of Chican@ English or accented English (it's not clear which) to characters who have less socially desirable traits reinforces stereotypes of ethnic dialects as inferior to standard English because the speakers are uneducated, have loose morals, and so forth.

Second, the emblematic use of Spanish creates a different issue. As it is often used along with Spanish-accented English, it creates another problem on top of the reproduction of negative stereotypes about people who do not speak standard English. Namely, it shows a performance of a completely unnatural way of speaking: it portrays Spanish speakers as largely speaking English to each other. The idea that dominant speakers of Spanish sit around speaking English to each other (with only the occasional use of Spanish endearments) is ridiculous. This representation does two things: first, it marginalizes Spanish, portraying it as a language which is not used for real content but simply for emotional overtones, even among native speakers; second, and more importantly, it creates a world in which this is a reasonable thing to expect of people – that is, it shows a world in which the norm is that Spanish speakers speak English to each other. This would not be so harmful if this was not already a serious suggestion made to immigrants. I have had conversations with people who feel that immigrants should speak English at home – for the benefit of their children, to practice their own English, etc. A focus group study in Ohio (Mughan, 2007) shows that although such opinions are not universal, they are not unusual in attitudes about immigrants in the US.

And it's true that some immigrants to the US do speak English at home, some or even all of the time. You probably know people who do not speak their first language to their children; I do, and many of them do this because they want their children to have the benefit of learning English when they are young. They sometimes regret it later. I also know many children who resent not being taught their heritage language. So it happens, but is this a reasonable expectation or desirable scenario? It can be harmful to one's sense of identity to abandon one's first language. Portrayals on the big screen, or even on the smaller television screen, of people doing exactly that, normalize this behavior and make Spanish seem expendable.

There is another pattern of bilingual discourse I have observed in films depicting Spanish speakers that Petruccio (2008) does not discuss – **asymmetrical codeswitching**. This portrayal is usually between members of different generations; the parents and/or grandparents speak Spanish and the younger generation answers in English (this has also been noted by Androutsopoulos, 2007: 220). Sometimes this is subtitled as in *Quinceañera* and *Real Women Have Curves*. In 'Spanglish' there are scenes in which the daughter is expected to translate for the mother. There is a certain accuracy to this portrayal; such intergenerational patterns of asymmetrical codeswitching are well-documented (Boeschoten, 1990; Fuller, 1997) and there is a body of literature that addresses the phenomenon of children translating for their parents (e.g. Tse, 1995; Weisskirch & Alva, 2002). But the problem with this portrayal of Spanish in these films is that the use of Spanish is not neutral. It is often the characters who are older, poor, uneducated and socially backward (e.g. sexist) that speak Spanish and the younger, more likeable, smarter characters who answer in English. This is also presented in a slightly different way in *American Family* as the parolee son Esteban speaks some Spanish to his son while his high-achieving siblings almost never speak Spanish. Again, we have the association of Spanish with characters who have inferior roles in society. This portrayal positions Spanish as an encumbrance in achieving social power as opposed to a positive part of the Latin@ experience.

At the same time we see that the use of Spanish is also necessary for authentic Latin@ identity. In some cases accented English will do but in film, as in real life (see the discussion on the construction of Latin@ identity in Chapter 2), Spanish is sometimes seen as necessary to 'prove' Latin@ status. Glancing for a moment to other media aside from television and film we see a particularly salient permutation of this in Christina Aguilera's production of a Spanish language album as part of the attempt to re-frame her as Latina. But the flip side of this is something we often see in television shows such as *George Lopez* or *Ugly Betty*: humor about the rejection of Spanish (i.e. assimilation into the Anglophone mainstream) abounds. For example George, defending himself against his grandfather's accusation that he is not passing on his Mexican heritage to his children, says 'I'm down with *la raza*' pronouncing the word 'raza' not with an /s/ sound as in Spanish but with a /z/ sound, as a non-Spanish speaking Anglophone would read the word. Betty claims in one episode, 'my Spanish really sucks'. Positioning these characters as not really speakers of Spanish makes them part of the mainstream and not part of the impoverished, violent world of the barrio. Their rejection of Spanish is portrayed as funny, not a loss.

TV representations of Latin@s for children: Spanish as a resource

In contrast to the films made for adult audiences, television programs aimed at young audiences have a vastly different portrayal of Latin@s. I will focus primarily on two television shows aimed at preschoolers: *Dora the Explorer* (2000–present) and *Maya and Miguel* (2004–2007). These are not the only television shows which have primarily Latin@ characters; for example, *Dragon Tales* (1999–2005) stars two Spanish-English bilingual children who travel to the land of dragons (where some of the dragons are also Spanish speakers). However this show revolves much more around the experiences of the children in their secret trips to visit the dragons and not a depiction of Latin@ life and thus will not be a focus of this discussion. I will not address films here except to note that there are few children's movies which focus on Latin@ families or communities aside from the *Spy Kids* series (2001, 2002 and 2003). In *Spy Kids*, as in *Dragon Tales*, the Latin@ heritage of the children is largely backgrounded. I will also make some reference to the Spanish speaking character in *Sesame Street*, Rosita, although that show focuses on diversity more generally and not the Latin@ experience specifically.

One of the stereotypes of Latin@s is the same in media aimed at adults and children – the prevalence of the extended family household in Latin@ families. Maya and Miguel live in a multi-generational household as their grandmother lives with them. Dora does not live in the same household as her grandparents but, a lá George Lopez, they live close enough that she can walk to their house, which she frequently does in her adventures.

There, however, the similarities end.

The families in *Dora the Explorer* and *Maya and Miguel* are all middle class. While the occupations of Dora's parents are not evident, Maya and Miguel's parents are small business owners (they run a pet store). Dora, Maya and Miguel live in middle class neighborhoods, and there is no indication that gangs exist in their worlds. Diversity is an important part of the communities they live in. The diversity in *Dora the Explorer*, which is aimed at a preschool audience, consists largely of animals or fantasy characters who function like humans: squirrels, cows, foxes, trolls and of course the monkey Boots, Dora's best friend and constant companion. In *Maya and Miguel*, their circle of friends is ethnically diverse; Maya's friend Maggie is visibly Asian, and is described on Wikipedia as

'Chinese American', where her other best friend Chrissy is described as 'Dominican American'. (Maya herself is described as 'Latin American', a strange way to describe a child who appears to have been born and raised in the US, so take these descriptions for what they're wiki-worth.) Miguel's best friend Theo is African American and his second best friend Andy is a White boy who was born with only one arm. Social class and gender/sexuality diversity are not made apparent in these depictions but ethnic diversity is paramount and the issue of the differently-abled is broached.

The gender roles are no more rigid than in any other children's show, meaning that while the mothers may cook and the fathers may mow the lawn, the expectations of the children are not heavily gendered, and boys and girls engage in some similar activities. For example, all children play sports. While Maya and Miguel do have close same sex friendships, they also operate in a social world in which both boys and girls are part of their social networks. Dora's friends, although rarely human, are depicted as both male and female. The clothing of these characters is not gender neutral but not overly feminine or masculine. Maya wears pants and t-shirts as does Miguel; the main difference between her appearance and Miguel's being that she wears more form-fitting tops and has a large ponytail. Dora wears a pink top and frilly anklets but paired with her quite serviceable t-shirt, shorts and sneakers, her clothes signal that she is a girl but do not constrain her behavior in any way. In this way, gender – like ethnicity – is presented as a trait of the characters but not something that influences their experiences or opportunities.

Ethnicity is rarely, if ever, explicitly referenced. Instead, language is used as an index for ethnicity. Spanish speakers are almost always Latin@ although non-Latin@s may also learn and use some Spanish. In the children's shows there are often overt or subtle attempts to provide a vehicle for learning Spanish. This is explicitly the case with Sesame Street's Spanish Word of the Day, and fairly overt in *Dora the Explorer* in which pauses are included for audience participation, some of which involves repeating Spanish words. Teaching viewers Spanish does not seem to be an aim of *Maya and Miguel* but it is also aimed at slightly older children who may be at an age where talking back to the TV seems babyish. However, the pattern of codeswitching used in all of these shows lends itself to being comprehensible to non-Spanish speakers while also providing the opportunity to acquire some common Spanish words. For example the grandmothers are always referred to as 'Abuela' and there is often repetition in both languages as illustrated in the theme song for *Dora the Explorer* with the line 'let's go. . .*vámanos*!'

Notably absent is the kind of asymmetrical codeswitching prevalent in the Latin@ dramas for adults. In *Maya and Miguel* everyone in their family mostly speaks English but uses a bit of Spanish. The Spanish used is emblematic in the same ways discussed by Petrucci, except, of course, for the lack of profanity. One recurring use of Spanish is that when Maya has an idea, she typically says '¡Eso es!' ('that's it!'). There are also occasional uses of the usual commands 'vamos, muchachos' ('c'mon, boys') and 'ándele' (which can be loosely translated as 'hurry'). The parents and grandmother also have Spanish-accented speech (although Maya and Miguel do not). Language is thus a strong marker of ethnic identity, with all other markers being less consistently a part of the performance of ethnicity. Their daily lives do not seem to be different from the non-Latin@s in their social sphere. Maya and Miguel do have a piñata at their birthday party, but this is a practice which is hardly exclusively for Latin@s, although it is associated with Latin@ culture.

The characters in *Dora the Explorer* tend to be constructed as fitting into one of three categories: bilingual, monolingual in English, or monolingual in Spanish. Dora and all of her family members (parents, grandmother and cousin Diego, who eventually has his own spin-off show) are bilingual. There are occasionally other Latin@ characters who are also bilingual, one memorable example being a wizard ('El Encantador') played by Ricardo Montalbán in one episode in 2002. He spoke some Spanish but mostly used his trade-mark Spanish-accented English. Many of Dora's friends are monolingual in English, such as her best friend the monkey Boots and Benny the Bull. Dora's nemesis Swiper the Fox is also an English monolingual as is her friend Isa the Iguana. However Tico the Squirrel is monolingual in Spanish; he is the only regularly appearing character who does not speak English, although often the problems that Dora must solve require her to use Spanish.

Dora's role, then, is a kind of bridge between English and Spanish speakers. Because the plot of each episode is a mission that Dora must complete the premise of the show lends itself well to her use of Spanish as a tool. For example in one episode there is a gate that they must command to open but the gate only speaks Spanish, so the viewing audience is encouraged to shout *abra* 'open' along with Dora.

In both of these programs bilingualism is portrayed as a resource and a positive individual trait, not a societal problem (Popp, 2006). There is no stigma attached to Spanish – no one is ever told to 'Speak American or get out'. Anglophones are not only portrayed as accepting of Spanish being spoken but they are generally eager to learn (e.g. Dora's friend Boots and Maya's friend Maggie are both depicted as learning Spanish). And although Spanish and/or Spanish-accented English does index a Latin@ identity, that identity is not one which is a burden or that lowers the social status of that person. It seems to largely index an experience in which grandmothers are close by and children have additional linguistic resources. Otherwise being Latin@ is much the same as being a member of any other ethnic group. True, the people so indexed tend to be brown-skinned (although, remember, these are cartoons) but this does not appear to be a relevant contrast with lighter-skinned characters in terms of social value. In short, it's a bilingual utopia, the epitome of the 'language as a resource' ideology about Spanish (De Casanova, 2007). This is also more or less the depiction of Spanish in a number of other children's shows and movies. In the three *Spy Kids* movies, Spanish sometimes comes in handy in conquering evil-doers who want to take over the world. In *Dragon Tales*, as mentioned above, Spanish is a great resource for communicating with Spanish-speaking dragons, and also, in recent seasons, a new immigrant neighbor. In *Handy Manny* (2006–present), the handyman Manuel and his trusty tools have many Spanish-speaking customers, so luckily Felipe the Phillips screwdriver is bilingual so he can translate for the English monolingual hammer, hand saw, etc. Spanish, we learn from these shows, is a useful tool.

Perhaps it makes sense that within this sanitized presentation of the American melting pot the Spanish varieties used are 'the voice from nowhere' – although American varieties of Spanish are spoken, they are not clearly identifiable as being from a particular country or region and the characters are usually not explicitly linked to particular Latin American countries. De Casanova (2007) calls this a 'generic Latino' image which is used to market the shows to as broad an audience as possible.

The notable exception to all of this is Rosita, a character on *Sesame Street*. In some ways the portrayal of Latin@ culture through Rosita's inclusion as a regular character on the show is not diametrically opposed to that of Dora or Maya and Miguel; one of her roles on the show is to teach Spanish, especially but not solely through her 'Spanish Word of the Day' segment. She is portrayed as living with a large extended family, including the ubiquitous *Abuela*. However in episode 4081, two children asking Rosita and Big Bird for directions laugh at Rosita's accent. Here is the description of the ensuing treatment of this topic from sesamestreet.com:

> Rosita begins to feel sad and embarrassed by her accent, and explains that she sounds this way because she is from Mexico and she can't help the way she talks. Rosita then tries to get rid of her accent in order to speak like everyone else, but since she can't, she decides that she would rather not speak at all. Big Bird, Gabi and Miles try to tell her that they love the way she speaks, and that everyone has a unique voice and way of speaking. They also sing a song called 'Music of the Street' to show Rosita that these unique differences are what makes up the beauty of the street! In the end, not only does Rosita realize that she should be proud of her accent, but she also teaches the two kids a couple words in Spanish! (Sesame Street, 2004)

While the ideology of 'Spanish as a resource' is not neglected in this episode, the essence of difference is addressed in ways that are not made apparent in *Dora the Explorer* or *Maya and Miguel*. The idea of prejudice is approached and although it is resolved in the end, it causes Rosita anguish along the way. And, significantly, the basic sociolinguistic concept of language discrimination is brought to light. It also stresses that the way we speak is part of who we are; we all want to feel pride in who we are but we don't have absolute control over how we talk any more than we can change our basic appearance. Here I refer back to Chapter 2. One of the things I said was that there is no one-to-one relationship between language and identity characteristics. One of the things we see very clearly in the uses of Spanish in children's shows is that there is a clear, simple connection between speaking Spanish and being Latin@. However, aside from speaking Spanish, Latin@s are portrayed as pretty much identical to everyone else in the mainstream US.

Disconnect

So you may be thinking to yourself, 'Some people are just never satisfied – on the one hand she complains that the films for adults set Latin@s outside of the mainstream and she doesn't like that but then she's equally critical of the children's shows that depict Latin@s as essentially the same as everyone else! What does she want?'

It is, admittedly, difficult if not impossible to portray any ethnic group in a way which does not exoticize them but also does not treat diversity as merely difference in appearance. This is my complaint about television shows for children like *Barney*; although the children in the shows are carefully selected to represent different ethnicities, the children's behaviors – perhaps especially their language use – never deviate from the middle class norm. The message sent loud and clear is that as long as you act right, it's okay to look different (and perhaps eat some different foods or listen to different music). This is not a message about embracing diversity; it's a message about assimilation. On the other hand it would also be offensive to bring children on to the show to represent particular non-standard ways of speaking – a Black child to speak **AAVE**, a Mexican American child to speak **Chican@ English**, a White kid from the mountains who speaks **Appalachian English**, and so forth. This could easily be interpreted as mocking people of these backgrounds. And what many of the films for adults I have criticized attempt to do, at least in part, is to portray the Latin@ experience as one which involves a struggle against discrimination as well as poverty and gang violence.

The children's shows, on the other hand, seek to provide role models for Latin@ children and expose Anglophone children to people of different backgrounds in ways that make them seem familiar and to present speaking Spanish as a positive thing (see Associated Press, 2006). And maybe this works; maybe the generation growing up now which was raised with *Dora the Explorer* will not have the same prejudices as their parents' generation. But I doubt it, because the missing element from this portrayal is that language is an integral part of identity and that while speaking Spanish can indeed be an important and useful resource for solving problems, it is more than that. It is also a cause for discrimination and a source of pride, a symbol of belonging in some contexts and of seemingly deviant behavior in others. 'Being Latin@' is also not just one experience but takes on many different variations. The ethnic lumping that occurs when characters are portrayed as participating in some sort of pan-Hispanic culture does not show respect for anyone's heritage.

Discussion questions and activities

1. Are there recent movies or television shows you have seen which depict Latin@s? How do they use language? Discuss the use of Spanish, standard English and 'accented' (Chicano or Learner) English and the identities of the characters.

2. What do you think is the impact of the depictions of Latin@s described in this chapter? Do representations of people in films and on TV really influence how we feel about them? Why or why not?

Recommended reading/viewing

Beltran, M. (2002) The Hollywood Latina body as site of social struggle: Media constructions of stardom and Jennifer Lopez's 'crossover butt'. *Quarterly Review of Film and Video* 19 (1), 71–86.

Johnson, M.A. (2000) How ethnic are US ethnic media: The case of Latina magazines. *Mass Communication and Society* 3 (2), 229–248.

My American Girls (documentary) (2001) Visit the website: http://www.pbs.org/pov/myamericangirls/POV, a production of American Documentary Inc.

Rojas, V. (2002) Do I see myself represented on Spanish Television? Latinas 'talk back' to Univision and Telemundo. Online at: http://www.portalcomunicacion.com/bcn2002/n_eng/programme/prog_ind/papers/r/pdf/r005se04_rojas.pdf.

The Bronze Screen (video) (2002) 100 Years of the Latino Image in American Cinema. Nancy De Los Santos: director, screenwriter and producer; co-directed by Alberto Dominguez and Susan Racho.

Part 2
Language Practices

5
Spanish Language Maintenance and Shift in the US

Objectives: To present the factors which influence the use of Spanish in the US and several frameworks within which they have been studied, and to provide an overview of Spanish language use in selected localities.

The first section of this chapter will address the possible outcomes of language contact with specific reference to Spanish speakers in the US. The next section discusses the concept of **diglossia** and the school of thought about separation of languages that is challenged in this text. Following this, I present research which looks at the factors that influence minority language use, presenting this information framed within two different theoretical models, **Ethnolinguistic Vitality** and **Social Network Theory**. The final section of the chapter contains overviews of the patterns of language maintenance and shift of particular groups of Spanish speakers in the US: Spanish in the southwest, Cuban Americans in Miami, Puerto Ricans in New York City, and Spanish in Chicago.

Introduction: Minority languages

Before focusing on Spanish, I want to first address the broader issue of what I mean by the term **minority languages** in the US and how minority languages come to exist in this context. I use the term minority language here to refer to all languages which are not the language spoken by the dominant majority; in the US, this means all languages other than English. There are, of course, contexts within the US in which languages other than English are socially dominant and spoken by the majority of the population in a certain area. For instance, in an ethnic neighborhood you might hear more Spanish, Chinese or Hmong than English; but in the wider community, these languages are still in the minority. Such situations and how they influence the long-term use, or **maintenance**, of languages will be discussed in this chapter.

As for how it comes to be that languages other than English are spoken in the US, I think the general answer to this is already obvious to you: people who spoke different languages colonized the US, so all of those languages, in addition to the ones that were already here and the languages of subsequent immigrants, have contributed to the linguistic repertoires of the people living in this country. The boundaries of the US are defined politically, not linguistically. Building on that basic understanding, here I will discuss the socio-political and ideological aspects of language diversity, and the consequences for language use.

There are two overarching reasons why people speak more than one language (Myers-Scotton, 2006: 45). One is close proximity; that is, when people who speak different languages live near each other and have regular contact. This is clearly the case with Mexico and the US, and this border region is one of the reasons that Spanish is an important language in the American southwest. This is intertwined with the other catalyst for multilingualism, displacement (which includes **conquest/colonization** and immigration). Some of what is now the US was Spanish-speaking territory due to Spanish colonization before it became part of the US through conquest; the current border between the US and Mexico was not historically a linguistic border between an English-speaking and a Spanish-speaking area.

Immigration is also common with neighboring countries, and so this reason for minority languages being present in the US is intertwined with close proximity. For Mexicans, especially, the close proximity to the US makes it an obvious choice if they decide to leave their country to look for other opportunities. And once a group of people has immigrated to a particular area of the US, others from their social networks in their country of origin may join them. The reasons for this are obvious; it is much easier to settle in a city or town where you know people who can help you – especially if you do not speak the majority language and are not familiar with the mainstream culture and political structure. Thus, we get populations of people who are not just from the same country but often from the same region or town, and frequently there are kinship relations between them as well. For example, in the Spanish-English bilingual classroom where I did research in a rural southern Illinois school, many of the Mexican American children had cousins in the school district; their families had come to this small community because they had relatives who could help them get settled.

Options in language contact: Factors and attitudes

Regardless of the reasons for being exposed to a second language, there are a limited number of possible outcomes: continue to only speak your first language (L1); learn the second language (L2) and continue to speak your L1; learn the L2 and stop speaking your L1. In the following sections, I'll discuss these outcomes in terms of Spanish minority language speakers in the US, the ideologies which surround them, and the realities of language use in Latin@ communities.

Keeping the L1 and 'refusing' to learn English

The first possible outcome of being exposed to a second language, as stated above, is to not learn that language (in this case, English) and stick with one's first language. This is a stereotype of Latin@ immigrants perpetuated by the media and based on false impressions and misconceptions about language and language learning, as well as blatant disregard for the facts about acquisition of English from both the past and present. I would like to address this stereotype and the misconceptions involved by looking at some statistics about language proficiency in the US and also discussion about it in public online venues.

It is clear that there is a strong stereotype about Latin@s, and Mexicans in particular, not learning English; this is reflected in the following post on topix.com, a website which says 'Take a stand on the issues you care about'. On April 8, 2011, American Man posted something with the heading 'Why can't mexicans speak English ????????':

> Spanish come this country and speak English
> Italians come to this country and speak English
> Germans come to this country and speak English
> Pollock's come to this country and speak English
> French come to this country and speak English
> Russians come to this country and speak English
> Chinese come to this country and speak English
> Japanese come to this country and speak English
> Korean come to this country and speak English
> Vietnamese come to this country and speak English
> Puerto Rican come to this country and speak English
> Irish come to this country and speak English
> People From Every Other Nationality In The Entire World Come To The United States of America and speak English!
> Why are mexicans The only Nationality that can't come to this Country and Speak English ?
> Maybe it's just because mexicans are Ignorant ?
> Why do we have to Cater to this one Nationality of Fruit Pickers and Lawn Care Specialist ? (Topix, 2011)

I would like to make two criticisms about the underlying assumptions of this commonly held opinion. My first point is that the claim that Latin@s do not learn English is simply untrue, and doubly untrue if we look beyond the first generation. The 2007 American Community Survey Report on 'Language use in the United States' (Shin & Kominski, 2010) indicates that of the 34,547,077 speakers of Spanish or Spanish Creole surveyed, only 10.7% were said to not speak English at all, and an additional 18.4% said they did not speak it well (see Figure 5.1 for the survey questions that these data are based on). While this results in 29.1% of the Spanish or Spanish Creole speakers in the US reporting they do not speak English well or very well, let's put these figures in context. First, these figures are based on self-reports. It's difficult to assess what it means when someone says they speak English 'well' or 'not well'; someone may be able to communicate but still feel they do not speak the language 'well'.

Second, it's important to look at who the speakers are that describe themselves in this way: they are mostly foreign born and are more likely to be in the higher age groups (over 40 or over 65). In other words, most of the people who do not learn English are older adults who have themselves immigrated to the US; younger immigrants and those born in the US generally speak English. I'll come back to this point below.

Sadly, knowledge about statistics for language learning doesn't seem to lead to a change in attitude. In a post on 'Yahoo! questions' on the topic of 'Why do we say Immigrants

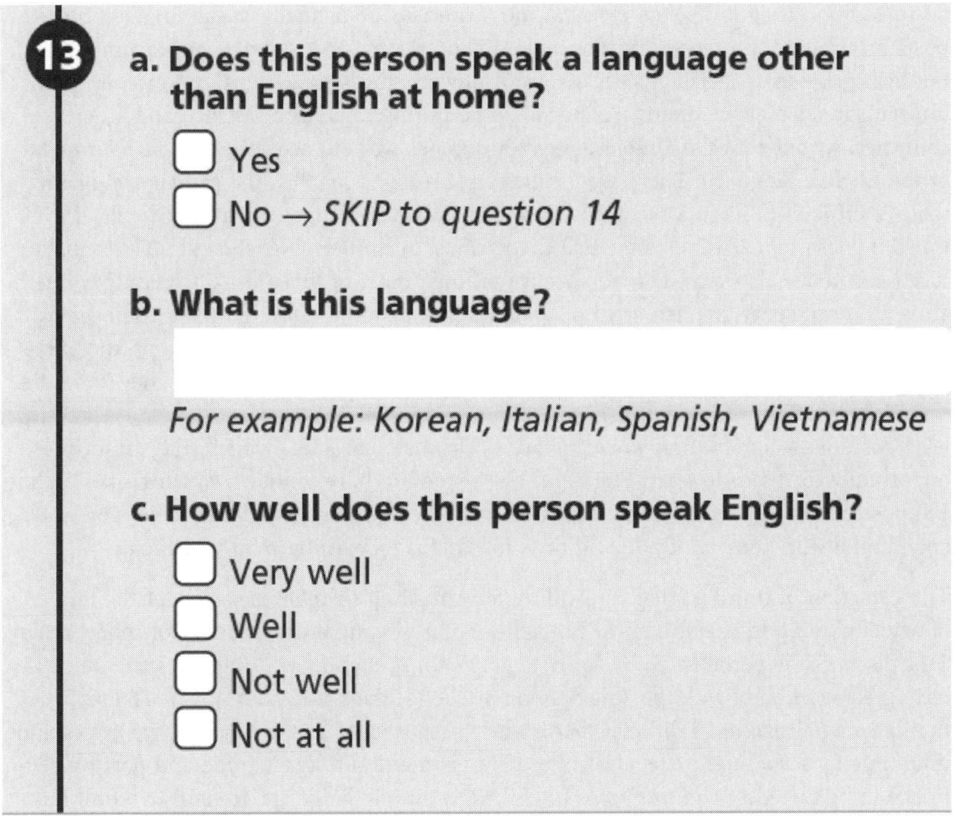

13 **a. Does this person speak a language other than English at home?**

☐ Yes

☐ No → *SKIP to question 14*

b. What is this language?

For example: Korean, Italian, Spanish, Vietnamese

c. How well does this person speak English?

☐ Very well

☐ Well

☐ Not well

☐ Not at all

Figure 5.1 *The questions on language from the 2007 American Community Survey*

don't want to learn English?' one writer notes 'For long-term immigrants, less than 3% are unable to speak English well. (National Academy of Sciences)' (Yahoo, 2009). This writer then goes on to say:

> I recently read a story where an immigrant came from some country (can't remember which one)... But she learned English within 1 years time. There is no reason that it should take anyone 10 years to know or be familiar with the English language of any country including the US. It's the illegals who take issue with learning English. That is why they refuse to learn English. Or don't attempt to learn it quickly. (Yahoo, 2009)

The expression 'refuse to learn English' is an interesting one; it implies that individuals have every opportunity and simply do not cooperate with the national agenda of teaching ESL. Another poster on this thread was vociferous in his objection to government funded ESL programs, because, as s/he maintained: 'They do not learn English, because they have no interest in knowing the language' (Yahoo, 2009).

So in addition to ignoring the fact that most Latin@s do, actually, speak English, these posts bring us to the second misconception about Latin@s and language learning: that not being able to speak English is a sign of unwillingness to learn. As we can see from the statistic cited above, there are indeed some immigrants, from Mexico and other countries, who live in the United States for decades without acquiring a basic command of the English language. There are a number of reasons for this, the primary one being that it's difficult to learn a second language as an adult. I suggest that it is rarely, if ever, unwillingness to learn English which is the cause of limited English skills. The statistics discussed above also provide a perspective on this: most of those who, according to the survey, do not speak English at all or do not speak it well are foreign born and over 65. They also tend to have lower levels of education. In other words, they came to the US as adults. They were poorly educated in their country of origin, which meant they had little opportunity there to learn English before emigrating; once in the US they have taken low level positions – agricultural work, factory work, custodial jobs – which may offer little opportunity for them to learn English. They also often have families, which makes taking ESL instruction outside of work more difficult; when you are struggling to support and spend time with your family, taking time for language learning may be difficult.

The depiction of immigrants as unwilling to learn English relieves society of the burden of actually trying to teach them; it is a self-serving discourse which does not reflect reality. This discourse is perpetuated by some organizations, such as US English, Inc., which have great credibility with the Anglophone public (Millard *et al.*, 2004: 23). The reality is that language learning is difficult, particularly if you have limited financial resources and little time to devote to it. It is also inherently threatening to one's pride and positive self-image to be forced to communicate in childishly simple language, to have to admit that you do not understand, and to struggle to pronounce things correctly while others laugh. It is degrading when people tell you to go back to Mexico (even if you are from Honduras) if you have difficulty speaking or understanding English. Considering the hostility some language learners encounter, it's not surprising that they might not seek out situations to speak English.

So, to summarize, I suggest that, first of all, the claim that most immigrants don't learn English is false, and second, for those that do not, the main reason is not lack of desire or motivation but lack of opportunity. This is partly because ethnic enclaves might allow for isolation from majority language speakers, partly because there is discrimination, partly because we do not live in a society where there are lots of inexpensive opportunities for adult education, and partly because adult immigrants are often busy with work and family and cannot easily take advantage of what opportunities do exist. Seeing any immigrant's lack of English proficiency as a sign of lack of desire to participate in US society is at best an exaggeration, and at worst perpetuating prejudice.

Another problem with the 'refusal to learn English' position has to do with a lack of understanding of the process of language learning. Even with great effort and lots of exposure, acquiring a language takes years, not months. Many monolingual US Americans feel that immigrants to this country should be able to speak English fairly immediately. There is no sense that perhaps some services provided in the minority language might be part of a transition to functioning in English. Many adults and children arrive in the US without speaking English and two years later are fluent; but the English Only zealots they encounter during their first year in the US might well cite them as another example of an immigrant 'unwilling' to learn the majority language.

Learning English and maintaining Spanish

This brings me to the second possible outcome of being exposed to a second language: you learn that language, and maintain your first language. But what exactly does it mean to maintain a language? As we'll see, there isn't a clear answer to this question. Many speakers of minority languages do not have a lot of opportunity to speak their first languages, but this may still be the language they feel most comfortable speaking and feel they speak best. So what is their 'dominant' language? There is no clear definition of 'dominance' in terms of language proficiency. So while some scholars of language contact do look at the structure of the minority language (this is in the next chapter), language maintenance and shift research is primarily concerned with how much, where, when, and by whom the minority language is used. So when we talk about language maintenance, we are not talking about a person's proficiency, but simply continued use of the minority language.

Acquisition of English and maintenance of Spanish is the pattern for many Latin@s in the US. If they are **first generation immigrants**, Spanish is their first language but they have also learned English; if they are **1.5** or **second generation immigrants**, they may speak both languages natively ('1.5 generation' immigrants are those who were not born in the US, but came at a young age and thus had the opportunity to acquire English before the **critical age**). In this chapter, continuing to speak Spanish is discussed under the term **language maintenance**. Maintaining both languages requires not just the opportunity to speak them but also the attitude that Spanish language maintenance does not prevent the learning of English, and speaking English does not mean that one must abandon one's heritage languages (Suarez, 2002).

As discussed in Chapter 1, there are often ideological impediments to bilingualism; it is seen as 'un-American' to speak a language other than English. Spanish is often seen as an index of an identity which is viewed as foreign, or a sign of a person with mixed loyalties. Such attitudes about Spanish language use can mean that English is used in more **domains**, meaning that the acquisition and maintenance of Spanish are limited.

Language shift: Losing Spanish

A third possibility is that people may learn the second language and lose their first language; this is called **language shift**. It is more likely for children than adults learning English as a second language to shift to English as their dominant or only language, simply because children, especially children under the age of about 11, generally learn languages more quickly and are more likely to attain native fluency (and, especially, native phonology) than adults. However, there is something we call **language attrition**, which is the loss of a language over the lifetime of an individual speaker. Here, I will focus on language shift, and in particular how the language of a community might shift from one language to another over generations.

One often-cited pattern of language shift in immigrant communities is that there are three generations to language shift (Myers-Scotton, 2006: 68). The first generation (the generation that emigrates) is dominant in the minority language, the second generation is bilingual, and the third generation is dominant in the majority language. Subsequent generations speak only the majority language. While this basic trajectory may frequently be the case, let's break it down and discuss how the actual experiences of minority language speakers might vary from this pattern.

There are many different personal scenarios which influence patterns of language use, and this is the problem with a general claim of three generations to language shift (see Villa & Rivera-Mills, 2009 for a more detailed discussion of this issue). First, not all immigrants have a spouse with the same linguistic background, and many do not settle into a lifestyle which allows them to maintain their first language as their home and community language. Some immigrants arrive in the US already able to speak English, and many become immersed in a community or family in which their first language is not spoken. For instance, many Spanish-speaking adult immigrants marry or live with English speakers who do not speak Spanish, and thus use English as their main language for communication in their private sphere as well as at work and in other public arenas. While Spanish speakers who have children with non-Spanish speakers may raise their children to speak Spanish, this is clearly more difficult to achieve if the parents do not speak Spanish to each other and only one parent speaks Spanish to the children.

Also, we are assuming that the 'first generation' immigrant is a fully grown adult; this is not always the case. While it is less common for children to emigrate on their own, circumstances may lead to a child or young adult being in the US without their family. In this case, they may be surrounded by English speakers, and may be likely to stop speaking Spanish.

So, there are a number of reasons why it might not be accurate to describe the first generation immigrant as 'dominant' in Spanish. This has a domino effect on the subsequent generations; the second generation is less likely to be bilingual if not raised in a household in which Spanish is the primary language, and there is then a decreasing likelihood that the third generation will have any knowledge of Spanish at all.

But let's assume that the first generation in a family follows the stereotypical pattern and speaks mostly Spanish in the home, and the second generation learns Spanish from them. The description of this second generation is commonly 'bilingual', but this is another term, like 'dominant', which is used in a lot of different ways. Many people often equate the term 'bilingual' with what language contact scholars might call a **balanced bilingual**, that is, someone who has equal proficiency in both languages. Although this is what is often thought of as a 'real' bilingual, few people who speak two languages are balanced bilinguals. Many people speak more than one language because they use their languages in different domains, so while perhaps they prefer Spanish in their private spheres, they are more comfortable speaking English when conversing about topics connected to school or work. They may be unfamiliar with the English words for certain foods or cultural practices that are particular to their home experience, but use the English words for technical terms or things they associate with US culture even when speaking Spanish. So balance is difficult to attain when one learns one's languages in different social contexts. For those bilinguals who are lucky enough to be educated in two languages, their language proficiencies may be more equal and equivalent, but it is still unlikely that they would have all of the same experiences in both languages.

Also, of course, members of the second generation, having been raised entirely in the US, are likely to end up having social networks comprised of other people from the US who may or may not share their linguistic background. And because of their exposure to English in public realms, they often adopt English as the language for peer interaction – and it is not uncommon for second generation siblings to speak English to each other. So, it is less likely that it will come naturally to them to speak Spanish to the next generation, and this is one reason why the third generation often does not continue to speak the minority language. For third generation heritage Spanish speakers, exposure to the minority language may come primarily from their grandparents, not their parents. So the extent of the contact between the first and third generations plays a major role in the language proficiency of third generation speakers.

Of course, this is assuming that these speakers are not embedded in a community in which Spanish is the dominant language, because while language learning begins in the home and with one's family, it continues and is sometimes primarily influenced by the language of the community with which one identifies. There are all sorts of language minority communities that foster the development and continued use of languages other than English in the US. In the next section, I will look at what aspects of communities contribute to bilingualism, and which tend to lead to language shift.

Diglossia versus sustainable languaging

In Chapter 1, we discussed monoglossic language ideologies as prevalent in popular thought about bilingualism; that is, the idea that languages can clearly be delineated and should be kept strictly separate. This ideology has also dominated scholarship on multilingualism. Fishman (1980, 1985, 1989, 1991; Fishman et al., 1971), a prominent researcher on language maintenance and shift, discussed bilingualism in terms of domains of language use and **diglossia**. Building on work by Ferguson (1959), Fishman defined diglossia as an enduring situation of bilingualism in which each language has stable and compartmentalized functions (Fishman, 1980). In a diglossic relationship, one of the languages is seen as the 'High' (H) language, and the other as the 'Low' (L) language; the H language is learned later (usually in school) and is therefore no one's mother tongue, but is used for formal functions in society.

Fishman then discussed the four possible scenarios within his framework: bilingualism with diglossia, bilingualism without diglossia, diglossia without bilingualism, and neither bilingualism nor diglossia. According to Fishman, bilingualism with diglossia is the only societal arrangement within which bilingualism would be preserved. In bilingualism without diglossia, Fishman says that languages in contact will compete for use in different domains and ultimately only one language will win. The long-term outcome of bilingualism without diglossia is, he claims, neither diglossia nor bilingualism – that is, without diglossia, a bilingual society will become monolingual. The final option, diglossia without bilingualism, is described as a political arrangement in which two monolingual entities are brought together into one political unit; the examples given include Switzerland, Belgium and Canada, which have territories that are dominant in different languages.

This framework gives rise to several questions. First, if the H variety in diglossia is not learned natively, but bilingualism only continues if coupled with diglossia, this implies that it is impossible to maintain bilingualism in societies in which people have 'native' competence in one or more languages. While there are surely many examples to refute this, one of them is a country that Fishman himself cites as exemplifying bilingualism with diglossia – Paraguay, where there is widespread bilingualism in Spanish and Guarani. Fishman assigns Spanish the H role, meaning that it should not be the first language of anyone, but studies in Paraguay have long shown that it is spoken as the home language for some members of the bilingual population (Choi, 2005; Rubin, 1968). Thus, it's not clear that Paraguay qualifies as a diglossic speech community, but bilingualism has nonetheless continued.

Which brings us to the second question: how long does bilingualism have to continue to be considered 'stable'? Fishman is vague about this, but does suggest more than three generations. Must the continued use be across generations within the same families, or merely within a community?

Third, by what criteria do we say that the population of, say, Canada, is monolingual? Although there are separate territories which are designated as Anglophone and Francophone, certainly there are many people who speak French and English in both (see, for example, Cardinal, 2004; Heller, 1999, 2002).

Fourth and finally, who gets to decide if languages are 'compartmentalized' in a diglossic relationship or not? Although classical versus regional varieties of Arabic have always been the lynchpin of the definition of diglossia, I suggest that the perception of the strict compartmentalization of these two dialects may have been influenced by the belief in diglossia. Recent research has revealed contexts in which two varieties of Arabic are juxtaposed within a conversation or monologue, a phenomenon which supposedly does not occur in diglossia (see, for example, Albirini, 2011 and Soliman, 2009 for discussions of this type of codeswitching).

The point I am making here is that while Fishman's framework has been widely accepted, it is really representative of an ideology about bilingualism, not irrefutable evidence about how language maintenance is to be achieved. And the ideology it represents is a monoglossic ideology.

There is of course an alternative ideology about multilingualism as it specifically relates to language maintenance, and that is what García (2011a) refers to as 'sustainable languaging'. Remembering the discussion from Chapter 1 about the fluid use of various elements of language (translanguaging), this is applied to the idea of maintenance. García writes:

> The difference between maintenance and sustainability is telling in itself. Maintenance refers to activities required to conserve as nearly, and as long, as possible, the original condition of something. Language maintenance is thus an effort to retain the language as spoken 'originally' by the group, before it came into contact with other languages, before the diaspora came into being. On the other hand, sustainability refers to the capacity to endure, but always *in interaction* with the social context in which it operates. The concept of sustainability contains in its core the grappling with social, economic, and environmental conditions by which systems remain diverse and productive over time.....Language sustainability refers to renewing past language practices to meet the needs of the present while not compromising those of future generations. (Garcia, 2011a: 7, italics in original)

Much of the research reviewed in the rest of this chapter was done within the monoglossic perspective. I do not wish to discount this research; it is a substantial and, by any set of criteria, valuable body of literature. However, I also wish to make clear as we go along that many of these studies reflect a particular dominant theoretical paradigm which influenced methodology and the interpretation of findings.

Ethnolinguistic vitality

Giles *et al.* (1977) discuss what they call **ethnolinguistic vitality** in terms of three categories of factors: demographic factors, status factors and institutional support. As we will see, these factors are not independent from each other, but are intertwined.

In the first category, **demographic factors**, there are a number of characteristics associated with the population which contribute to the likelihood of language maintenance. First, the raw number of speakers is important as well as the geographical distribution of those speakers; languages tend to be more easily maintained if there are a large number of speakers, especially if they densely populate an area. Isolation or segregation of the minority group, something which is often seen as a negative factor in the 'melting pot' of the US, is a positive factor for language maintenance. If minority language speakers have little contact with speakers of the majority language, they will maintain their minority language more easily. Finally, practices of **exogamy** or **endogamy** also influence language maintenance; if speakers of a minority language marry people who do not speak their language, it is less likely that the language will be passed down to the next generation.

Status factors include factors about how the minority language is viewed both within the minority group and by members of the mainstream. Within the minority group, the importance of the language in terms of group identity is paramount. This may or may not coincide with **overt prestige**; in many cases, **covert prestige** of a way of speaking is the most important element in language maintenance. If a variety has covert prestige, speakers will continue to speak it because it plays a crucial role in constructing their in-group identities. Overt prestige provides different, more instrumental motivations for language maintenance. A minority language with overt prestige may have more institutional support (see below) and also be more readily accepted by the mainstream population. For majority language speakers, the association of the minority language with a prestigious group will foster tolerance and even desire to learn the language, as will the perception of the language being useful for employment or education opportunities. Ehala (2011) claims that the most important factor in ethnolinguistic vitality is the emotional attachment of minority language speakers to a collective minority group identity – in other words, high status within the group for the minority language. However, again we must note that such factors do not exist in a vacuum; these positive views of the language contribute to institutional support, particularly educational opportunities, for the minority language.

Institutional support is the final category of factors noted by Giles *et al.* (1977); the types of institutional support available for the minority language play an important role in the continuation of language use on the community level. The institutions generally considered are media (radio and TV in particular), schools, religious institutions and government agencies and services. Various studies have stressed the importance of specific institutions in language maintenance. Moring *et al.* (2011) put emphasis on the media as an important vehicle for language retention; Salmons (2005) suggests that local control of education and religious institutions is critical to language maintenance.

However, the availability of support for language maintenance from such institutions is clearly not independent from the demographics or status of the minority population. If there are a large number of speakers of the minority language in a particular area, the members of the group itself are more likely to have the resources to create community media and religious institutions. Also, the local, state or federal government may recognize that significant populations should be provided with services such as driver's license tests and election ballots in the minority language, or translation services for courtroom interactions. Further, as will be discussed in more detail in Chapter 7, bilingual education may be an option if the population is large enough. In many cases, opportunities for education in the minority language are created by the minority language community members themselves outside of the public school system, much like minority language church services are organized or local radio shows might be created to appeal to a large market of minority language speakers.

The picture that emerges from looking at Giles *et al.*'s framework is that language maintenance occurs most frequently when there are large, but socially isolated, populations of minority language speakers who view their language as integral to group identity, and the status of the language is high enough in the wider community that media, education and government services are provided in their group language. Further, the group would ideally also have created community resources such as religious institutions which function in the minority language.

However, there is no one set of factors which guarantees language maintenance or destines a language to shift, and other studies have looked at correlations between non-causal factors and language maintenance for further insights. Here, I include just a few examples of research on this topic done on Latin@ communities. According to Linton (2003: 2), 'Cuban or Puerto Rican ancestry, living with a Spanish-dominant person, having children in one's household, and working in a service- or health-related job all increase the odds of bilingualism.' Although these are not presented as causal factors, we can see how some of them overlap with Giles *et al.*'s factors, which ARE presented as causal. For instance, living with a Spanish-dominant person clearly increases the likelihood that Spanish will be spoken in the home. The discussion below about language maintenance in Cuban or Puerto Rican origin communities will come back to the point of the features of these communities and support of bilingualism.

Another study looking at a correlation between distance from the Mexican border and Spanish maintenance (Bills *et al.*, 1995) can also be fit into the ethnolinguistic vitality framework; proximity to the Mexican border may contribute to the availability of services in Spanish, the status of Spanish, and the density of Spanish-speakers in the community.

However, while these factors clearly play a role in language maintenance and shift, it is also important to recognize that embedded within the idea of 'status' are many attitudinal factors and ideologies about language that also influence language maintenance. Minority languages are not always maintained even when there is plenty of opportunity for speakers to continue to speak them, and this has to do with other social factors. For instance, in Chapter 1 we discussed ideologies about Spanish in the US, and it was shown that there is an association between speaking Spanish and lower socio-economic class status. This association is based on the value of integration and assimilation, and the ideology that true Americans are monolingual in English; thus socio-economic success is only thought to be derived from abandoning Spanish. It is perhaps unsurprising, then, that Bills *et al.* (1995: 21) found a correlation between language maintenance and low income and educational levels for US Latin@s in the southwest. The ideological climate about Spanish in the US leaves room for the interpretation of the causal relationship as being that maintaining Spanish dooms one to a working class existence, although there is no evidence that this is the case. More recent work outside of the southwest (Jenkins, 2009; McCullough & Jenkins, 2005) suggests that this correlation is weakening, but other research on Latin@s across the US (Lutz, 2006, which looks at data from Hispanic youths from the National Education Longitudinal Study, NELS 88) shows that a negative correlation between speaking Spanish and higher income exists, but there is variation by national origin. In particular, while Mexican Americans with higher income are LESS likely to speak Spanish, Cuban Americans with higher income are MORE likely to speak Spanish. While Lutz cautions against making too much of these claims and calls for further research on the topic, she also aptly points out that 'In the Cuban case, this is likely related to an ethnic economy that allows for socio-economic mobility while also preserving Spanish' (Lutz, 2006: 1427). This could also be put in terms of status; Spanish holds a higher status in Cuban American communities (perhaps because of the on-average higher levels of education among emigrants from Cuba), and thus speaking Spanish is less stigmatized and not perceived as a threat to middle class standing. In short, we see that the factors of language and social class are intertwined, as opposed to one clearly causing the other, but ideologies which link Spanish and poverty discourage speakers from continuing to speak Spanish.

Lutz (2006) also notes some interesting correlations between racial identity, gender and Spanish language use in her data. Girls were significantly more likely to use Spanish than boys, a finding which is replicated and discussed in many other studies (see Lutz, 2006: 1427–1428 for discussion and references). This seems to be linked to gendered social networks, a topic that will be addressed in more detail in the next section. Girls appear to interact more with parents and other community members who are likely to be the 'keepers' of the minority language, and also to be more loyal to the minority language in ways that are less clearly part of their social networks.

As far as racial identity is concerned, people with Hispanic backgrounds who identified as 'Black' were less likely to speak Spanish than those who identified as 'White' or 'Other' (Lutz, 2006: 1424). The variable of racial identity was intertwined with gender; girls who identified as 'Other' were the most likely to have high levels of Spanish proficiency, with boys who identified as 'Black' the least likely. One interpretation of these data is that in the US, being perceived as 'Black' is, as discussed in Chapter 2, often seen as at odds with being Latin@, even more than being perceived as 'White'. Latin@s are stereotypically believed to be racially 'Other', so an appearance and identification as such is most compatible with speaking Spanish. Here, again, we see that ideologies about language and 'race' influence linguistic practices.

Missing from this discussion is the use of **bilingual discourse** or translanguaging; instead, all of this literature on language use is framed in terms of the use of Spanish and English as separate codes. According to Fishman's ideas about diglossia, bilingualism would not endure in communities in which there is a great deal of translanguaging. However, studies on language maintenance have generally not looked at bilingual discourse as a linguistic practice, but instead observed or surveyed speakers about their language use, defined in terms of one language or the other, in particular domains.

There are a number of fruitful lines of research which could be followed to integrate the sustainability perspective into future work. For instance, research on ethnolinguistic vitality could investigate the status of Spanglish as an in-group code, examining how it is used in various institutions and how this might influence, and be influenced by, everyday modes of interaction. There are salient examples of bilingual radio and TV programs, for instance (see, for example, the section of 'Do You Speak American' featuring Patricia Lopez on her television show 'Mex to the Max'); it would be interesting to note if this visibility of bilingual discourse correlated with more acceptance of it. Further, what would studies correlating social factors such as gender, social class and race to language use find if instead of binary options about code choice, research participants were asked about how they use bilingual discourse? The picture of language maintenance and our ideas about ethnolinguistic vitality might look very different if the focus shifted away from different domains for Spanish and English.

Language maintenance and social networks

Social Network Theory is based on the assumption that speakers acquire and develop speech patterns from the people with whom they interact regularly, with different types of ties between speakers carrying more or less influence. This approach has most frequently been used in the field of sociolinguistics to look at social and ethnic dialect features, but there is also a growing body of research which looks at the role that social networks play in bilingual communities, and in particular in the acquisition and maintenance of minority languages (Stoessel, 2002; Wei & Lee, 2002). This body of literature is less rooted in the concept of languages being used separately in different domains than most research on language maintenance. At least some studies incorporate analyses of codeswitching which might be compatible with a perspective of translanguaging. Before delving into this literature, however, I would like to provide a very brief overview of the basic concepts of social network theory as it is used in the study of sociolinguistics.

There are different types of social networks, and these different types of networks are related to different patterns of language use. One of the features of social networks that appears to be an important influence on language use is network **density**. You have a dense social network if all of the people in your network have ties to each other; you have a loose social network if you tend to have ties to people who do not know each other, or who are not friends. **Multiplexity** is another important feature. Multiplex networks are networks in which each tie represents several different types of relationship, for example, your sister-in-law is also your neighbor and colleague. Individuals with dense and multiplex social networks are shown to use the most vernacular features, and these are also the types of networks within which minority languages are most commonly maintained (Milroy, 2002).

Early research which applied Social Network Theory to language choice data focused on minority group language use. Milroy and Wei (1995) showed that social networks as a variable were better predictors of language choice in different interaction types than demographic categories of age group, generation, sex or other static factors. This research did not look solely at the use of separate languages, but also found that different patterns of codeswitching were used by speakers associated with different networks (e.g. fluent **intrasentential codeswitching** among teens in a bilingual network contrasts with the monolingual speech of their parents' network). More recently, work within this framework by Raschka et al. (2002) builds on these findings, showing that maintenance of a minority group language can also be tied to language use within non-family and peer networks.

Other recent work within Social Network Theory has examined the role of social networks in second language acquisition as well as in first language maintenance. Smith (2002), Stoessel (2002) and Wiklund (2002) all show that social networks which involve contact with speakers of the minority language, whether it is the first or second language, are a key factor in the development and maintenance of proficiency in that language. While these results are unsurprising, they do more than provide empirical support for commonsensical assumptions; they also specify what types of network ties contribute in what ways to language learning. For example, Smith (2002) claims that network density is not a prerequisite for communicative competence; instead, language skills may be nurtured through many weak ties.

Spanish language maintenance and shift in the US

Given these different ways of looking at language maintenance, we can now move on to examine studies of particular Spanish-speaking communities in the US. Important factors discussed thus far in this chapter that we will re-visit in these case studies include ideological or status factors (what are the ideas about and attitudes towards Spanish, and bilingualism, in the community) as well as how the social networks of the speakers – which are influenced by the demographics and institutions of the community – provide opportunities for Spanish use and translanguaging, or impetus for shift to English.

Case studies of language maintenance and shift in different communities: Variables and consequences

The following sections provide overviews of different Latin@ communities across the United States. Because of the wealth of studies on language maintenance in Latin@ communities, these discussions do not represent a comprehensive summary of all of the literature on this topic, but rather a selection of studies which exemplify some of the issues and themes in the research on Spanish language maintenance and shift in the US.

Spanish in the southwest

Although Spanish speakers in the American southwest come from various countries, the majority are Mexican or Mexican American. Thus for many of the studies carried out on language maintenance in this region, the focus is on Mexican and/or Chican@ Spanish.

The Mexican American population in the US can be described as consisting of three different groups: permanent immigrants, short-term immigrants and cyclical immigrants (Valdes, 1988). In the southwest, this situation is further complicated by the fact that some heritage Spanish speakers are not immigrants; their Spanish-speaking ancestors were residents of the area long before it was US territory. These different experiences and lengths of stay in the US clearly impact the language proficiencies and preferences of individuals. However, societal bilingualism in the US southwest can generally be characterized as influenced by continued in-migration and proximity to the ancestral country of origin.

This complex set of variables is taken into account in the proposed model of Villa and Rivera-Mills (2009), which talks about language shift as a non-linear process; that is, individuals may stop using Spanish when they are young, but then re-acquire or re-activate Spanish in later phases of their lives. These authors put a lot of focus on the choice of partner in the transmission of Spanish; **linguistic endogamy** (marrying someone within the ethnolinguistic group) greatly affects what language(s) will be spoken in the home and thus passed on to the next generation. Also, bilingual education may encourage language maintenance and alter the course of language shift.

On a more micro-level, Velázquez (2009) examined the attitudes and actions of parents (primarily mothers) in El Paso, Texas, regarding passing on Spanish to their children. Although all of the parents in her study felt that Spanish was important, this did not necessarily translate into the investment of time and effort necessary for the next generation to become fluent speakers. Further, despite some positive views about Spanish, Velázquez also found evidence of some attitudes about the learning and use of the Spanish language and the status of its speakers which were less conducive to language maintenance. Overall, most of the mothers interviewed did not perceive Mexican Americans as having status or power in the political or public realm, and some felt that bilingualism was not a source of cultural capital that could lead to socio-economic success. In fact, some of the mothers felt that learning Spanish might hinder their children's achievements in learning and becoming highly proficient in English. However, it should also be noted that all of the research participants gave estimates of how much of the El Paso population was Latin@ that were at the same level as or higher than those reflected in census data. The general attitude was that most, if not all, Latin@s spoke Spanish, and many non-Latin@s also had at least rudimentary skills in the language as well. Thus we see an attitude that the language is robustly present in the community, despite the admitted dominance of English in most contexts.

Another recent study of Spanish in El Paso (Achugar, 2008) shows a somewhat different picture of this community. In this research, data from prominent individuals at the university and from newspaper articles show that there is a strong theme of resistance to normative monolingualism as an ideology. A key aspect of Spanish language status in this competing ideology is that it is legitimate in the public sphere and a valuable resource in such contexts.

Another Texas community which has been studied in these terms is San Antonio (Garcia, 2003; Schecter & Bayley, 2002). In both of these studies, San Antonio is compared to Californian communities – the San Francisco area by Schecter and Bayley, and Los Angeles by Garcia. Both comparisons show that San Antonio has a Latin@ majority, as compared with Latin@ minorities in the California contexts, and that the Latin@ population in San Antonio is primarily Mexican American, while the Latin@ population is more diverse in the California contexts. There are also multiple minority languages in both Los Angeles and San Francisco, which means that resources for minority languages might potentially be divided. Also, the Latin@ population in San Antonio has been living there, and maintaining Spanish while also learning English, for generations; this is less the case in the California locations. Finally, California is officially an English Only state, while Texas is not, thus socio-politically the ideology of normative monolingualism is stronger in California.

Garcia's study indicates that while Spanish may be maintained in both San Antonio and Los Angeles, probably for different reasons, in San Antonio it has gained status and usefulness in the public sphere, while in Los Angeles there is continued in-migration of Spanish speakers. Comparing this to Schecter and Bayley's study forces us to acknowledge that the type of research done on the community also makes a difference in the findings. Garcia's article is an overview of the two communities, both of which she has been or is a resident of; she relies on her experiences, statistics and historical accounts of the role of Spanish in these two locales. Her research provides an overview of the factors that contribute to language maintenance in each city. In contrast, Schecter and Bayley's book-length treatment of the topic has different methodologies and goals; in addition to an overview of the social and linguistic situation for Spanish speakers in these two communities, they also provide case studies of particular families, looking at their patterns of language use and attitudes about Spanish and English. Consequently, the influences on language maintenance they find are of a more personal nature. For example, a residence isolated from English speakers and where only Spanish is spoken in the home, a situation which is possible in either location, contributes heavily to learning Spanish before English and the continued use of Spanish by the children once they begin school and learn English. Other factors are less individual and linked more to the wider community, but are also not specific to either Texas or California: the availability of some sort of Spanish-language education, having an extended family or local community within which Spanish is spoken, and access to Spanish language media (e.g. telenovelas, radio stations) all contribute to language maintenance.

Moving to a territory between Texas and California, namely Arizona, Cashman (2009) looks at the larger sociopolitical context and dominant language ideologies as factors in language maintenance, focusing on the opposing (although nonetheless simultaneously present) forces of internalization and resistance. She describes Arizona as anti-immigrant and anti-bilingual, due to legislation limiting bilingual education options and opportunities for immigrants, and a pervasive attitude of 'language panic', which, she says, 'has the effect (and perhaps the intention) of focusing the anxieties of the public on a selected language (and by extension its speakers), holding the language (and its speakers) as responsible for society's ills' (Cashman, 2009: 57). This panic is not exclusively found among non-Latin@s; Latin@s also internalize this ideology, and turn away from Spanish. Competing with this is the language pride of Spanish speakers in Arizona, which has led to the creation of Spanish-language media, dual language schools, and other grassroots movements. The result is that along with panic and pride come both maintenance and shift as individuals and communities respond differently to hegemonic ideologies.

The southwestern US, although often thought of as the primary region of this country where Spanish is spoken, is neither uniform across the (admittedly quite large) area, nor does it exhibit linear language shift or stable maintenance. Instead, there are dynamic forces which influence how languages are used, including a range of factors from legislation to strength of family ties.

Cuban Americans in Miami

The literature on Spanish language use in Miami brings out aspects of the sociolinguistic situation which are clearly different from other Latin@ communities. These differences are linked to the reasons for immigration and demographic features of the Cuban American population in Miami, as well as the presence of Spanish speakers from various Latin American countries. Emigrants from Cuba tend to be educated and middle class, and generally have left their country for political reasons; this clearly distinguishes them from poor and uneducated emigrants who have come to the US to find work as agricultural, domestic or factory workers. Further, US immigration policies have favored middle class Cubans (González, 2001; Novas, 2008). In the US, despite the difficulties of the immigrant experience, the language barrier, and discrimination, Cuban Americans tend to be college educated (70%) and employed in white collar jobs (50%) (Ramirez & de la Cruz, 2002, cited in Porcel, 2006: 94). Cuban Americans are highly involved in local, regional and national politics, leading to their positioning as a relatively powerful social group. This means, in terms of the factors of ethnolinguistic vitality, that they rank high on all counts – there is a concentrated population of Spanish speakers, many Spanish language institutions, and relatively high regard for Spanish and its speakers, at least within the Cuban American community (Lopez Morales, 2000; Lynch, 2000a; Porcel, 2006). Further contributing to the demographics which are believed to contribute to language maintenance is the fact that during the 1990s Nicaraguans, Colombians, Puerto Ricans, Dominicans, Mexicans, Hondurans, Peruvians, Salvadorans and other nationalities flooded into the Miami area. Dade County, as well several other major municipalities in the surrounding area, became approximately 50% 'Hispanic' according to census figures (Lynch, 2000a: 273).

Many studies indicate that Spanish is flourishing in the Miami area. In particular, there are a number of studies which focus on the development of the Cuban American variety of Spanish in Miami. Such analysis of change usually involves the examination of inter-generational differences; in other words, this work relies on the idea that Spanish continues to be spoken by the next generation. While contact with English is in some cases posited as a source of particular features of the Spanish varieties spoken in this area, such developments are not discussed as if they are in conflict with the maintenance of the minority language. For example, Alvord (2010a, 2010b) examines intonation patterns in Miami Spanish, finding some continuity but also some intergenerational differences. Lynch looks at both the development of the subjunctive (Lynch, 2000b) and the use of final /s/ marking on verbs (Lynch, 2009), again looking at development in the Spanish dialect over generations.

At the same time, and in some cases by the same authors, there is a theme in the literature about the question of language maintenance. Lynch (2000a, 2000b) is most optimistic about the promise of Spanish in the Miami area, but even earlier studies such as Resnik (1988) point out that although Spanish is spoken outside the confines of the ethnic group boundaries, Cuban Americans share many values with the mainstream population, leading to assimilation into Anglophone society. Other studies (Castellanos, 1990; Porcel, 2006; Portes & Schauffler, 1994) portray the situation as one of transitional bilingualism, with the young people dominant in English. Porcel (2006) states that the apparent paradox – that while there is the greatest potential for minority language maintenance within the Cuban American community in Miami, there is also the least inclination to maintain the language – is not a paradox at all; despite the relatively high status of Spanish, favorable demographic factors and institutional support, Spanish is no match for English in terms of overall status and the resources devoted to its promotion. There is no definitive word on Spanish in Miami for future generations, but watching this situation unfold will provide important information about what factors carry the most influence for language maintenance.

Puerto Ricans in New York City

Much of the research on Puerto Rican origin Spanish in New York City looks at particular structural aspects of the variety, often with a comparison to varieties spoken in Puerto Rico. For example, Flores-Ferrán (2002, 2004) discusses the use of subject personal pronouns in New York City Puerto Rican Spanish, arguing that the high rate of occurrence relative to other varieties of Spanish largely mirrors patterns of use in Puerto Rico, and does not indicate transfer from English. As with the studies of Cuban origin varieties of Spanish in Miami, such studies often do not directly address the possibility of language shift but assume continued transmission of the language.

Zentella (1997) combines ethnographic and sociolinguistic methods to present a description of the full spectrum of language use in a Puerto Rican community, *el bloque*, over a period of more than a decade. She outlines the community repertoire not just in terms of using Spanish and English, but also different varieties of each language, and bilingual discourse ('Spanglish'). The codes spoken in *el bloque*, as reported by Zentella (1997: 41), include Popular Puerto Rican Spanish, Standard Puerto Rican Spanish, English-dominant Spanish, Puerto Rican English, AAVE, Hispanized English and Standard New York City English.

Regardless of the variety of Spanish, the question remains as to what extent these codes continue to be spoken. English-dominant Spanish, as the term suggests, is spoken by children who have English as their dominant language, which suggests language shift. While Zentella's profiles of different families showed a great deal of variation in the amount of Spanish used in different households – the most important variable being if there was a Spanish-dominant adult who motivated the children to use Spanish – there was a clear tendency for children to use English among themselves. As these children grew older, the community of *el bloque* disintegrated and the network within which Spanish was maintained was no longer present. While those who learned Spanish in their youth did not forget how to speak it, or even necessarily stop speaking it entirely, the prospects for passing Spanish on to future generations seemed slim. In some cases, young parents expressed a desire to have their children speak Spanish, or even had a confident certainty that they would, but they did not provide a Spanish-speaking environment for them. For the participants in Zentella's research, then, language shift seemed to be underway. It is important to note, however, that, as in the Mexican American communities discussed above, in a broader context the language may continue to be spoken because of continued in-migration from Puerto Rico; but there is little evidence that it survives more than a generation or two once speakers are established in New York City (García *et al.*, 2001; Zentella, 1997).

Unlike the situation for speakers of Spanish in Miami, where there are many favorable factors supporting the minority language, the situation of Spanish in the Puerto Rican neighborhoods of New York City does not seem favorable in terms of the factors we have discussed. The speakers tend to be low in status in the larger community, as is their language; and while there may be covert prestige attached to speaking Spanish, the social networks of the speakers are often not dominated by other Spanish speakers. In other words, despite the relatively large number of Puerto Ricans living in New York City, they do not have the type of isolated and concentrated community that fosters language maintenance (although as noted by García *et al.*, 2001, this does not mean a loss of ethnic identity). Further, the institutional support is not strong; bilingual education tends to be transitional, and for the participants in Zentella's study was not consistently available as a mechanism for encouraging language maintenance but was primarily a vehicle for transition to English.

Spanish in Chicago

According to the 2010 census, 28.9% of Chicago's residents identify as 'Hispanic' (United States Census Bureau, 2012). This places Chicago as having the fifth largest Latin@ population in the US, after New York City, Los Angeles, Houston and San Antonio. According to data provided by Potowski (2004, 2009) from the 2000 census, 70% of the Latin@ population in Chicago is Mexican American and 15% Puerto Rican. López (2009), also relying on data from the 2000 census, notes that despite the predominance of Mexican American and Puerto Ricans, Cuban Americans and members of other minority groups from Central and South American are also well represented. There are four communities in Chicago which have a Latin@ population of over 70%, and many others with a substantial number of Latin@ residents (Farr, 2011). Thus in terms of raw numbers and population density, Chicago is not an unfavorable place for Spanish maintenance. In terms of the status of the speakers, it is very mixed; while there are many Latin@ professionals, politicians and elected officials, there are also many Latin@ factory workers and kitchen crews (Potowski, 2004).

Institutional support is present in the form of bilingual schools, churches, newspapers and media (see http://www.cal.org/twi/index.htm for a list of bilingual schools, http://www.abyznewslinks.com/uniteilch.htm for the Chicago News Media guide, and http://www.ethnicchurch.com/filter/spanish.aspx for the Ethnic Christian Church director.)

Work on Spanish language maintenance in Chicago provides a picture of language use which shows that young people tend to speak more English to each other, and use English language media, but continue to speak Spanish to the older generation (Potowski 2004; Ramirez, 1991). Thus a shift to English over generations in a single family is common, but there is a relatively steady influx of Spanish-speaking immigrants who ensure that the language continues on a societal level.

An additional aspect of Spanish in Chicago which should not go unmentioned is the contact between speakers of two distinct dialects, Mexican Spanish and Puerto Rican Spanish. Although animosity between these two groups of speakers is often reported (Rúa, 2001), there is nonetheless contact between groups resulting in children with one Mexican and one Puerto Rican parent. Often referred to as 'MexiRicans' (Potowski, 2008a, 2008b), these children are exposed to two linguistically and culturally different worlds through the two sides of their families. Potowski's work shows that the Spanish dialect of the mother is often dominant over that of the father in the speech of the children, but ethnic identification is fluid and may shift across interactions (Potowski, 2008a, 2008b, 2009; Rúa, 2001). There is only a small body of research on this group of Spanish-English bilinguals, so it is not clear if their dual affiliations influence language maintenance and shift, although Torres (2010) has noted that language shift appears to be accelerated in Puerto Rican communities.

Conclusion

Some of the themes which emerge from these vignettes of Spanish-speaking communities illustrate how differences across communities matter, while others show that there are similarities across communities regardless of country of origin, location in the US, or factors in terms of demography, status and institutional support.

One factor which proves to be an important variable in language maintenance is the opportunity to have Spanish language education (this will be discussed in greater detail in Chapter 7). This factor is intertwined with others: the resources of the community (often related to social class), status of the language and its speakers within that community, and density of the minority language-speaking population.

One of the overarching themes is perhaps a simplistic one: Spanish language maintenance is difficult in this English-dominant country, even in communities which provide bilingual education and social networks of Spanish speakers. Part of this difficulty is that the ideology of English dominance can be internalized by Spanish speakers; another part is that many people do not accurately assess the focus on Spanish which is necessary to transmit the language to the next generation. Often, because they themselves learned Spanish in the home, they assume their children will, but both the home experience and the wider community may be markedly different for the children than it was for the parents. Often, this means that the children do not learn Spanish, or learn far less than anticipated by the parents, especially if there is no opportunity for bilingual education in the community.

Despite these practical and ideological considerations contributing to language shift, there has been an increase in the number of Spanish speakers in the US. This is primarily because of continued in-migration from Latin America (Lipski, 2004).

There are two important directions for future research which are indicated here. First, there is a growing body of research about Latin@s in the 'new Diaspora', which refers to areas of the US which have recently become home to more immigrants from Latin America, such as the south (Beck & Allexsaht-Snider, 2002; Gibson, 2002; Wortham et al., 2009). Watching how Spanish and English speakers interact in these areas will be an important part of future research on Latin@s in the US.

Further, because most of the research on language maintenance and shift is not heteroglossic in perspective, there is little research which explores the long-term effect of transnational identities and translanguaging. While bilingual discourse is acknowledged in many studies, it is, if anything, sometimes assumed to be detrimental to maintaining Spanish. It can be hoped that future studies will look beyond a domain analysis and instead focus on the possibility of sustainable translanguaging.

Discussion questions and activities

1. Wolford and Carter (see recommended reading) address the issue of the role of sociolinguists in public discourse about Spanish in the US. What can and should you do, as someone who is informed about the issues, in terms of educating the public about this topic?
2. What possible problems do you see with using census data and self-report studies to assess language maintenance? What other ways can you think of to collect data on minority language use?

Recommended reading/viewing

Bayley, R. and Bonicci, L.M. (2009) Recent research on Latinos in the US and Canada, Part 1: Language maintenance and shift and English varieties. *Language and Linguistics Compass* 3 (5), 1300–1313.

PBS (2004) *Do you speak American?* Episode 3. McNeil Lehrer Productions, PBS.

Wolford, T.E. and Carter, P.M. (2010) Spanish-as-threat ideology and the sociocultural context of Spanish in South Texas. In S.V Rivera-Mills and D.J. Villa (eds), *Spanish of the US Southwest: A Language in Transition* (pp.111–132). Norwalk, CT: Iberoamericana Vervuert Publishing Corp.

6

Linguistic Consequences of Spanish-English Bilingualism in the US: 'Spanglish' and Chican@ English

Objectives: To introduce students to the basic structural aspects of language contact, and to look at some features of contact varieties of Spanish and English which have developed in the context of Spanish-English bilingualism in the US.

I begin this chapter with a discussion of the nature of language mixing in general, the tradition of research on this subject, and the use of the term 'Spanglish', which has often been used to refer to a language which is a mixture of Spanish and English. The next section introduces some phenomena which often occur in language contact. The third section of this chapter will move on to structural borrowing, that is, what beyond words has been borrowed from English into Spanish in the US. After a summary of this topic, I will then look at the other side of the language contact coin: what happens to English varieties in bilingual communities? Research on what has been called Chican@ English will be discussed in this final section.

Introduction

There are two main difficulties in writing this chapter. First, a lot of the material requires at least some knowledge about language or linguistics. If you haven't taken a grammar course or an introduction to linguistics course, some of the details of this chapter may be unclear to you. However, the text is designed to give the reader a broad understanding about what happens to languages in contact, so the aim is for the big picture to become clear even if the details are fuzzy.

Second, almost all of the research discussed here is carried out within what we have discussed in previous chapters as a monoglossic paradigm for bilingualism; that is, the languages are viewed as two distinct, monolithic entities. This chapter is an attempt to re-frame this research within a heteroglossic perspective, asking the question, what structures are used in translanguaging?

Although the focus of this chapter is structural, we cannot separate linguistic forms from their social functions. The social context of language contact has a great influence on the structural outcome (Thomason & Kaufman, 1988; Winford, 2003). I am going to use the term **language contact phenomena** here to refer to all of the linguistic forms that occur when two (or more) languages are in contact. Definitions and examples of these different phenomena will be presented in the next section, but first I would like to reiterate two points central to the study of language contact phenomena. First, as has been stressed in previous chapters, it is natural for all speakers to use forms which are assigned to different languages in their speech; it is the strict separation of these codes into discrete languages which is unnatural. Thus, it is not surprising that US Spanish is different to Spanish spoken in other cultural contexts; languages in contact invariably influence each other, and usually in asymmetrical ways (Fairclough, 2003; Lipski, 2007b). Although language change is often characterized as language deterioration, today's 'bad grammar' and 'mixed language' are the standard constructions and vocabulary of tomorrow.

Second, despite the common occurrence of translanguaging, mixed codes are usually assigned negative value in the dominant society, especially if the mainstream population is not multilingual. In many cases multilinguals themselves also have negative attitudes about language contact phenomena. It is thought that languages should remain 'pure' and linguistically distinct. As Rodriguez (2007: 38) writes about contact between Spanish and English, 'Spanglish's critics view Spanglish as a dirty dialect that threatens to pollute Spanish and English.' Translanguaging is often viewed as a sign that a speaker cannot speak either language, that is, it is seen as a sign of linguistic deficiency (Myers-Scotton, 2006: 10).

In contrast to that popular misconception, the discussion here will begin with the assumption that translanguaging is not only a natural practice but it also serves an important social function. In this case, use of elements from both Spanish and English is an act of identity; it is a means of constructing a bilingual, bicultural ideology that is a challenge to essentialist, hegemonic ideas about monolingualism, national belonging and, in many cases, racial categorizations. Rodriguez (2007: 29) writes:

> Spanglish is therefore more than a long-term racial miscegenation process occurring among Latinos in the US, and definitely more than the evolution of a language that fuses English and Spanish. It is, in fact, about the evolution of an identity that is finally disconnected – liberated, really – from one race, one place, one space, one language, one vision, one history, and so on.

This is echoed by Morales (2002: 6–7):

> When I speak of Spanglish, I'm talking about a fertile terrain for negotiating a new identity. . . .At the root of Spanglish is a very universal state of being. It is a displacement from one place, home to another place, home in which one feels at home in both places, yet at home in neither place. It is a kind of banging-one's-head-against-the-wall-state, and the only choice you have left is to embrace the transitory (read transnational) state of in-between.

My aim in citing these authors is to set the scene for the following discussion of linguistic traits by keeping the meaning of and motivation for bilingual discourse alive. While we can discuss the linguistic features of utterances in technical terms, I do not want to lose sight of the fact that what I call translanguaging – also called Spanglish, or Spanish-English bilingual discourse – is a dynamic form of communication which develops out of particular cultural contexts.

Although recent research stresses a more fluid and less binary view of heteroglossia, the use of elements assigned to two different codes is often discussed in terms of being a deviant mixture of two distinct entities, and this is hardly unique to Spanish and English. In popular discourse, we have terms like 'Dinglish' (a mixture of *Deutsch* (German) and English) and 'Chinglish' (a Chinese-flavored variety of English). Researchers on bilingualism have also long recognized this, and decades before the term translanguaging came into use, scholars have come up with terms for the pervasive use of two or more languages in discourse. Auer (1984: 9) discusses 'the creation of a new code',

Myers-Scotton (1993: 119) describes what she calls 'codeswitching as an unmarked code', and Gafaranga and Torras (2002: 11) refer to 'language alternation as the medium'. All of these terms address the use of elements of two (or more) languages as a frequent occurrence, socially meaningful, and a code unto itself. Work on translanguaging and heteroglossia build on these perspectives, and this is the school of thought within which we find most of the research (and popular texts) on 'Spanglish'.

Before continuing, the use of the term 'Spanglish' should be problematized. Although often used in a derogatory manner to indicate that the language being spoken is not a 'real' language, the term Spanglish has also been adopted by many speakers of US Spanish; there are a number of popular books with the word 'Spanglish' in their titles (see the list in the recommended reading section later), and there are various bumper stickers, t-shirts and other artifacts of popular culture that show that the term is used to mark an in-group way of speaking. However, there are also detractors who point out that this term carries ideological baggage (Otheguy, 2009). Otheguy and Stern (2010) present an argument against using the term Spanglish for oral varieties of Spanish spoken in the US, arguing in part that it is not a hybrid language and the term is misleading. They continue:

> We reject the use of the term Spanglish because there is no objective justification for the term, and because it expresses an ideology of exceptionalism and scorn that actually deprives the North American Latino community of a major resource in this globalized world: mastery of a world language. Thus on strictly objective technical grounds, as well as for reasons of personal and political development, the term Spanglish is to be discarded and replaced by the term Spanish or, if greater specificity is required, Spanish in the United States. (Otheguy & Stern, 2010: 85)

Otheguy and Stern are certainly correct that the use of this term is a recognition of exceptional status, and that by any name – Spanglish, translanguaging, codeswitching, language mixing, etc. – it is not an exceptional practice. Their point is that Spanish in the United States is not exceptional, it is simply another dialect of Spanish; and this is a valid point, as there are hundreds of varieties around the world which have changed and adapted to new environments and are used in similar ways. Yet the crux of the matter here is socio-political, not linguistic, and in many cases the use of the term Spanglish is a celebration of the heteroglossic nature of linguistic performance. The choice is between rejecting Spanglish as a derogatory term which stigmatizes what is a natural linguistic process (as suggested by Otheguy & Stern, 2010) or participating in co-opting a term which has been used in a derogatory manner by the dominant group to create minority group solidarity and challenge monoglossic ideologies (Cruz & Teck, 1998; Santiago, 2008; Stavans, 2003; Stavans & Albin, 2007). Both of these positions are valid, and I do not wish to pass judgment on which position has more merit. Therefore, in the following discussion, I will continue to use the term Spanglish if that is the term used by the authors whose work I am discussing; but as a descriptive term, I will use 'US Spanish', or 'contact variety of Spanish' in cases where 'Spanish' seems to require more description.

Stavans (2000, 2003) draws parallels between 'Ebonics' and Yiddish and Spanglish. (Instead of 'Ebonics', which is the term Stavans uses, in this discussion I will use the term African American Vernacular English (AAVE), which is more common in sociolinguistic circles.) These are relevant comparisons. Like AAVE, Spanglish is a way of speaking which is considered non-standard, and is something which has developed as a way of speaking within an ethnic group; although it is used by others, and aspects of it may make their way into mainstream US English varieties, it is essentially a means of constructing in-group identity. However, there are important distinctions between AAVE and Spanglish. Most obviously, although AAVE may well have a **Creole origin**, it is not a recent mixture of two languages which are perceived as distinct entities, as Spanglish is. Thus the common criticism of AAVE is that it is 'bad English', while the criticism of Spanglish is that it is not 'pure Spanish'.

Stavans (2000) also makes the point that Spanglish is not limited to use by poor or uneducated speakers, while he claims AAVE is; I have two criticisms of this distinction. First, his depiction of AAVE as being spoken by African American youth, particularly in the ghetto (Stavans, 2000), is inaccurate. Although Stavans recognizes that AAVE is not merely a collection of slang words, but that it is a code with its own structural integrity, he seems to be otherwise unacquainted with both the age variation (e.g. Rickford, 1999; Wolfram & Thomas, 2002) and social class variation (e.g. Linnes, 1998; Weldon, 2004; Wolfram, 2007) of AAVE. Second, while he aptly points out all of the myriad users of Spanglish – 'people in all social strata, from migrant workers to politicians, academics, and TV anchors regularly use it, both in the United States and south of the Rio Grande' (Stavans, 2000) – I would suggest that this is not necessarily the most common view of Spanglish. Spanglish is often equated with uneducated speakers and its use is often considered to be detrimental to the academic or professional success of the speakers (see also Lipski, 2007a on this topic). Further, even those who go on record as being proponents of Spanglish do not present it as a fully legitimate language. In an article in the *New York Times*, journalist Lizette Alvarez claims that Spanglish is 'the best of both languages' (Alvarez, 1997: 483), but also says that it has 'few rules' and that Spanglish is often spoken 'with a sense of humor' (Alvarez, 1997: 484). In other words, it is not a real language, just a way of playing with language. In an article speaking out against Spanglish, Echevarria (1997), in a *New York Times* article titled 'Is "Spanglish" a language?', first describes it has having 'crossed over from the street to Hispanic talk shows and advertising campaigns', but then claims:

> The sad reality is that Spanglish is primarily the language of poor Hispanics, many barely literate in either language. They incorporate English words and constructions into their daily speech because they lack the vocabulary and education in Spanish to adapt to the changing culture around them. (Echevarria, 1997)

So although there are important distinctions between AAVE and Spanglish, I would suggest that they share the trait of being stereotyped as inferior ways of speaking which relegate their speakers to ghettos. The reality of the use of both of these varieties is more complex, but they are assigned similar negative connotations in popular culture.

The parallel to Yiddish made by Stavans brings out other important aspects of the social context of Spanglish. First, Stavans notes that both Yiddish and Spanglish are language mixtures which never had a unified standard but are comprised of regional varieties mixed with another code. In the case of Yiddish, varieties of German, Hebrew, Russian, Polish and other Slavic languages come together to form a code; in the case of Spanglish, many varieties of Spanish are in contact with many varieties of American English. And in both cases, what emerges is a transnational code, a code which defies categorization not just because of its linguistic traits but also because of its mobility and social flexibility.

In the next sections, I will address how to describe some of the linguistic features of translanguaging among Latin@s in the US. I will first discuss a number of different ways in which two languages can be structurally combined, and then address the possibilities for structural convergence; that is, the borrowing or integration of more than just words from one language into another.

Language contact phenomena defined

In Haugen's (1950) landmark work, the author outlines a number of possible patterns of influence of one language on another. These terms and categories are relevant for describing the structure of US Spanish. First, we have what is commonly called a **loan-word** or a **borrowing**, and this is a word taken from one language and used in another. We will call the language which incorporates an element from another language the **recipient language**, and the language from which the element is taken the **donor language**. One of the aspects of borrowing that linguists discuss is **phonological integration**; if a word is phonologically integrated, the sounds of the recipient language are used; if it is not phonologically integrated, sounds from the donor language are preserved. But despite this cut-and-dried sounding criterion, phonological integration of loanwords is not fixed but variable. It depends first on the sound correspondences between the two languages; if the languages have a similar phonological system, integration is easier. However, phonological integration also depends on the level of bilingualism (especially in terms of phonology, or what is commonly thought of as 'accent') of the individual speakers. That is, if I speak English with a 'Spanish accent', then obviously the Spanish loanwords I might use in English will also use Spanish phonology. Thus phonological integration of loanwords can be a subjective matter.

However, in order to be considered a loanword, and not part of bilingual discourse, borrowings must be used by monolinguals of the recipient language. The process of borrowing is generally thought to be that words from Language X are first used by X/Y bilinguals in bilingual discourse; when particular words are also adopted by monolingual speakers of Language Y they are considered borrowings. The underlying idea about the process of language contact and change is that what begins as the translanguaging of bilinguals becomes established and these words or structures are also used by other speakers of the recipient language.

Once they are used by monolinguals of the recipient language, most borrowings are phonologically integrated, with sounds from the donor language which are not present in the recipient language replaced (Winford, 2003: 47). For example, the word *taco* has been borrowed into English as a cultural loanword; but the **unaspirated** /k/ sound used in Spanish has been replaced by the **aspirated** /kʰ/ of English. Similarly, the loanword *troca* 'truck' in US Spanish uses an unaspirated /k/, not the aspirated /kʰ/ of the English source word, and also uses a Spanish flap /r/ instead of the English retroflex /ɹ/.

In some cases, what Haugen called **hybrid loanwords** are formed; typically these are compound words which are half in the donor language and half in the recipient language. Weinreich (1967: 52) cites *home plato* 'home plate' and *pelota de fly* 'fly ball' as examples from Spanish in the US.

Another type of language contact phenomena noted by Haugen and others is the **calque**, also known as a **loan translation** (Haugen, 1950: 214; Myers-Scotton, 2006: 218; Otheguy, 1993). Calques are literal translations, often idiomatic phrases or metaphors. Haugen notes that the English term 'skyscraper' was translated literally into several languages to refer to tall buildings (*cf.* Spanish *rascacielos*). Perhaps the best known, or most frequently cited, calque in Spanish in the US is *llamar para atrás* for 'call back'; standard Spanish employs the words *volver al llamar* 'to return the call' (Fernández, 1983: 19).

Another phenomenon is what Haugen calls **semantic loans** or **loanshifts** (Haugen, 1950: 214, 219; Myers-Scotton, 2006: 218). These are words from the recipient language which have taken on a different meaning because of their phonological similarity to words from the donor language. For example, Smead (2000: 162) notes the use of *colegio* ('school' in most Spanish varieties) to mean 'college' in US Spanish, and Ardilla (2005: 72) notes the use of *ganga* (which means 'sale' or 'bargain' in other varieties) to mean 'gang'.

But language contact does not just result in using words and phrases from all sources, but also grammatical structures and phonology. In the following section, research addressing the possible influence of English on Spanish grammar will be addressed. In the subsequent section, research on the possible influence of Spanish on English, in what is commonly called Chican@ English, will be discussed.

Structural borrowing

For Spanish in the US, there are several themes in the findings on structural borrowing. First, while many studies show changes that are linked to English influence, there does not seem to be 'radical restructuring' (e.g. Silva-Corvalán, 1994; Zapata *et al.*, 2005). That is, basic word order and important grammatical categories have not changed. Second, several researchers suggest that the changes are a means of lightening the cognitive load by using structures which are common to both languages (e.g. Montoya, 2011; Nava, 2007; Silva-Corvalán, 1994; Toribio, 2004). Third, many authors agree that although language contact may not be the sole or direct cause of the features which emerge in contact varieties of Spanish, language contact accelerates changes which are already underway and promotes simplification (e.g. Gutierrez, 1994; Orozco, 2007; Silva-Corvalán, 1994).

In the field of contact linguistics and, especially, historical linguistics, there has long been a tendency to avoid claims of language contact as the source of language change in favor of explanations which show general principles of language development (e.g. simplification). I believe that this tendency is rooted in a perspective that language contact in general, and translanguaging in particular, is not part of 'normal' language development. While I do not agree with this perspective, it is clearly reflected in much of the research discussed in the rest of this chapter.

Various studies have examined whether varieties of Spanish in contact with English show increased use of subject-verb word order, which is not mandatory in Spanish declaratives. Both Silva-Corvalán (2004: 141–5) and Nava (2007) show that although subject-verb order is the most common order in all varieties of Spanish, bilingual speakers in the US, especially those who are dominant in English, produce higher rates of subject-verb word order. This does not indicate a dramatic change in Spanish syntax, but rather the reduced use of variation in word order for **pragmatic** reasons.

A similar story can be found in the analyses of the use or non-use of subject pronouns. Spanish is notoriously what is called a **pro-drop** language; the subject pronouns can be 'dropped' because verbs mark the person and number, so the use of a pronoun provides only redundant information (except for the **grammatical gender** of the subject in some cases). Subject pronouns are thus used for pragmatic reasons, for example emphasis or contrast. So while the **unmarked** version of 'I love you' would be *te quiero* (you-obj love/1pSG; see key to abbreviations at the end of the chapter), it is also possible to say *yo te quiero*, with an overt 1st person singular subject pronoun (i.e. *yo* 'I'). With the overt pronoun *yo*, there is emphasis on the subject. For example, in response to the lament *nadie me quiere* 'nobody loves me', one might respond *yo te quiero* '*I* love you'.

The point here is that use of subject pronouns is variable in Spanish. In English, obviously, this is not the case; while we do use telegraphic speech in some contexts (e.g. 'will be back soon'), in conversation the unmarked case is the use of subject pronouns (e.g. 'she was alone'; compare with Spanish *estaba sola* 'was/3pSG alone/F').

There are various positions in the literature about whether Spanish speakers in the US use more subject pronouns due to influence from English; one of the critical issues to be addressed here is, more than whom? What is the relevant comparison? Another issue is, even if there is more use of subject pronouns, can we show that this is due to influence from English?

Silva-Corvalán (1994: 162f) notes that the bilingual speakers in her study do not use a higher percentage of subject pronouns overall than monolingual Spanish speakers, although they may have different constraints on their pronoun production (that is, they use pronouns in different contexts, and for different pragmatic reasons, than speakers of other Spanish varieties). On the other hand, Otheguy *et al.* (2007) note an increase in subject pronoun use over generations in New York Spanish speakers which they attribute to contact with English and the development of a unique contact variety (involving contact between Caribbean and Mainland varieties of Spanish as well as English influence). Research by Montrul (2004) also claims influence from English leading to an increased use of subject pronouns, but not in her category of 'advanced heritage speakers', who scored higher on a Spanish proficiency test. Those categorized as 'intermediate heritage speakers' produced high rates of subject pronouns and, as in the other studies, seemed to have different constraints on the use of these pronouns. This study thus implies that the higher rate of use of pronouns is connected to a lower overall proficiency in Spanish. This analysis rests heavily on a monoglossic viewpoint of bilingualism, as it looks at the production of monolingual Spanish as the goal of the speaker.

This perspective is also adopted in research done by Flores-Ferrán (2002, 2004) which argues that English is not the influencing factor. Her research looks at the subject pronoun use of speakers of Puerto Rican Spanish in New York City (NYC) in comparison with speakers in Puerto Rico, and also examines if the variable of amount of contact with English of the NYC speakers can be correlated with subject pronoun use patterns. She finds that the rates of pronoun use by NYC Spanish speakers are not significantly higher than those reported in studies in Puerto Rico; it should be noted that Caribbean Spanish varieties notoriously have higher rates of overt subject pronoun use than other Latin American varieties of Spanish, which is a factor in the comparison of rates across studies. Although the native-born group of New York Puerto Rican Spanish speakers in Flores-Ferrán's study did produce the most overt subject pronouns, there was a not a linear progression of increase in pronoun use with an increase of exposure to English. Thus Flores-Ferrán concludes that there is insufficient evidence to argue for the influence of English on the Spanish spoken by these speakers (Flores-Ferrán, 2004: 71).

Despite Flores-Ferrán's argument, the idea that contact with English causes speakers to choose Spanish constructions which have equivalents to English runs strong in the literature on US Spanish. In addition to the features of subject pronoun expression and word order discussed above, Koontz-Garboden (2004) makes this claim for the use of the progressive form (see example (1)), Montoya suggests this for possessive constructions (see example (2)) and Silva-Corvalán also presents this explanation for the lack of use of the complementizer *que* 'that' in contexts in which it would not be required in the equivalent English sentence (see (3)).

(1)   e.g. *el sol estaba brilliando* 'the sun was shining'; cf. *el sol brillaba*
        (Koontz-Garboden, 2004: 1298)
(2a)   *Ella es muy acomplejada con su acento* (FJOTLMNC)
        She is very self conscious about her accent
(2b)   *Ella es muy acomplejada con el acento*
        *She is very self conscious about the accent (Montoya, 2011: 113)
(3)   Yo creo Ø inventaron el nombre
        I believe [that] they invented the name (Silva-Corvalán, 1994: 136)

Simplification can be seen most notably in the loss of tense-mood-aspect forms, that is, on the marking of verbs (Lipski, 1993; Lynch, 2000b; Montrul, 2007; Silva-Corvalán, 1994, 2004). In extreme cases, speakers of some US varieties of Spanish have a streamlined system which includes only present, **preterit** and **imperfect** morphology and **phrasal future tense marking** (e.g. *voy a comprar* 'I'm going shopping' as opposed to *compraré* 'I will shop'); there is little use of the **conditional** and **subjunctive** moods. While it is true that English lacks markers for the conditional and subjunctive moods, it is important to note that the tenses that are commonly used by Spanish speakers in the US do not align neatly with the tense system of American English. English does not have imperfect morphology, but that form is not lost in contact varieties of Spanish. Thus, if English is the catalyst for these changes, the influence is not a matter of transfer of features but instead that language contact accelerates simplification.

Concluding remarks about structural aspects of US Spanish

This chapter thus far has shown how US Spanish has been influenced by English, or, how translanguaging has become an established part of the performance of US Spanish. Most saliently, words and phrases from English are used in Spanish. In some cases, while the lexicon remains Spanish, the structure of English influences the grammar of an utterance. Over time, some varieties become somewhat simplified, for example, with a reduction in the verbal **morphology** or with a decline in pragmatic variation. These changes are not directly or solely the result of language contact, but are part of the ongoing change all languages undergo; yet bilingualism is part of the environment which conditions these changes.

In the next section, we will examine the flipside of US Spanish: how English develops in the context of bilingualism. The vast majority of the work done on English in Latin@ communities is done on Mexican American communities, thus this section will focus on what is called Chican@ English.

Chican@ English

What researchers have called 'Chicano English' or 'Mexican American English' (Martínez, 2006) is a variety of English spoken in Chican@ communities by dominant speakers of English. It is a variety of English associated with members of this particular ethnolinguistic group, but it is not simply a 'Spanish accent' in English; some speakers of Chican@ English do not speak Spanish at all. So Chican@ English should not be confused with 'learner English'; it's an ethnic variety, not a non-native variety (Bayley & Santa Ana, 2004; Fought, 2003; Metcalf, 1979; Ornstein-Galicia, 1984; Penfield & Ornstein-Galicia, 1985; Santa Ana, 1993; Santa Ana & Bayley, 2004).

Whether you know it or not, you are probably familiar with other ethnic varieties of American English, or at least stereotypes of them. AAVE (or what is sometimes called 'Ebonics') is an ethnic variety of English; it is a way of speaking English that is associated with African Americans. You are probably also familiar with depictions of Italian American varieties of English, if nothing else, from television shows and movies about the Mob; things such as 'youse guys' and pronouncing *these* and *those* as 'dese' and 'dose' are part of the stereotypical marking of someone as of Italian descent. Most of these people don't speak Italian; their families have been in the US for generations, but they speak a variety of English that has features of the non-native varieties spoken by their ancestors.

How does this happen? Well, we're not clear on the details – this is something that needs further study – but basically, the accent and structures of non-native speakers of English are picked up by speakers who have English as their first language, because they associate those features of English with membership of the ethnic community. This does not always happen, however. Many individuals who are raised by parents who have strong accents in English, in communities where many of the adult speakers have these same accents, nonetheless acquire a non-ethnically-marked variety of English. That is, they speak English the same way as other native speakers outside of their ethnic group in their communities. This happens in many Chican@, Puerto Rican, Cuban American, Dominican American, etc. etc., communities across the United States, as well as in countless non-Latin@ minority language contexts. But in some cases, an ethnic variety of English develops. There is no easy answer as to why this happens in some cases and doesn't in others; it's a complex situation in which speakers must have ample motivation to mark their ethnic identity through language, but are not, usually, learning the ethnic language. So in the case of Chican@ English, it would develop among speakers who want to identify themselves as Chican@, but do not necessarily speak Spanish.

This is a rather simple description of the social motivations, and I am NOT implying that Latin@ speakers of mainstream varieties of English are trying to deny that they are Latin@, or that speakers of Chican@ English are never speakers of Spanish. It's much more complicated than that. As researchers, we have not yet had the opportunity to track exactly how varieties such as Chican@ English develop. So what follows is not a conclusive description or explanation of Chican@ English, but some observations and ideas about its development and use.

One of the things researchers have tried to document is the features of Chican@ English; what makes it distinct from other American English dialects? In terms of morphology and **syntax**, or the grammar of the dialect, the literature indicates few features which are unique to Chican@ English (Bayley & Santa Ana, 2004; Fought, 2003; Penfield & Ornstein-Galicia, 1985). Many features of **non-standard** American English dialects are found in Chican@ English, including **multiple negation** (also called negative concord), as in (4); **regularization** of irregular past tense verbs, as in (5); absence of 3rd person singular –*s*, as in (6); and absence of past tense marking, as in (7).

(4) Thing **ain't** gonna **never** change in L.A. **no** more (Fought, 2003: 97)

(5) when she **striked** me with that... (Bayley & Santa Ana, 2004: 376)

(6) If somebody **come** up and **push** me then I'll probably have to push 'em back or something (Bayley & Santa Ana, 2004: 376)

(7) I saw some girl, she **look** pretty (Bayley & Santa Ana, 2004: 376)

In addition, features of colloquial speech of other American English dialects are also used by speakers of Chican@ English, such as 'be like' as a **quotative**, as in (8), or 'like' as a focus particle, as in (9), or **resumptive pronouns**, as in (10).

(8) When people want to fight me **I'm like** 'well okay, well then I'll fight you' (Bayley & Santa Ana, 2004: 379)

(9) She was **like** a real think lady (Bayley & Santa Ana, 2004: 380)

(10) I know this lady that **she** used to live here (Bayley & Santa Ana, 2004: 380)

Bayley and Santa Ana also report the use of features that are usually associated with AAVE, such as **habitual** *be* or **zero copula** (see examples 11 and 12); however, these uses are reportedly quite infrequent. It is interesting to note, however, that the zero copula examples Bayley and Santa Ana cite come from San Antonio speakers who have little contact with African Americans, and live in a city in which African Americans are only 7% of the population. In contrast with Bailey's description of the use of AAVE by Domini-can Americans (Bailey, 2001, 2002) and Zentella's discussion of the use of AAVE by Puerto Ricans in New York City (Zentella, 1997), whose studies involve speakers who have regular contact with AAVE speakers, the features in the San Antonio speakers' language seem to be taken not from AAVE but have developed as part of Chican@ English.

(11) You **be** doing a classwork in class, and she used to tell me: 'do this' (Bayley & Santa Ana, 2004: 377)

(12) I see so many people dying of diseases and I Ø just tired of it (Bayley & Santa Ana, 2004: 377)

While all of these features occur in the speech of Chican@s in these studies, it's not clear that these features are clearly different from the other local varieties in the communities studied. There are also other features cited in the literature which appear to be specific to Chican@ English, but it is unclear that they are the majority pattern – that is, they may not be used by the majority of the speakers, or frequently by any particular speakers, so it's difficult to assess their importance in the description of Chican@ English. Also, they are often fairly subtle linguistic features, ones that non-linguists are unlikely to notice as markers of ethnicity. For example, Fought (2003) discussed the use of 'could' rather than 'can' when talking about ability, as in the example 'Nobody believes that you **could** fix anything' (Fought, 2003: 100). Similarly, Wald (1987) discusses the use of 'tell' to intro-duce questions, as in 'I **told** Elinore: "Is that your brother?"' (cited in Bayley & Santa Ana, 2004: 381).

So on the whole, there are few morpho-syntactic features of Chican@ English which are uniquely part of this dialect, and none that can be clearly linked to Spanish (Fought,

2003: 102). In this way, the dialect is not clearly different from the local mainstream dialects. However, the phonology of Chican@ English is much more distinctive to hearers. Although earlier studies include many features (Penfield & Ornstein-Galicia, 1985: 36), many of which I believe would also be part of a 'Spanish accent', or the speech of a Spanish-speaking English Language Learner, the more recent work by Santa Ana and Bayley (2004) and Fought (2003) have a much more streamlined list of features. Dialectologists traditionally put a lot of focus on **vowel systems**, and therefore one area of interest in Chican@ English is the production of vowels. Two differences from local dialects cited by both Fought and Santa Ana and Bayley include less frequent **vowel reduction** and **monophthongization**. An example of vowel reduction in other American dialects is the use of the 'uh' sound for the long 'e' in words like *because*. In casual speech, this is rarely pronounced 'bee-cuz'; the vowel in the first syllable is reduced to 'uh' [ə] ('buh-cuz'). If Chican@ speakers were doing this less, it would mean that they would use pronunciations like 'bee-cuz' more frequently. Monophthongization is when a vowel, for example like the vowel in *least*, is pronounced as an 'e' ([i]) without a following glide. For many speakers of US English varieties, this vowel is not simply a long 'e' sound but an 'e' sound followed by a glide into 'y' [j]. Chican@ English speakers often do not use this glide, but produce the 'e' sound without it (Fought, 2003: 64).

One of the issues addressed in the research on this variety has been whether Chican@ English speakers are participating in local **sound changes** involving vowels. The answer is yes and no; participation in local sound changes is dependent on affiliation with the local mainstream community. In Fought's work in California, the local mainstream accent is apparently associated with European American identity, and is therefore used primarily by Chican@ English speakers who are middle class and not affiliated with gangs. Chican@ English speakers who are working class and have gang affiliations avoid sounding like their White, middle class peers and thus do not participate in ongoing sound changes (Fought, 1999, 2003). Konopka and Pierrehumbert (2008) found that the speakers in their study (speakers of what they called 'Mexican Heritage English' in Chicago, most of them not Spanish speakers) were not participating in /æ/ **raising**, a salient feature of the **Northern Cities Vowel Shift** and part of the local dialect. They posit that this is dependent on alignment with the wider community. In other words, as discussed in Chapter 2, these speakers use linguistic resources to construct their social identities; in this case Chican@ English is used to construct identities which are not aligned with mainstream social groups.

Generally speaking, the consonants of Chican@ English tend to mirror those of the other American English dialects, with the exception of the pronunciation of /t/and /d/ and in some cases 'th' sounds (Santa Ana & Bayley, 2004). Produce a 't' sound; notice that your tongue is on what's called the alveolar ridge, the spot right behind your top teeth; the same for a 'd' sound (if you are a speaker of most American English dialects, anyway). Chican@ English speakers will produce these sounds with the tongue slightly farther forward, touching the top teeth. In some cases, this is also how they will produce 'th' sounds, which, by speakers of most dialects of American English, are produced with the tongue in an **interdental position**, that is, between the upper and lower teeth (Fought, 2003: 67–8).

Aside from this minor distinction from other American English dialects, the other important feature of Chican@ English consonants is not how they are produced but if they are deleted. What is called **consonant cluster reduction** is often found in Chican@ English, especially deletion of /t/ and /d/ when they follow other consonants. For instance, the words *last week* might be pronounced 'las' week' (Santa Ana & Bayley, 2004: 425). This is, as you have probably already recognized, a feature which is common in rapid and colloquial speech in many dialects of American English. It is not, of course, categorical in anyone's speech; I might say 'last week' and 'las' week' within the same conversation. I also might say 'fol' clothes' (*fold clothes*) but 'fold up' in the same conversation, because I am more likely to delete the final 'd' when the next word starts with a consonant sound than a vowel sound. Santa Ana (1996) presents the argument that the details of this **variation** are different in Chican@ English than in other dialects of American English, and that the patterns of 't' and 'd' deletion can be traced back to the Mexican Spanish phonological system.

What is arguably most noticeable about Chican@ English is its **intonation** (Metcalf, 1979: 7, 10). Santa Ana and Bayley (2004) outline a number of patterns of the rise and fall of pitch which distinguish Chican@ English from other American English dialects. First, Chican@ English has, in general, more patterns with what they call 'glides', which means a gradual rise or fall in pitch, as opposed to abrupt rises or falls, which are called 'steps'. (Think of this as the difference between a ramp and stairs.) The syllable in which the gradual rise in pitch occurs is also often lengthened, and the cumulative effect of this is emphasis. This contrasts with other dialects of American English which use stress on a syllable, not a rise in pitch, for emphasis. This difference could be depicted something like this:

(13) He was CHOKing on it (stress on the first syllable of the word 'choking'; typical of most American English dialects)
He was chooo↑king on it (lengthened 'o' sound and gradual rising pitch; typical of Chican@ English)
(adapted from Santa Ana & Bayley, 2004: 427)

While this difference might give someone's speech a slightly ethnic flavor, more noticeable is the contrast in final pitch contours. In other dialects of English, there is a step down in pitch at the end of statements, and a step up in pitch at the end of questions. (Try saying 'That sounds good' and 'Did she answer?' yourself to see if you can hear this.) In Chican@ English, both questions and statements tend to have a glide up and then down at the end (although the contour of the entire sentence is not the same, the end segments are). In particular this contour in statements is something that is readily recognized as a marker of ethnicity, and incorporated into stereotypes of Mexicans. Santa Ana and Bayley note that Speedy Gonzales, a cartoon character, is in general a caricature of a Mexican and part of this depiction is his intonation. Go to http://www.youtube.com/watch?v=oUWVJu96aLo and watch a Speedy Gonzales cartoon to see what this sounds like. You may recognize this way of speaking as having the same intonation used to represent banditos and peasants in Hollywood westerns (Santa Ana & Bayley, 2004: 429).

It should be noted that most of the studies of Chican@ English look at this variety in one locality, a major exception being Metcalf (1979), who briefly summarizes research on Chican@ English, carried out by himself and other researchers, from a variety of locations: six different cities in California, Arizona and Las Vegas and several towns in Texas. He notes different phonological patterns in these different varieties, leading us to believe that however Chican@ English developed, it is deeply localized.

Wherever Chican@ English develops, its presence indicates the construction of a Chican@ identity that has been cumulatively constructed in a community. While not a conscious choice, ethnic dialects, like minority languages, are a means of identifying as part of a particular social group. As discussed in Chapter 2, however, we need to keep in mind that every code has multiple meanings. With Chican@ English, the element of choice is also lessened; no one chooses the local dialect they learn in the home. However, we all have some control (although perhaps not conscious control) over the extent to which we continue to use that dialect, or incorporate features of other dialects we hear into it, and it is here that language use is an act of identity.

Much work remains to be done on Chican@ English; in particular, varieties that are spoken in different areas of the country have not been well documented, and many of the grammatical features have not been studied **quantitatively**. Until this is done, it is difficult to ascertain how common some of the cited features are, and thus how important they are to the definition of the dialect.

What is clear, however, is that Chican@ English can be used to construct a Chican@ identity. In a study by Frazer (1996), non-Latin@ college students could readily recognize the speech of 'Hispanics' (the term used in this study) from that of non-Hispanics. This indicates that certain ways of speaking would lead to a speaker being labeled as 'Hispanic' by others, regardless of how s/he might self-identify. Significantly, the features of Chican@ English which occurred in the speech of the most speakers in this study (n=11) were the prosodic features, i.e. the patterns of intonation discussed above. Little work has been done within the social constructionist framework for the study of identity on Chican@ English; this will be a productive area for future research.

Discussion questions and activities

1. The issue of whether or not to use the term 'Spanglish' is parallel to the controversies about the use of the word 'queer' for recent scholarly trends (e.g. Queer Linguistics, Queer Theory), and in-group use of the word 'gay' for homosexual men and lesbians. On the one hand, these words have been used as insults and for that reason many wish to avoid them; on the other hand, there is power in embracing the words and making them symbols of in-group solidarity. Note that although 'gay' is used in a derogatory way by some (e.g. 'That's so gay', meaning 'That's stupid/ugly/etc.'), it has also become a relatively neutral term in public arenas, for example in the discussion about so-called 'gay marriage'. In what ways is 'Spanglish' similar to and different from the words 'queer' and 'gay', and do you advocate use or avoidance of the term? Why?

2. Does your speech (in the language you spoke at home as a child) sound the same as your parents? If there are differences, what do you think contributed to the development of the way you speak?

Recommended reading

Cruz, B. and Teck, B. (1998) *The Official Spanglish Dictionary: Un User's Guide to More Than 300 Words and Phrases That Aren't Exactly Español or Inglés.* New York: Fireside.

Morales, E. (2002) *Living in Spanglish: The Search for Latino Identity in America.* New York: St. Martin's Press.

Rodríguez, A. (2007) *Diversity.* Mountain View, CA: Floricanto Press.

Santa Ana, O. (1993) Chicano English and the nature of the Chicano language setting. *Hispanic Journal of Behavioral Sciences* 15 (1), 3–35.

Santiago, B. (2008) *Pardon my Spanglish: One Man's Guide to Speaking the Habla ¡Porque Because!.* Philadelphia: Quirk Books.

Key to abbreviations for grammatical glosses

F   feminine grammatical gender
Obj: objective case
1pSG   first person singular
3pSG   third person singular

7
Latin@ Education in the US

Objectives: To review the issues underlying the education of Latin@s, whether they are monolingual in Spanish, monolingual in English or bilingual, and to become acquainted with assessments of the effectiveness of different program types.

This chapter begins with a general introduction to the issues surrounding the schooling of Latin@ children in the US, and then, in the next section, focuses on different types of programs designed to educate students who are English language learners, what the most effective programs are, and why. The final two sections present summaries of research on the schooling of Latin@s which focus on language ideologies and social identities in the educational context, tying the topic of education into the material covered in earlier chapters.

Introduction

There has long been cause for concern about Latin@ children in the US educational system. Latin@s, and particularly those of Mexican descent, have a high dropout rate from high school (Gándara, 1995; Gutierrez *et al.*, 2000). According to research carried out by the Pew Research Center, 41% of Latin@s aged 20 and older in the United States do not have a regular high school diploma, versus 23% of Blacks and 14% of Whites in the same age group. High school dropout rates are almost double for foreign-born than US-born Latin@s (Fry, 2010: ii).

In research on the success of minorities in schooling in the US, Ogbu and Simons (1998) refer to 'voluntary' and 'involuntary' minorities. Two examples of involuntary minorities are African Americans, whose ancestors were brought to the US against their will, and Native Americans, who were the majority before they became a minority through colonization. Voluntary minorities are those who themselves, or whose ancestors, came to the United States in search of better opportunities. Generally speaking, immigrants are voluntary minorities, but Ogbu qualifies that guest workers, refugees and undocumented migrants are not voluntary minorities, because they did not choose freely or come to the United States to improve their status (Ogbu & Simons, 1998: 164).

The point of this classification is that the factors which influence how members of particular minority groups do in school are the result of the specific experiences of the minority group. If we define the majority culture in the US as the culture of the descendants of European immigrants, then the minority groups who came to the US under the circumstances most similar to that of European immigrants are those most likely to succeed. Since the bulk of European immigrants came in search of a better life in the New World, voluntary minorities are thus more likely to succeed in mainstream US schools.

So, where do Latin@s fit into this dichotomy? The answer is that there are many different backgrounds and experiences of Latin@s in the US. Some Latin@s are clearly voluntary minorities who have immigrated to the US legally with the goal of improving their lot in life. However, in the southwestern United States, there are many Latin@s whose ancestors have lived in this territory since before it became part of the US; they are involuntary minorities. There are still others who came as guest workers, refugees or undocumented migrants, in many cases without the intent to stay or the means to integrate into US society. Here we see the first issue with the education of Latin@s: this is not a homogeneous group. It is a broad category which encompasses native and non-native speakers of English, native and non-native speakers of Spanish, people in a range of occupations and with different socio-economic standing, people with different attitudes towards education and schools.

It would be impossible to address the experiences of all Latin@s in this chapter, so while I strive to incorporate studies from different locations, and with Latin@s of different national backgrounds, income levels and abilities in English, there is a focus in this chapter on English language learners, and especially those who come from less educated backgrounds. The reason for this focus is that studies on different populations have shown that children whose parents are educated on average tend to do better in school, for the simple reason that schools are designed with their linguistic and cultural preferences, practices and abilities in mind (Heath, 1982; Lareau, 1987, 2000). The challenge in our schools is how to serve children who do not come from this middle class background, and within this group I will focus on Latin@ children who do not speak English as their first language.

The next section of this chapter will give a taxonomy of different types of programs used to educate speakers of minority languages and the features of these programs; then I will present studies which evaluate their effectiveness. The subsequent section will delve into ideologies about language which influence the implementation of different types of educational programs for Latin@s, with links back to the concepts discussed in Chapter 1. The last section will then draw on ideas developed in Chapter 2 about identity, and address how identity issues are paramount in education.

Education of Latin@s in the US: History and program types

This section will focus largely on the education of children who have Spanish as their dominant language and the role language proficiencies in Spanish and English can play in the classroom. However, I do not want to lose sight of the fact that the issues involved in the education of Latin@s are not just about what language to use in the classroom. There is also the larger issue of how we, as a society, view the role of schools in socializing children and transmitting culture, and what norms for socialization and what aspects of culture are part of the educational system. These things are at issue in the education of monolingual children, too, especially but not only if they speak a non-standard variety of English.

Also, to the extent that the education of Latin@s IS about what language is used, this is an issue that is not merely about educational effectiveness, but is also about language ideologies and social identities. A monoglossic ideology about languages runs very strong in all educational programs, and essentialist ideas about Latin@ identity also influence curricular choices.

A short history of educational policies in the US regarding the language(s) of education

It's a common perception that education in the US has always been in English, but this is far from true. Children were educated in many different languages (e.g. German, Italian, Polish) in their local communities even after English had become the de facto national language, and there were bilingual education programs in the latter half of the 19th century (Baker, 2001: 184; García, 2009a: 163). It was not until the turn of the 20th century that the official move towards schooling in English began. In 1906, the Nationality Act was passed, which required immigrants to speak English to become naturalized US Americans. This act did not directly dictate the language to be used in schooling, but it did begin a trend in which the focus was on child literacy rather than child labor, which in turn led to a focus on English in schools (Baker, 2001: 184). It was not until over 10 years later, in 1919, that the Americanization Department of the US Bureau of Education adopted a resolution specifically recommending that all schools be conducted in English, and even at that point it was not the law (Baker, 2001: 184).

There have been, and continue to be, ups and down in the importance placed on foreign language teaching in high school and college education, but there is little actual policy about what must be taught, or what federal funds will pay for. One exception is the 1967 Bilingual Education Act, enacted as Title VII of the Elementary and Secondary Education Act, which authorized the use of federal funds for the education of speakers of languages other than English (García, 2009a: 169). The Supreme Court decision in Lau versus Nicholas in 1974 went a step towards dictating what type of education must be provided for English learners, as shown in the following excerpt from the decision:

> There is no equality of treatment merely by providing students with the same facilities, textbooks, teachers and curriculum; for students who do not understand English are effectively foreclosed from any meaningful education. (Baker, 2001: 186)

This was further strengthened by the 1974 amendment to the Bilingual Education Act which required schools receiving federal grants to include teaching in a student's home language and culture to foster the child's progress through the educational system.

All of this was undermined in the turnaround during the Reagan administration (1981–1989), which was largely hostile to bilingual education and began the move towards English immersion programs (Baker, 2001: 187–188). In 1998, despite research showing the effectiveness of bilingual education (see Green, 1998), Proposition 227 was passed in California, which stated that 'all children in California public schools shall be taught English by being taught in English' (Proposition 227, 1998). A similar proposition was passed in Arizona in 2000, and in Massachusetts in 2002. There was some resistance to this wave, however, when a similar amendment was voted down in Colorado (Baker, 2001: 183). But in 2002, with the No Child Left Behind Act, bilingual children were officially left behind and the focus moved to turning them into monolingual children (Crawford, 2008).

Despite this growing lack of federal and state support for or approval of bilingual education, or perhaps because of it, there continues to be a rise in dual language programs; Baker gives the figure of 33 dual language schools in the US in 1990 compared with 225 in 2000 (2001: 219), and the Directory of Bilingual Two-Way Immersion Programs in the US lists 422 programs, and these are only those that have chosen to register on the website (Two-Way Immersion, n.d.). It is important to note that since the beginning – the beginning being the establishment of the Coral Way Spanish English bilingual program in Dade County, Miami, in 1963 – such programs have been the result of local organization, not federal programs. The next section will outline different approaches to bilingual education, leading to an explanation of why dual language programs, and not other types of programs, tend to develop out of grassroots movements.

Educating English language learners: Program types

There are many different ways to categorize bilingual education programs. Baker (2001) talks about weak strong forms of bilingual education, while García (2009a: 115–117) presents the dichotomy of **subtractive bilingualism** versus **additive bilingualism** as well as **monoglossic**, **diglossic** and **heteroglossic** beliefs which underlie bilingual curricula. There is one central question at the heart of all of these different terms: is the aim of the program to foster bilingualism, or to simply transition the child to speaking the mainstream language, with little concern for the minority language? And if bilingualism is the goal, what is the ideology about what it means to be bilingual? These questions will be addressed for each of the program types discussed below. Please note that while these program types are not specific to the US, I frame the discussion, for the sake of simplicity and to keep to the focus of this text, as being about Spanish speakers in the US.

Submersion

It is a misnomer to call programs in this category 'bilingual education', because neither the goals nor the methods have anything to do with bilingualism. This term is usually used in cases in which there is little to no special programming for English learners; they are placed in mainstream classrooms and given the same instructions as Anglophone students. Of course, many individual teachers use various methods to help these students, in some cases including a focus on and appreciation of bilingualism (see Brunn, 1999 for examples and discussion of this) but there is no official program in place with this goal. The goal of the curriculum and structure of such programs is to foster English language learning and assimilation to monolingual norms in education as quickly as possible.

Transitional bilingual education programs: Early exit

The aim of transitional bilingual education programs, like submersion, is English language learning and assimilation. The goal is for children to stay in these programs a short time, usually 1–2 years, and then be placed in the mainstream, monolingual classrooms. The use of the child's first language is usually seen as a means of helping them to continue to do grade-level content material until they have learned English; the goal is not to foster literacy in Spanish or to recognize the culture of the minority language students.

Although codeswitching into Spanish to aid comprehension might be used in these programs, or into English during Spanish instruction to introduce vocabulary that will be needed as the students transition into the mainstream classrooms, such instances of bilingual discourse are not part of the basic philosophy of transitional programs. (This also holds true for the late exit program, discussed in the next sub-section.) Rather, such bilingual discourse may be used for instruction at the discretion of the teacher. In some cases (e.g. as reported in García, 2009a: 222–3), teachers will develop writing practices which allow the students to use resources in both of their languages as they develop English proficiency. For the most part, however, classes are held in either Spanish or English, not in both.

Transitional bilingualism programs: Late exit

So-called 'late exit' programs also have the long-range goal of assimilation, but with more recognition of the importance of first language literacy and bilingualism. As discussed above, despite more focus on bilingualism, the curriculum is designed with classes to be taught in either English or Spanish, and any use of translanguaging as a resource is implemented by individual teachers.

One difference to early exit programs is more focus on the Latin@ experience in the US. Because these programs use the home language as well as the majority language for up to six years, they often incorporate more than merely the language but also include cultural aspects of the minority group in the curriculum.

Immersion and other maintenance programs

Immersion is not to be confused with submersion; submersion generally means not having a special program at all for English learners. Immersion is traditionally aimed at speakers of the MAJORITY language with the goal of bilingualism and biliteracy in the majority language and the minority language taught in the school. In North America, the most famous immersion programs are French immersion programs in Canada. These schools are designed to serve Anglophone children, but have the goal of English-French bilingualism, with the understanding that the children will continue to learn and speak English in their homes, and French will be mastered in school.

What has become more common (although still rare) in the US is what are called **dual immersion** (or **two-way immersion**) programs. These programs serve both minority language students AND majority language students, with the goal being that all students will be bilingual and biliterate in these two languages. They are generally maintenance programs, meaning that the goal is the maintenance of bilingualism. Although there are programs in many different language pairs, the most common are probably Spanish-English and Chinese (either Cantonese or Mandarin)-English; the following discussion will focus on Spanish-English programs, which are being developed all over the country. There are different ways to design these programs, with one main variable being the amount of time that is spent in each language. In the US, we often speak of '90:10', '80:20', '50:50' programs, which are references to the amount of time which is devoted to teaching in Spanish and English, respectively. The use of more Spanish than English in many of these programs is based on the assumption that, since the children live in an English-dominant society, they will have more exposure to English in their daily lives outside of school; also, special subjects (Music, P.E., Art, etc.) at the school are usually taught in English, and the language used among the children on the playground and for casual interactions also tends to be English.

As will be discussed further in the section on language ideologies in bilingual education below, these programs, although they promote bilingualism, do so in a monoglossic framework. That is, the languages are usually used separately in instruction in one language or the other, and the children are classified as being **'native' speakers** of one language or the other.

Another type of program which is designed to maintain bilingualism is what is called the **heritage language** program. These programs are designed to create and maintain bilingualism among members of (ethno)linguistic minority groups. There are a number of programs which would fall into this category which serve Native American populations; there are also programs for Latin@ children which are called heritage language programs, as well as for other immigrant languages in the US (Baker, 2001: 208–209). The focus in these programs is clearly on the maintenance of the minority language and culture. Although, as in all other cases, how language is used in the classroom may vary depending on the individual teacher; because the goal of heritage language programs is acquisition/maintenance of the minority language, this is often viewed as something best achieved by the use of Spanish, not bilingual discourse.

Effectiveness of bilingual education programs

Assessing the most effective way to educate children is not a straightforward matter. One of the first issues is, what is an appropriate way to measure student achievement? In the US today, curricula are often measured by standardized test scores; these tests are always in English, so there is already a bias against bilingual children. A related issue is the timeframe within which high achievement is expected; while children in submersion may do better than children in dual language programs after one year, a more important consideration is how children in these different programs do after six years of schooling. Another important issue when programs are compared is the population of children; there are many variables which might influence how well children do in school, which have nothing to do with the language(s) in which they are educated (e.g. socio-economic class and educational level of their parents, or the age of arrival of immigrant children). And finally, studies looking at the effectiveness of bilingual education need to clearly define what type of program is being assessed. Combining early exit and dual immersion programs into one category of 'bilingual education' does not lead to a meaningful comparison to submersion.

So, I'll cut to the chase here: research shows that maintenance bilingual education is more effective in educating minority language children than ESL programs or transitional bilingual programs, and this is when 'effectiveness' is measured in terms of standardized test scores. In the following pages I will discuss the research on the effectiveness of bilingual education, the methodologies used and the specific findings. But first, I want to state clearly that ALL of the comprehensive studies done by qualified researchers, which compare maintenance bilingual programs with early exit or submersion programs, show that the kids in the maintenance programs do better in the long run (i.e. by sixth grade). The reasons cited for this are consistent: it's easier to learn to read in a language you know (surprise!), and literacy skills transfer; it takes years to develop academic competency in a second language, and only maintenance programs allow for that; and finally, children flourish when their home experiences (i.e. language and cultural practices) are recognized and respected. Because many of the studies I will cite have been carried out with the purpose of evaluating the effectiveness of educational programs in helping children achieve higher test scores on standardized tests they take in English, the obvious is sometimes left unstated: these children not only do better in school, they can do academic tasks in two languages. In this era of globalization, this argument is finally beginning to hold some weight.

But not everywhere. In post-Proposition 227 California, there seems to be rejoicing about the decrease in biliteracy. There have been some reports – not, significantly, reports by researchers on English learner education, but by journalists and politicians – which tout the success of Proposition 227 and English Only programs. But education experts (e.g. Butler *et al.*, 2000; Crawford, 2003; Garcia & Curry-Rodríguez, 2000) have all argued that there is no evidence that Proposition 227 has made a difference in the achievement of

English learners in the state; while test scores have increased, they have increased for ALL students in California, most likely because teachers have become more adept at teaching to the test. There are no studies carried out by language education experts which show that the move to English Only education has been effective in educating English language learners.

Why, you may well ask, if studies consistently show that bilingual education is effective, and we have a growing awareness that bilingualism is valuable, are maintenance programs not supported by federal and state policies and funding programs? That's a question I can't answer; it puzzles me too. All of the possible answers trouble and sadden me. My best guess is that most people don't really understand what's involved in dual immersion programs, and because they equate 'bilingual education' with 'remedial education for immigrant children', they don't grasp the benefits. (And in cases like the effects of Proposition 227, they don't correctly interpret the data.) There may also be **xenophobia** at work here; many US Americans, as discussed in Chapters 1 and 5, have the attitude that immigrants should simply learn English, and they are not willing to consider that bilingual education is an effective way to do that because it also has the – undesirable, in their minds – effect of supporting minority group language and culture. In short, I suspect that the ideology of normative monolingualism is so deeply ingrained that most people do not question it, even when faced with data that show the benefits of bilingualism.

I am going to focus my review of the literature on research carried out in and after the 1990s, after the emergence of more dual language programs in the US, but it is relevant to note that studies from the 1970s showed that bilingual programs were more effective than monolingual English programs (Baker, 2001: 232). A 1983 study (Baker & de Kanter, 1983) looking specifically at transitional programs did not find them to be more effective than monolingual English programs; although these findings were sometimes interpreted to mean that submersion is equally effective compared to transitional bilingual education, it is important to note that the authors state specifically that ESL instruction can be effective 'if the teaching is done right' (Baker & de Kanter, 1983: 51). This study was criticized for the implicit value of assimilation assumed in simply assessing transitional and English Only programs. A study published a few years later (Willig, 1985) showed the effectiveness of bilingual education, noting that all so-called bilingual education is not created equally, which is a point which becomes the focus of later studies.

In the remaining review of literature on the effectiveness of bilingual education, I will focus on the difference between programs which seek to immerse or transition children quickly to English, versus programs that also develop Spanish literacy. So my emphasis in the following discussion is on the difference between programs which seek to foster bilingualism and those which seek the best way to teach English to minority language children.

In the early 1990s, results from what is commonly referred to as the Ramírez Research (including what is often called 'the Ramírez Report' (Ramírez et al., 1991), which was submitted to the US Department of Education) appeared. This research was the result of an eight-year longitudinal study of over 2300 Spanish speaking children from 554

Kindergarten to sixth grade classrooms in five states (New York, New Jersey, Florida, Texas and California). It compared three types of programs: what were called 'structured immersion' programs, which were entirely in English; early exit programs, which included instruction in Spanish about one-third of the time; and late exit programs, which moved from 75% Spanish in first grade to a bit over half of the instruction in Spanish in second grade. The findings clearly show that by the sixth grade, the children in the late exit programs were performing at higher levels (according to standardized tests) in mathematics and English language skills. One of the clear implications of this study is that the claim that it is 'time on task' that makes a difference – that is, the more time the child is exposed to English, the faster and better they will learn – is patently false. Also, it is equally clear that instruction in the home language does not impede learning English, as anti-bilingual educators had claimed (Ramírez, 1992; Ramírez et al., 1991).

The next large-scale research program assessing the effectiveness of bilingual education for the education of Spanish-English bilinguals in the US was done by Thomas and Collier (1995, 1997, 2000, 2002). This study compared students in eight different types of programs: 90:10 dual language programs, 50:50 dual language programs, 90:10 one-way developmental bilingual education programs, 50:50 one-way developmental bilingual education programs, 90:10 transitional bilingual education programs, 50:50 transitional bilingual education programs, English as a Second Language (ESL) taught through academic content, and the English Mainstream (i.e. submersion). The programs were located in five urban and rural research sites in the northeast, northwest, south-central and southeast US. Their findings, based on a five-year study looking at 210,054 student records for K-12 students, found conclusively that the most effective programs are those which are maintenance bilingual programs. Further, they found that the more time spent on instruction in Spanish, the better the children tended to do – that is, while students in programs which were 50:50 (Spanish to English) did well, students in 90:10 programs did even better. They stress in their report that a key aspect of these programs is the maintenance aspect; the minimum length of time a child needs to attain academic proficiency in a second language is four years (Thomas & Collier, 2002: 319). Children who are moved into mainstream programs before this length of time suffer with regard to their academic achievement. Those schooled in bilingual programs not only excel during their time in the bilingual program, but also go on to outperform their monolingually-schooled peers in English Only high school curricula. In sum:

> The strongest predictor of L2 student achievement is amount of formal L1 schooling. The more L1 grade-level schooling, the higher L2 achievement. Bilingually schooled students outperform comparable monolingually schooled students in academic achievement in all subjects, after 4-7 years of dual language schooling. (Thomas & Collier, 2002: 320)

These results may seem astounding at first glance, as if there is something magical about bilingualism which transforms students into high achievers. And while I do believe there is something special and wonderful about being able to speak more than one language, even I cannot leave my readers with the impression that it is the wave of a bilingual wand that does the trick. The truth of the matter is complex, but much of it can be summed up with a reiteration of the issues I mentioned above: first language development is key to the development of a second language, literacy skills transfer, and the social environment of the classroom matters. Thomas and Collier stress this last point:

> Schools need to create a natural learning environment in school, with lots of natural, rich oral and written language used by students and teachers (L1 and L2 used in separate instructional contexts, not using translation); meaningful, real world problem-solving; all students working together; media-rich learning (video, computers, print); challenging thematic units that get and hold students' interest; and using students' bilingual-bicultural knowledge to bridge to new knowledge across the curriculum. (Thomas & Collier, 2002: 321)

These findings are consistent with another concurrent study examining data from 18 schools (Lindholm-Leary, 2001). This research found that dual language students outperformed transitional bilingual education students in both English and mathematics by sixth grade, and also had higher Spanish proficiency. In a comparison with California norms, the dual language students showed higher performance in both reading and mathematics and very positive attitudes about their schools, teachers and classrooms – something which contributes to academic success and low attrition rates.

And in case you are wondering, the children in these dual language classrooms who do not come from Spanish-speaking backgrounds do well in school, too (Lindholm-Leary, 2001). In some cases, these students may be a self-selected population who would do well in school anyway; that is, the parents who choose to enroll their Anglophone children in a two-way immersion program are often educated and middle class and their children have an advantage in school because they come from a home environment where there is time and money to invest in education. There is little research done on this half of the two-way immersion classroom population, but it is clear that in terms of academic achievement, there is no disadvantage, and there is the advantage of early language learning.

More recent research reviewing studies of the education of English language learners in US schools confirms this finding. In the long run, dual language programs are most effective for academic achievement, including effectively fostering achievement in literacy and math but also in terms of contributing to lower dropout rates and positive attitudes towards school (Genesee et al., 2005).

So perhaps the magic of bilingual education isn't (just) about language learning, but about a good overall curriculum and learning environment. Thomas and Collier, citing earlier work by Baker and Prys Jones (1998), note that one aspect of the programs that they sought to assess was parental engagement, which is a contributing factor to student success (Thomas & Collier, 2002: 311). This brings us back to an earlier point: the impetus for dual language programs. They are usually locally organized and implemented, sometimes in response to state mandates about bilingual education, but always as part of the community's perception of the needs of the local student population. In my community in southern Illinois, as the Spanish-speaking population in the elementary schools began to rise, a group of people from the university and the community joined together to educate people in the region – teachers, school administrators and parents – about the benefits of dual language education. Illinois has a law that dictates that any school building which houses 20 or more students classified as having Limited English Proficiency and speaking the same home language MUST offer some sort of bilingual education, but dual language programs are not specified; an early-exit program would suffice to satisfy the policy. When the school district reached this critical level of Spanish-speaking students in the building that houses Kindergarten and first grade classes, they decided to implement a dual language program. The program has been positively received by parents in the school district, both those who have Spanish as their heritage language and those who have English (or some other language) as their home language, and the program now continues into the fifth grade, with plans to offer some Spanish language content instruction in the middle school. As a parent of a child in the program, I can attest to the fact that yes, there is something magical about bilingualism; children learn a second language in ways that seem supernatural to adults, and are prime candidates for developing ideologies about bilingualism which can successfully compete with normative monolingualism. But at the same time, the success of the program has not come about as a result of an incantation; it has come about because it has dedicated teachers, involved parents and the support of the administration. And – literacy skills transfer, first language development is an integral part of second language learning, and everyone learns better in an environment in which they feel their ways of speaking and being are valued.

I do not want to minimize the cost in time and money of implementing and maintaining a bilingual education program. It is also important to recognize that dual language programs are not the only way to create an environment which values pluralism and the languages and experiences of the students. But in terms of effectiveness, the research is clear: dual immersion is best. And in addition to better serving English language learners, it fosters bilingualism among all of the children, regardless of their home language.

Ideologies in language education

I discussed the ideology of normative monolingualism at length in Chapter 1. To briefly recap this discussion, this ideology includes two parts: first, that monolingualism is the right and natural state for a particular political region – in this case, the US; second, if individuals do speak two languages, they should keep them strictly separate. In this section, I will relate that ideology to the education of Latin@s, and also discuss the connected ideologies of English hegemony, subtractive acculturation and elite versus immigrant bilingualism, as well as ideologies about diversity and plurality, heteroglossia and the value of Spanish. The educational implications of these ideologies, in terms of both policy and practices, will be addressed.

Although research has shown that there are differences across program types in how well certain curricula serve the student population, there is one thing all of the programs discussed above have in common: they ALL revolve around the monoglossic principle of dealing with Spanish and English in separate contexts. Although all of the models of education for minority language children can potentially incorporate the use of translanguaging as a resource in the classroom, this is not an explicit tenet in any form of bilingual education. There are aspects of the descriptions which hint at this by advocating pluralist values. For instance, Thomas and Collier advocate 'using students' bilingual-bicultural knowledge to bridge to new knowledge across the curriculum' (2002: 321), but also, earlier in their summary, discuss the use of 'natural' language use, which they seem to equate with the use of languages in separate contexts. As has been discussed in recent research (e.g. Fuller, 2010; García, 2009b: 146), 'natural' language use by bilinguals often, even usually, includes bilingual discourse. While research has shown the merits of using both languages in instruction (Becker, 2001; Canagaraja, 2011; García, 2008, 2009b, 2011b; Jacobson, 1988; Nichols & Colon, 2000), this has yet to permeate into the ideologies which usually underlie bilingual education programs and curricular design.

As discussed in Chapter 1, the policy outcome of the ideology of normative monolingualism is English Only legislation. One of the aims of such policy is to get rid of bilingual education, and in some cases this ideology results in the complete lack of services for English language learners (Beck & Allexsaht-Snider, 2002), although lip service is given to promoting English as a way of ensuring equality. Normative monolingualism dictates that English is and should be the dominant language in US society and schools; often, this ideology holds even when there is a bilingual program, even a dual language program designed to create and maintain bilingualism (Fitts, 2006). In some cases, the hegemony of English may be largely external to the bilingual program and is in part brought about by aspects of the educational program beyond the control of bilingual educators; for instance, that special subjects are taught in English, or that the children's lives outside of school are largely played out in English and thus English is the dominant language on the playground (Fuller, 2007, 2009; Fuller et al., 2007; Pease-Alvarez & Winsler, 1994; Potowski, 2004, 2007). The hegemony of English often encroaches unnoticed into the bilingual domain of dual language programs. Students and teachers may use more English than Spanish regardless of the percentage of time officially designated for English or Spanish (DePalma, 2010: 57).

Also, patterns in the bilingual discourse may relegate Spanish to a peripheral status, for example, if English is used for the main message and Spanish for less important supporting information (e.g. Pease-Alvarez & Winsler, 1994; Self, 2005). DePalma (2010) describes the conscious efforts of one kindergarten teacher to construct Spanish as a 'power language' by incorporating the use of Spanish into contexts other than activities dictated by the curriculum, but this was ultimately perceived as taking time away from achieving academic goals. Another study which speaks to the conflict between using Spanish and conforming to classroom expectations is Hayes (2005), who looked at play interactions in a kindergarten classroom in a dual language program. She found that the most talk (in any language) was found in the negotiations of the play frame, and while the children did use Spanish in these contexts, it was at odds with the teacher's desire to avoid conflicts. This study speaks to the issue of the type of language interaction that is required for language learning, and that all types of language use are not necessarily deemed appropriate in the classroom.

Another ideology that contributes to normative monolingualism is the idea of **subtractive acculturation** (which subsumes what is called subtractive bilingualism in some of the literature). This is the idea that learning English and adopting US cultural practices means losing the minority language and culture; this is in opposition to additive bilingualism, when one learns a second language but maintains the first. The concept of subtractive acculturation, instead of simply subtractive bilingualism, is meant to acknowledge that language is part of an intricate cultural system, and that the goal of subtractive approaches to education is not simply to turn the children into English monolinguals, but into fully-fledged members of the US mainstream culture. This ideology rests on the belief that assimilation keeps America strong whereas diversity (of language or cultural practices) weakens it. As discussed in Chapter 1, there are many holes in this logic, but it is a strong and widely held belief. And subtractive acculturation is a negative process for those who are being acculturated; no one wants to be treated as if their home language and lifestyle are irrelevant and wrong. An assimilationist ideology can be alienating for children who believe that their cultural and linguistic heritage is of value (Patthey-Chavez, 1993), and damaging if it convinces them that it isn't.

With regard to Latin@s in particular, this ideology involves the fiction that former immigrants assimilated and worked hard to contribute to society, but that current Latin@ immigrants demand privileges – such as bilingual education – and lack motivation (Bigler, 1996). There are many reasons why this is an unfair portrayal of US history and Latin@s. Earlier immigrants did not all learn English immediately, there were huge differences in the national economy then and now which contributed to the success and integration into society for earlier immigrants, and there is also a lack of equivalence in the experience of European immigrants and Latin@ immigrants because of racial discrimination. Being classified as non-White in the racial system of the US makes integration and membership in the mainstream more difficult. Beck and Allexsaht-Snider (2002: 43) note that in what has been called the 'new Latino diaspora' of the south, the difficulty of assigning Latin@s to a category in the Black-White binary racial system has led to the further alienation of children in the educational system.

There are also ideologies about bilingualism itself that contribute to educational policies and practices. One major dichotomy which is relevant here is the distinction between **elite bilingualism** and immigrant bilingualism. In the US, elite bilingualism is found when Anglophones speak another language; this is viewed as a positive achievement and, increasingly, as a resource for participating in the global economy. So elite bilingualism is a good thing; it is not connected with lack of participation in the mainstream culture – quite the contrary: it is assumed to be a ticket to success in that sphere.

Immigrant bilingualism is when speakers of minority languages, such as Spanish, learn English. While learning English is good, little value is placed on maintaining Spanish. In this context, speaking a language other than English is suddenly a liability; it is linked to lack of participation in the mainstream culture. This is illogical and downright biased; it assumes that immigrant bilingual children need to just focus on learning English, and are not candidates for participating in the multilingual global economy. The curricular outcome of this is that there is a focus on foreign language learning to create elite bilingualism, but not maintenance of and literacy in immigrant languages. In other words, while Spanish is taught as a foreign language everywhere, there are fewer classes offered for speakers of Spanish as a native (or heritage) language. García (2008: 37) writes, 'It is clear that the US school system is in no way developing the potential bilingualism that the sheer number of Latino students would make possible.' This is because Latin@s speaking Spanish and English is immigrant bilingualism, which is ideologically inferior to elite bilingualism.

The flipside of this ideology is noted by Fitts (2006), whose work in a dual language program in Colorado showed that even in this context some ideologies about bilingualism were counter-productive to the professed goals of the program. Although lip service was given to the idea that everyone at the school was bilingual, some people – namely, Latin@s – were MORE bilingual. Thus 'real' bilingualism was only possible for those who had a language other than English as their heritage language. This focus on immigrant bilingualism is misguided, given what I said earlier about the preference for elite bilingualism; the program might serve its students better by attempting to blur the line between these two phenomena. Further, ideas about bilingualism that run counter to ideologies of pluralism (discussed more, later) are present in the parallel monolingualism view, that is, the view that languages should be kept separate and not mixed; this is a frequent downside to the dual language program philosophy (Baker, 2001: 216ff).

Another ideological problem in education rests in the values assigned to Spanish. Freeman (2000) discusses a dual language program in which there was difficulty with the implementation of the bilingual curriculum because of deep-seated prejudices against Spanish as the language of education; Worthy et al. (2003) note that even in an environment supportive of bilingualism, maintenance of the minority language is challenged by the pressures of the dominant, monolingual society. García criticizes the term 'heritage language' because it implies that Spanish is a thing which is related to the past, not something which is relevant for the future. This makes 'Spanish for heritage language speakers' courses seems less relevant, as if Spanish is learned out of nostalgia, not because it is of value in contemporary life. We have already discussed the attitudes about Spanish not being considered valuable because it is seen as undermining participation in mainstream culture. While we also see a discourse about Spanish as a resource, which makes Spanish more valuable, this commodification of linguistic and cultural diversity is often seen as being in opposition with Spanish as an important part of cultural heritage and identity (Leeman & Martínez, 2007; Ricento, 2009). What seems to be missing from the official discourse about the value of Spanish is that it is important for the emotional development of Spanish speakers and is an essential aspect of their social identity which should be respected.

Another important issue involved in ideologies about the value of Spanish has to do with the variety of Spanish; varieties with regional and especially lower social class connotations are brought from Latin American countries to the US, and these varieties are often criticized by speakers of European Spanish or more standard Latin American varieties. In addition, US varieties (e.g. Chicano Spanish), as discussed in the last chapter, are often dismissed as illegitimate hybrids which are not real languages. Negative feedback from teachers about the variety of Spanish spoken by children can be as detrimental to the motivation and success of children as negative attitudes about Spanish or bilingualism in general.

Often, the educational policy outcome of these ideologies is that there is no actual policy about educating English language learners, which leaves children at the mercy of the attitudes and abilities of the individual teachers (Beck & Allexsaht-Snider, 2002; Brunn, 1999; Gibson, 2002). While caring teachers can certainly make a difference, and some teachers will incorporate positive attitudes and practices surrounding diversity into their classrooms without policies mandating them, this rather arbitrary approach to educational quality does not serve most children well. Also, Valdes (2001) presents a poignant picture of how one teacher, who despite clear goodwill towards her students, fails in her attempts to teach them English because of institutional and pedagogical shortcomings.

Resistance to the hegemony of English and the de-valuing of Spanish can be seen in ideologies and practices which value cultural and linguistic plurality. For instance, Mirón and Inda (2004), in their research on Latin@ English learners, report that students felt they had a right to construct cultural citizenship in the US through their use of English, but also claimed the right to be bilingual without this negating their national belonging. Similarly, in Bigler (1996) the story told by Latin@ voices was one of stressing the value of their bilingualism, in contrast with the assimilationist perspectives of the others in their community.

In many cases, an ideology of valuing linguistic pluralism means that bilingual discourse is used and accepted and an effective means of communication (Jacobson, 1988). Brunn (1999), in a discussion of teacher strategies for educating the new influx of Latin@ language learners in their classrooms, shows how some teachers adopted a 'bilingual is best' approach which made use of both languages for the social and academic achievement of the children. Hadi-Tabassum (2002) discusses the construction of a 'third space' by children in a dual language program, and Shannon (1995) discusses a bilingual classroom in which the teacher encouraged the use of bilingual discourse in the acquisition of English literacy. Becker (2001) shows that codeswitching positively correlates with variables related to enhanced narrative skills and was thus a positive strategy used by children in academic contexts; research by Nichols (2000) and Nichols and Colon (2000) also show the benefits for English literacy of maintaining and using Spanish. García (2009a, 2009b, 2011b) discusses the use of translanguaging, which she describes as '*multiple discursive practices* in which bilinguals engage in order to *make sense of their bilingual worlds*' (García, 2009a: 45, italics in original). This includes codeswitching, but also other kinds of bilingual language use such as translation, and she stresses that there are no clear-cut boundaries between languages. In educational contexts, this means that students are able to make use of all of their linguistic resources to complete academic tasks.

What many of these studies bring out is the agency of individual teachers in creating an environment which is encouraging of bilingualism. Palmer (2007) notes that bilingualism was valued within the bilingual classroom, despite lack of recognition of the value in the wider community of the school, and that the responsibility for challenging the hegemonic discourses of normative monolingualism and subtractive acculturation lies with teachers. When teachers conform to the hegemonic ideology of English monolingualism, bilingual children have few ways to make use of their bilingual skills (Beck & Allexsaht-Snider, 2002; Brunn, 1999; Gibson, 2002).

So, under what circumstances is there likely to be support for bilingual education, and resistance to assimilationist ideologies? Linton (2004) addresses this issue with specific attention to dual language programs. Her research indicates that school district and parent demographics are the factors which correlate with the successful implementation of dual language programs, but contrary to popular beliefs, racial and economic diversity are not deterrents to program effectiveness. She writes:

> ...Spanish-English dual language programs are most likely to exist in relatively large, urban school districts, where there are enough Spanish and English speakers to balance the classrooms, and not too many other language LEP students. Given the above, parent education is relatively high, and parents (at least mothers) are able to spend time at school. (Linton, 2004: 62)

In terms of language policies which favor dual language programs, it is no surprise that English-Plus statutes exert a positive effect, but there is a surprise in the correlation between anti-bilingual education campaigns within the state with higher numbers of dual language programs (Linton, 2004). While this last may seem counter-intuitive, it speaks to the nature of the development of dual language programs as part of grassroots movements which work against dominant ideologies.

However, it must also be noted that despite the positive attitudes of teachers towards Spanish, or the presence of dual language programs, language shift to English is often the reality for the students (e.g. Pease-Alvarez & Winsler, 1994; Potowski, 2004, 2007). As discussed in Chapter 5, maintenance of a minority language relies on a number of factors, and value of the language and education, although important, are in themselves not enough to perpetuate bilingualism.

The role of identity in Latino education

A common metaphor used by proponents of bilingual education is 'language as a resource'; maintaining Spanish while learning English is thus presented as a means to achieve upward mobility. An increase in this attitude from 1970 to 2000 was found in Leeman and Martinez's (2007) study on Spanish textbooks; even Spanish for heritage language speakers is increasingly framed as a resource, not part of cultural identity. This perspective, while focusing on one positive impact of language maintenance, ignores the significance of language as a means of identity construction, and the importance of this in the educational setting (Weisman, 2001). This section presents research on the role of identity in the education of Latin@s.

Overwhelmingly, there are studies which report the loss of motivation, self-esteem and overall language skills with the loss of Spanish (e.g. Beck & Allexsaht-Snider, 2002; Quiroz, 2001; Valenzuela, 1999; Weisman, 2001). Latin@ students whose language and cultural backgrounds are not valued in the school feel that they themselves are not valued, and this can only have a negative impact on their education.

There are many ways in which social identity is constructed through language choice in the classroom. One aspect of identity has to do with language proficiency; positioning oneself as bilingual can be a source of power. In Fuller (2007) one student in a transitional bilingual education program, Antonio, constructed himself as a bilingual while constructing a fellow student as a Spanish monolingual and the researcher as an English monolingual; this positioning put him in a position of authority. This type of linguistic identity is also mentioned in a study by Vann et al. (2006). In this classroom, one particular student was constructed as a proficient bilingual by the teacher, other students and especially himself. In both of these cases, this positioning was part of a larger identity construction as a good student. Cammarota (2004) also discusses how academic achievement can be used by Latinas to resist subordination due to gender discrimination. The opposite of this is shown in Cuero (2009), when a Latino boy is not perceived as a good student because his behavior did not conform to school expectations, although his grades and test scores were equivalent to students who were perceived as good students. Another twist on this scenario is presented by Potowski (2007) in her description of a girl, Melissa, in a dual language classroom who insisted on speaking Spanish (not, incidentally, her first language) with her peers in Spanish class, an unpopular move in the English-dominant peer group. This led to less social talk being directed at her by other students and, consequently, Melissa was more often left out of deviations from the assigned task. The end result was a more studious identity for Melissa. This willingness to swim against the tide to maintain (and improve) Spanish proficiency is seen in a somewhat different manifestation in the speaker Miguel in Fuller (2007). Miguel's strong preference for Spanish is deemed a means to construct a Mexican identity, which contrasts with the more bilingual (Mexican American) identities of the other children. However, Miguel also used language choice to construct the identity of a good student, and this meant using whatever the language of instruction was, whether it was English or Spanish. It is likely that this was also part of Melissa's strategy, and that she did not use Spanish during English instruction.

The gendered aspects of the construction of ethnic identity are highlighted in a study by Meador (2005), who looked at the identity construction options of Mexican immigrant girls in the rural southwest. Because 'good student' identities were viewed as being determined by English proficiency and participation in competitive sports (i.e. 'jock' status), and the Mexican immigrant girls were assumed not to be jocks or fluent English speakers, the identities ascribed to them were limited and precluded being seen as 'good students'.

Gender roles are tied to ethnicity and language choice in a study done by Cook-Gumperz and Szymanski (2001). In the classroom analyzed in this article, which contained many Latin@ students, the concept of 'family' is used by the teacher to encourage groups of children to help each other and work together. The use of Spanish in this classroom reinforces the link to the home context, and the children do indeed seem to take on roles that mirror those they might have at home. In particular, the girls in the classroom often take on roles as group facilitators and foster collaboration in the groups. At the same time, power struggles tend to be between girls who are vying for these leadership positions, and codeswitching is one of the linguistic tools used to construct powerful identities.

In another study (Vann et al., 2006) the teacher was also shown to reify the distinction between boys and girls in the classroom, contributing to positioning the girls as bystanders more than participants, which inevitably disadvantaged the girls in terms of academic achievement. Further, the teacher constructed the children as future employees at the local meat-packing factory, consigning them to a lower socio-economic status. Again, there are inevitable consequences in terms of educational success from creating such low expectations for students; it should be noted that some of the students in this classroom resisted being put into this frame.

Another study which shows the construction of social class along with 'race'/ethnicity is Valdés (2011). This case study of two middle class third generation Latina girls looks at the role of education in the development of their ethnolinguistic identities. These girls grew up in an English-dominant home (their father was a second language learner of Spanish, and their mother spoke both English and Spanish, her heritage language, to them) but regularly had Spanish-speaking babysitters through their preschool years and thus had daily exposure to Spanish. The girls then both attended a dual language program in which most of the children were Latin@ and English language learners. Although there were some signs of integration and adoption of a Latina identity for both girls, their social class status tended to separate them from the working class immigrant children who comprised the majority of their school's population. Their identification as 'White' was also a means of establishing themselves as members of the middle class mainstream, which was at odds with being 'Latina', something associated more with newly arrived immigrant girls.

Despite these dynamic descriptions of students' language preferences and proficiencies, both ESL and bilingual programs are structured in ways that label children in static ways which belie their ever-changing identities. Fitts (2006) reports instances in a dual language program in which the children were asked to identify themselves as native speakers of either English or Spanish, but not both, although lip service was given to the idea that everyone at the school was bilingual. In my own child's dual language program, the teachers have told me that they work to avoid such categorizations, but I know from my own experiences that it is sometimes difficult – even for me, someone who is hyper-sensitive to the need to avoid such limiting identifiers for the children. In terms of programmatic choices, classrooms which integrate children of different language backgrounds and L2 classifications for all subjects are ideologically more in tune with the idea of creating an inclusive bilingual space than programs which separate children for literacy instruction according to their 'native' language.

However, as I have said above, bilingual education is not the only context in which Latin@ students, or any students, can feel valued and develop academic skills. To turn back to earlier comments about teacher agency, there is a theme in research about the disengagement of Latin@ students from the educational process. One particularly poignant study done by Quiroz (2001) examines student essays titled 'Who Am I?' done in eighth and 11th grades. The students showed increasing disillusionment with the school system and loss of faith that the teachers wanted to help them, and these feelings spurred lack of academic motivation and ambition. Quiroz's observations of teachers included them having breakfast or selling real estate instead of teaching their classes, signs of lack of caring and dedication that surely were not lost on the students. There were also other themes that showed that the students' home cultures were in conflict with the school; for instance, the role of the families of these children was integral to their scholastic success, but the motivating potential of families was not recognized or made use of in this school. Overall, this study supports the contention that students do not reject education per se – they realize that education is important for their futures – but they resist and reject the alienating experiences they have in school. This leads to either dropping out or minimal participation. Quiroz's study builds on the earlier research of Valenzuela (1999), which describes a school serving Mexican American students in Texas. She argues that through a lack of adequate funding, appropriate curriculum and caring about the students, schooling is a subtractive process for these children. The school 'reproduces Mexican youth as a monolingual, English-speaking, ethnic minority, neither identified with Mexico nor equipped to function competently in America's mainstream' (Valenzuela, 1999: 3). This author argues that the primary cause for the students' lack of success is a school system which creates divisions between groups of students and between students and teachers. Without meaningful relationships between the participants of the educational process, the teachers and administration cannot create a curriculum which is designed to serve the student body. This leads students to feel that the teachers don't care about them, and thus they cease to care about schooling, leading to lack of academic success. Valenzuela's analysis revolves around the concept of 'caring', and shows how both the teachers and the students charge each other with the responsibility for student failure through 'not caring'. In this study, 'caring' on the part of the teachers and administration would involve allowing students some options in identity construction through both linguistic and cultural flexibility in the curriculum.

Conclusion

While it is clear that policies and programmatic decisions do make a difference in the quality of education received by Latin@ students, there is no one type of program which can effectively combat hegemonic ideologies which devalue bilingualism, promote subtractive acculturation, and equate Whiteness with high status. Within dual language programs as well as within submersion programs, these ideologies are sometimes perpetuated and the linguistic, and thus identity, choices for Latin@ children are limited by negative consequences. In particular, the high dropout rate for Latin@ children, particularly foreign-born children, needs to be addressed in terms of ideologies of subtractive acculturation which hamper student success.

I do not, however, intend to paint a bleak and hopeless picture; quite to the contrary, I believe that through consciousness raising about the ideologies which influence educational programs and policies, and critical consumption of discourses about 'race', ethnicity, social class and minority languages and their speakers, we can create better opportunities for education in the US – for Latin@s, and for everyone.

Discussion questions and activities

1. Is it the job of students to adapt to educational practices in order to be successful, or is it the job of the educational system to adapt to the populations they serve to help them achieve success? What are the implications, in terms of curriculum and classroom practices, for each of these options?
2. What are the pros and cons of the term 'heritage language' in educational contexts?

Recommended reading

Castillo, J.M. (2003) Teaching Spanish to heritage speakers: Issues of language and identity. *Geolinguistics* 29, 51–57.

Ek, L.D. (2009) 'It's different lives': A Guatemalan American adolescent's construction of ethnic and gender identities across educational contexts. *Anthropology & Education Quarterly* 40 (4), 405–420.

Fuller, J.M. (2009) Multilingualism in educational contexts: Ideologies and identities. *Language and Linguistics Compass* 3 (1), 338–358.

Fuller, J.M. (2009) Teaching & learning guide for: Multilingualism in educational contexts: identities and ideologies. *Language and Linguistics Compass* 3/5: 1374–1378.

Gándara, P. and Contreras, F. (2009) *The Latino Education Crisis: The Consequences of Failed Social Policies*. Cambridge, MA: Harvard University Press.

Murillo, E.G. Jr., Villenas, S.A., Galván, R.T, Muñoz, J.S., Martínez, C. and Machado-Casas, M. (2010) *Handbook of Latinos and Education: Theory, Research, and Practice*. New York: Routledge.

Ogbu, J.U. (1995) Cultural problems in minority education: Their interpretations and consequences – Part one: Theoretical background. *The Urban Review* 27 (3), 189–205.

Ogbu, J.U. (1995) Cultural problems in minority education: Their interpretations and consequences – Part one: Case studies. *The Urban Review* 27 (4), 271–297.

Van Deusen-Scholl, N. (2003) Toward a definition of heritage language: Sociopolitical and pedagogical considerations. *Journal of Language, Identity & Education* 2 (3), 211–230.

Wiley, T. and Wright, W.E. (2004) Against the undertow: Language-minority education policy and politics in the 'age of accountability.' *Educational Policy* 18 (1), 142–168.

References

Achugar, M. (2008) Counter-hegemonic language practices and ideologies: Creating a new space and value for Spanish in southwest Texas. *Spanish in Context* 5 (1), 1–19.

Adventus blogspot (2006) 'What you mean "we", white man?' June 26, accessed August 1, 2012. Online at: http://rmadisonj.blogspot.com/2006/06/what-you-mean-we-white-man.html.

Albirini, A. (2011) The sociolinguistic functions of codeswitching between Standard Arabic and dialectal Arabic. *Language in Society* 40 (5), 537–562.

Alcoff, L.M. (2000) Is Latina/o identity a racial identity? In J. Gracia and P. De Greiff (eds) *Hispanics/Latinos in the United States: Ethnicity, Race, and Rights* (pp. 23–44). New York: Routledge.

Alcoff, L.M. (2008) Mapping the boundaries of race, ethnicity, nationality. *International Philosophy Quarterly* 48 (2), 231–238.

Alvarez, L. (1997) It's the talk of Nueva York: The hybrid called Spanglish. *The New York Times*, March 25, 483–387.

Alvord, S.M. (2010a) Miami Cuban Spanish declarative intonation. *Studies in Hispanic and Lusophone Linguistics* 3 (1), 3–39.

Alvord, S.M. (2010b) Variation in Miami Cuban Spanish interrogative intonation. *Hispania* 93 (2), 235–255.

American Anthropological Association (1998) Statement on 'Race', May 17, accessed August 1, 2012. Online at: http://www.aaanet.org/stmts/racepp.htm.

The American Heritage New Dictionary of Cultural Literacy (2005), accessed August 2, 2012. Online at: http://dictionary.reference.com/browse/ethnicity.

Androutsopoulos, J. (2007) Bilingualism in the mass media and on the internet. In M. Heller (ed.) *Bilingualism: A Social Approach* (pp. 207–230). New York, NY: Palgrave Macmillan.

Answerbag (2009) 'Should Oregon pass the English Immersion Measure?' Accessed August 20, 2010. Online at: http://www.answerbag.com/debates/oregon-pass-english-immersion-measure_1855505.

Anzaldúa, G. (1999) *Borderlands – La Frontera* (2nd edn). San Francisco: Aunt Lute Books.

Ardilla, A. (2005) Spanglish: An Anglicized Spanish dialect. *Hispanic Journal of Behavioral Sciences* 27 (1), 60–81.

Arizona Daily Wildcat (2000) 'Editorial: Mock Spanish not racist, just natural', March 2. Online at: http://wc.arizona.edu/papers/93/110/03_1_m.html.

Associated Press. (2006) 'Latino characters commonplace in kids' TV', March 1. Online at: http://today.msnbc.msn.com/id/11504591/ns/today-entertainment/t/latino-characters-commonplace-kids-tv/.

Attinasi. J. (1979) Language attitudes in a New York Puerto Rican community. In R. Padilla (ed.) *Ethnoperspectives in Bilingual Education Research* (pp. 408–461). Ypsilanti. MI: Eastern Michigan University.

Auer, P. (1984) *Bilingual Conversation*. Amsterdam: Benjamins Publishing Company.

Baez, J.M. (2007) Towards a latinidad feminista: The multiplicities of latinidad and feminism in contemporary cinema. *Popular Communication* 5 (2), 109–128.

Bailey, B. (2000) Language and negotiation of ethnic/racial identity among Dominican Americans. *Language in Society* 29 (4), 555–582.

Bailey, B. (2001) The language of multiple identities among Dominican Americans. *Journal of Linguistic Anthropology* 10 (2), 190–223.

Bailey, B. (2002) *Language, Race, and Negotiation of Identity: A Study of Dominican Americans*. New York: LFB Scholarly Publishing.

Bailey, B. (2007) Heteroglossia and boundaries. In M. Heller (ed.) *Bilingualism: A Social Approach* (pp. 257–274). New York, NY: Palgrave Macmillan.

Baker, C. (2001) *Foundations of Bilingual Education and Bilingualism* (3rd edn). Clevedon: Multilingual Matters.

Baker, C. and Prys Jones, S. (1998) *Encyclopedia of Bilingualism and Bilingual Education*. Clevedon: Multilingual Matters.

Baker, K.A. and de Kanter, A.A. (1983) *Bilingual Education*. Lexington, MA: Lexington Books.

Baktin, M. (1981) *The Dialogic Imagination*, translated by C. Emerson and M. Hosquist. Austin, TX: University of Texas Press.

Baron, D. (1990) *The English Only Question: An Official Language for Americans?* New Haven: Yale University Press.

Barrett, R. (2006) Language ideology and racial inequality: Competing functions of Spanish in an Anglo-owned Mexican restaurant. *Language in Society* 35 (2), 163–204.

Barron, D. (1996) 'Urban legend: German almost became the official language of the US; The legendary English-Only vote of 1795', March, accessed August 1, 2012. Online at: http://watzmann.net/scg/german-by-one-vote.html.

Barth, F. (1969) *Ethnic Groups and Boundaries*. Long Grove, IL: Waveland Press.

Baugh, J. (2003) Linguistic profiling. In S. Makoni, G. Smitherman, A.F. Ball and A. Spears (eds) *Black Linguistics: Language, Society, and Politics in Africa and the Americas* (pp. 155–168). New York: Routledge.

Bayley, R. and Santa Ana, O. (2004) Chicano English: Morphology and syntax. In B. Kortmann, K. Burridge, R. Mesthrie, E.W. Schneider and C. Upton (eds) *A Handbook of Varieties of English, Vol. 2: Morphology and Syntax* (pp. 374– 390). Berlin: Mouton de Gruyter.

Beck, S.A.L. and Allexsaht-Snider, M. (2002) Recent language minority education policy in Georgia: Appropriation, assimilation, and Americanization. In S. Wortham, E.G. Murillo Jr. and E.T. Hamann (eds) *Education in the New Latino Diaspora: Policy and the Politics of Identity* (pp. 37–66). Westport, CN: Ablex Publishing.

Becker, R.R. (2001) Spanish-English code switching in a bilingual academic context. *Reading Horizons* 42 (2), 99–115.

Bejarano, C.L. (2005) *¿Qué onda? Urban Youth Culture and Border Identity*. Tucson, AZ: University of Arizona Press.

Beltrán, M. (2008) When Dolores Del Rio became Latina: Latina/o stardom in Hollywood's transition to sound. In A.N. Valdivia (ed.), *Latina/o Communication Studies Today* (pp. 27–50). New York: Peter Lang.

Berg, C.R. (1990) Stereotyping in films in general and of the Hispanic in particular. *The Howard Journal of Communications* 2 (3), 286–300.

Berg, C.R. (2002) *Latino Images in Film: Stereotypes, Subversion, & Resistance.* Austin, TX: University of Texas Press.

Bhatt, R.M. (2008) In other words: Language mixing, identity representations, and third space. *Journal of Sociolinguistics* 12 (2), 177–200.

Bigler, E. (1996) Telling stories: On ethnicity, education and exclusion in upstate New York. *Anthropology & Education Quarterly* 27 (2), 186–203.

Bills, G.D., Hernández-Chávez, E. and Hudson, A. (1995) The geography of language shift: Distance from the Mexican border and Spanish language claiming in the southwestern U.S. *International Journal for the Sociology of Language* 114, 9–27.

BlackHistory.com (2008) 'One Drop Rule'. Accessed August 1, 2012. Online at: http://www.blackhistory.com/cgi-bin/blog.cgi?blog_id=63228&cid=56.

Blackledge, A. and Pavlenko, A. (2001) Negotiation of identities in multilingual contexts. *International Journal of Bilingualism* 5 (3), 243–257.

Blackledge, A. and Pavlenko, A. (2002) Introduction. *Multilingua* 21, 121–140.

Boeschoten, H. (1990). Asymmetrical code-switching in immigrant communities. In *Papers for the Workshop on Constraints, Conditions and Models* (pp. 85–100). Strasbourg: European Science Foundation Network on Codeswitching and Language Contact.

Bourdieu, P. (1991) Chapter 1: The production and reproduction of legitimate language. In J. B. Thompson (ed.) *Language and Symbolic Power* (translated by G. Raymond and M. Adamson) (pp. 43–65). Cambridge, MA: Harvard University Press.

Brunn, N. (1999) The absence of language policy and its effects on the education of Mexican migrant children. *Bilingual Research Journal* 23 (4), 319–344.

Bucholtz, M. and Hall, K. (2004) Language and identity. In A. Duranti (ed.), *A Companion to Linguistic Anthropology* (pp. 369–393). Oxford: Blackwell Publishers.

Bucholtz, M. and Hall, K. (2005) Identity and interaction: A sociocultural linguistic approach. *Discourse Studies* 7 (4–5), 585–614.

Bucholtz, M. and Hall, K. (2008) Finding identity: Theory and data. *Multilingua* (27), 151–163.

Butler, Y.G., Orr, J.E., Gutiérrez, M.B. and Hakuta, K. (2000) Inadequate conclusions from an inadequate assessment: What can SAT-9 scores tell us about the impact of Proposition 227 in California? *Bilingual Research Journal* 24 (1–2), 141–154.

Cammarota, J. (2004) The gendered and racialized paths of Latino and Latina youth: Different struggles, different resistances in the urban context. *Anthropology and Education Quarterly* 35 (1), 53–74.

Canagaraja, S. (2011) Translanguaging in the classroom: Emerging issues for research and pedagogy. *Applied Linguistics Review* 2, 1–28.

Cardinal, L. (2004) The limits of bilingualism in Canada. *Nationalism and Ethnic Politics* 10 (1), 79–103.

Cashman, H. (2005) Identities at play: Language preference and group membership in bilingual talk in interaction. *Journal of Pragmatics* 37 (30), 1–15.

Cashman, H. (2009) The dynamics of Spanish maintenance and shift in Arizona: Ethnolinguistic vitality, language panic and language pride. *Spanish in Context* 6 (1), 43–68.

Castellanos, I. (1990) The use of English and Spanish among Cubans in Miami. *Cuban Studies/ Estudios Cubanos* 20, 49–63.

Center for Applied Linguistics (CAL) (1992) 'English Plus', accessed August 1, 2012. Online at: http://www.cal.org/resources/archive/digest/1992englishplus.html.

Center for Applied Linguistics (CAL) (1997) 'Official English and English Plus: An update', accessed August 1, 2012. Online at: http://www.cal.org/resources/digest/lewello1.html.

Center for Applied Linguistics CAL (2012) Accessed August 1, 2012. Online at: http://www.cal.org/twi/directory/ for a list of two-way-immersion programs in the US.

Centers for Disease Control and Prevention (2003) US standard certificate of live birth. Online at: http://www.cdc.gov/nchs/data/dvs/birth11-03final-ACC.pdf.

Chancer, L.S. and Watkins, B.X. (2006) *Gender, Race and Class: An Overview*. Oxford: Blackwell Publishing.

Chávez, R. (2003) Ethnic stereotypes: Hispanics and Mexican Americans. In P.M. Lester and S.D. Ross (eds) *Images That Injure* (pp. 93–102). Westport, CT: Praeger Publishers.

Choi, J. (2005) Bilingualism in Paraguay: Forty years after Rubin's study. *Journal of Multilingual and Multicultural Development* 26 (3), 233–248.

Cohen, R. (1978) Ethnicity: Problem and focus in Anthropology. *Annual Review of Anthropology* 7, 379–403.

Cook-Gumperz, J. and Szymanski, M. (2001) Classroom 'families': Cooperating or competing – Girls' and boys' interactional styles in a bilingual classroom. *Research on Language and Social Interaction* 34 (1), 107 –130.

Cortés, C.E. (1997) Chicanas in film: History of an image. In C.E. Rodriguez (ed.) *Latin Looks: Images of Latinas and Latinos in the U.S. Media* (pp. 121–141). Boulder, CO: Westview Press.

Crawford, J. (2003) Numbers game: Challenging the fallacies about Proposition 227. *The Bilingual Family Newsletter* 20 (2). Online at: http://www.languagepolicy.net/articles/numbers.htm.

Crawford, J. (2007) Language legislation in the U.S.A. Online at: http://www.languagepolicy.net/archives/langleg.htm.

Crawford, J. (2008) The Bilingual Education Act, 1968–2002: An obituary. *Advocating for English Learners: Selected Essays*. Online at: http://www.languagepolicy.net/books/AEL/Crawford_BEA_Obituary.pdf.

Creese, A. and Blackledge, A. (2010) Translanguing in the bilingual classroom: A pedagogy for learning and teaching? *The Modern Language Journal* 94 (i), 103–115.

Cruz, B. and Teck, B. (1998) *The Official Spanglish Dictionary: Un User's Guide to More Than 300 Words and Phrases That Aren't Exactly Español or Inglés*. New York: Fireside.

Cuero, K.K. (2009) Authoring multiple formas de ser: Three bilingual Latino/a fifth graders navigating school. *Journal of Latinos and Education* 8 (2), 141–160.

De Casanova, E.M. (2007) Spanish language and Latino ethnicity in children's television programs. *Latino Studies* (5), 455–477.

Del Valle, S. (2009) The bilingual's hoarse voice: Losing rights in two languages. In R. Salaberry (ed.) *Language Allegiances and Bilingualism in the US* (pp. 80–109). Bristol: Multilingual Matters.

DePalma, R. (2010) *Language Use in the Two-Way Classroom: Lessons From a Spanish-English Bilingual Kindergarten.* Bristol: Multilingual Matters.

Echevarria, R.G. (1997) Is 'Spanglish' a Language? *New York Times* Op-Ed, March 28.

Editorial: The Candidate from Xenophobia. (2010) *New York Times* April 29, A30.

Ehala, M. (2011) Hot and cold ethnicities: Modes of ethnolinguistic vitality. *Journal of Multilingual and Multicultural Development* 32 (2), 187–200.

eHow (n.d.) 'How to become bilingual', *eHow.com*, accessed August 1, 2012. Online at: http://www.ehow.com/how_4775726_become-bilingual.html#ixzzouKm6B7f2.

Errington, J. (2000) Ideology. *Journal of Linguistic Anthropology* 9 (1–2), 115–117.

Facebook (n.d.) 'I should not have to press 1 for english', accessed August, 2012. Online at: http://www.facebook.com/pages/i-should-not-have-to-press-1-for-english/189057582033.

Fairclough, M. (2003) El (denominado) Spanglish en Estados Unidos: Polémicas y realidades. *Revista internacional de lingüística iberoamericana* 1 (2), 185–204.

Farr, M. (2006) *Rancheros in Chicagoacán: Language and Identity in a Transnational Community.* Austin: University of Texas Press.

Farr, M. (2011) Urban plurilingualism: Language practices, policies, and ideologies in Chicago. *Journal of Pragmatics* 43, 1161–1172

Ferguson, C. (1959) Diglossia. *Word* 15, 324–340

Fernández, R.G. (1983) English loanwords in Miami Cuban Spanish. *American Speech* 58 (1), 13–19.

Fishman, J.A. (1980) Bilingualism and biculturism as individual and as societal phenomena. *Journal of Multilingual and Multicultural Development* 1, 3–15.

Fishman, J.A. (1985) *The Rise and Fall of the Ethnic Revival.* New York: Mouton Publishers.

Fishman, J.A. (1989) *Language and Ethnicity in Minority Sociolinguistic Perspective.* Clevedon: Multilingual Matters.

Fishman, J.A. (1991) *Reversing Language Shift: Theoretical and Empirical Foundations of Assistance to Threatened Languages.* Clevedon: Multilingual Matters.

Fishman, J.A, Cooper, R.L. and Ma, R. (1971) *Bilingualism in the Barrio.* Bloomington, IN: University of Indiana Press.

Fitts, S. (2006) Reconstructing the status quo: Linguistic interaction in a dual language school. *Bilingual Research Journal* 29 (2), 337–365.

Flores-Ferrán, N. (2002) *A Sociolinguistic Perspective on the Use of Subject Personal Pronouns in Spanish Narratives of Puerto Ricans in New York City.* Munich: Lincom-Europa.

Flores-Ferrán, N. (2004) Spanish subject personal pronoun use in New York City Puerto Ricans: Can we rest the case of English contact? *Language Variation and Change* 16, 49–73.

Fought, C. (1999) A majority sound change in a minority community: /u/-fronting in Chicano English. *Journal of Sociolinguistics* 3 (1), 5–23.

Fought, C. (2003) *Chicano English in Context*. New York, NY: Palgrave Macmillan.

Fought, C. (2006) *Language and Ethnicity*. Cambridge: Cambridge University Press.

Frazer, T. (1996) Chicano English and Spanish interference in the Midwestern United States. *American Speech* 71 (1), 72–85.

Freeman, R. (2000) Contextual challenge to a dual-language education: A case study of a developing middle school program. *Anthropology & Education Quarterly* 31 (2), 202–229.

Fry, R. (2010) Hispanics, high school dropouts and the GED. Pew Research Center. Online at: http://pewhispanic.org/files/reports/122.pdf.

Fuller, J.M. (1997) Co-constructing bilingualism: Non-converging discourse as an unmarked choice. In A. Chu, A-M.P. Guerra and C. Tetreault (eds) *SALSA (Symposium About Language in Society – Austin) IV Proceedings* (pp. 68–77). Austin, TX: University of Texas Linguistics Department.

Fuller, J.M. (2007) Language choice as a means for shaping identity. *Journal of Linguistic Anthropology* 17 (1), 105–129.

Fuller, J.M. (2009) How bilingual children talk: Strategic codeswitching among children in dual language programs. In M. Turnbull and J. Dailey-O'Cain (eds) *First Language Use in Second and Foreign Language Learning* (pp. 115–130). Bristol: Multilingual Matters.

Fuller, J.M. (2010) Gendered choices: Codeswitching and collaboration in a bilingual classroom. *Gender and Language* 4 (1), 181–208.

Fuller, J.M., Elsman, M. and Self, K. (2007) Addressing peers in a Spanish-English bilingual classroom. In K. Potowski and R. Cameron (eds) *Spanish in Contact: Educational, Social, and Linguistic Inquiries* (pp. 135–151). Amsterdam: John Benjamins.

Gafaranga, J. and Torras, M.C. (2002) Interactional otherness: Toward a redefinition of codeswitching. *International Journal of Bilingualism* 6 (1), 1–22.

Gal, S. (1998) Multiplicity and contention among language ideologies: A commentary. In B.B. Schieffelen, K. Woolard and P. Kroskrity (eds) *Language Ideologies: Practice and Theory* (pp. 317–322). Cambridge: Cambridge University Press.

Gal, S. and Irvine, J. (1995) The boundaries of languages and disciplines. How ideologies construct difference. *Social Research* (62), 996–1001.

Gándara, P. (1995) *Over the Ivy Walls: The Educational Mobility of Low-Income Chicanos*. New York: SUNY Press.

Garcia, E.E. and Curry-Rodríguez, J.E. (2000) The education of limited English proficient students in California Schools: An assessment of the influence of Proposition 227 in selected districts and schools. *Bilingual Research Journal* 24 (1–2), 15–35.

Garcia, M.E. (2003) Speaking Spanish in Los Angeles and San Antonio: Who, when, where, why. *Southwest Journal of Linguistics* 22 (1), 1–21.

García, O. (2008) Teaching Spanish and Spanish in teaching in the USA: Integrating bilingual perspectives. In C. Helot and A-M. Meijia (eds) *Forging Multilingual Spaces: Integrating Majority and Minority Bilingual Education* (pp. 31–57). Bristol: Multilingual Matters.

García, O. (2009a) *Bilingual Education in the 21st Century: A Global Perspective.* Oxford: Wiley-Blackwell.

García, O. (2009b) Education, multilingualism and translanguaging in the 21st century. In T. Skutnabb-Kangas, R. Phillipson, A.K. Mohanty and M. Panda (eds) *Social Justice Through Multilingual Education* (pp. 140–158). Bristol: Multilingual Matters.

García, O. (2009c) En/countering indigenous bilingualism. *Journal of Language, Identity, and Education* 8, 376–380.

García, O. (2010) Languaging and ethnifying. In J.A. Fishman and O. García (eds) *Language & Ethnic Identity, Vol. 1: Disciplinary & Regional Perspectives* (2nd edn) (pp. 519–534). Oxford: Oxford University Press.

García, O. (2011a) From language garden to sustainable languaging: Bilingual education in a global world. *NABE Perspectives* 34 (1), 5–9.

García, O. (2011b) The translanguaging of Latino kindergarteners. In K. Potowski and J. Rothman (eds) *Bilingual Youth: Spanish in English-Speaking Societies* (pp. 33–55). Amsterdam: John Benjamins Publishing Company.

García, O., Morín, J.L.and Rivera, K. (2001) How threatened is the Spanish of New York Puerto Ricans? In J. Fishman (ed.) *Can Threatened Languages Be Saved?* (pp. 44–73). Clevedon: Multilingual Matters.

Genesee, F. Lindholm-Leary, K., Saunders, W. and Christian, D. (2005) English language learners in U.S. schools: An overview of research findings. *Journal of Education for Students Placed at Risk* 10 (4), 363–385.

Gibson, M.A. (2002) The new Latino diaspora and educational policy. In S. Wortham, E.G. Murillo Jr. and E.T. Hamann (eds) *Education in the New Latino Diaspora: Policy and the Politics of Identity* (pp.241–252). Westport, CN: Ablex Publishing.

Giles, H., Bourhis, R. and Taylor, D. (1977). Towards a theory of language in ethnic group relations. In H. Giles (ed.) *Language, Ethnicity and Inter-group Relations* (pp. 307–348). New York: Academic Press.

Golash-Boza, T. (2006) Dropping the hyphen? Becoming Latino(a)-American through racialized assimilation. *Social Forces* 85 (1), 27–33.

González, J. (2001) *Harvest of Empire.* New York: Penguin Books.

Green, J.P. (1998) A meta-analysis of the effectiveness of bilingual education. Online at: http://www.hks.harvard.edu/pepg/PDF/Papers/biling.pdf.

Gutierrez, M.J. (1994) Simplificiation, transfer, and convergence in Chicano Spanish. *Bilingual Review/Revista Bilingue* 19 (2), 111–21.

Gutierrez, K., Baquendano-Lopez, P. and Alvarez, H.H. (2000) The crisis in Latino education. In C. Tejeda, C. Martinez and Z. Leonardo (eds) *Charting New Terrains of Chicana(o)/ Latina(o) Education: Themes of Urban and Inner City Education* (pp. 213–232). Cresskill, NJ: Hampton Press.

Guzmán, I.M. and Valdivia, A.N. (2004) Brain, brow, and booty: Latina iconicity in U.S. popular culture. *The Communication Review* 7, 205–221.

Hadi-Tabassum, S. (2002) Language, space and power: A critical ethnography of a dual language classroom. Doctor of Education dissertation, Teachers' College, Columbia University.

Hakimzadeh, S. and Cohn, D. (2007) *English Usage among Hispanics in the United States.* Washington: Pew Hispanic Center.

Haugen, E. (1950) The analysis of linguistic borrowing. *Language* 26 (2), 210–231.

Hayes, R. (2005) Conversation, negotiation, and the word as deed: Linguistic interaction in a dual language program. *Linguistics and Education* 16, 93–112.

Heath, S.B. (1982) What no bedtime story means: Narrative skills at home and school. *Language in Society* 11, 49–76 .

Heller, M. (1999) *Linguistic Minorities and Modernity: A Sociolinguistic Ethnography.* New York: Longman.

Heller, M. (2002) Globalization and the commodification of bilingualism in Canada. In D. Block and D. Cameron (eds) *Globalization and Language Teaching* (pp. 47–63). New York: Routledge.

Hernandez, T.K. (2002) Multiracial matrix: The role of race ideology in the enforcement of antidiscrimination laws, a United States-Latin America comparison. 87 *Cornell Law Rev.*1093.

Hill, J.H. (1995) Mock Spanish: A site for the indexical reproduction of racism in American English. Online at: http://language-culture.binghamton.edu/symposia/2/part1/index.html.

Hill, J.H. (1998) Language, race, and white public space. *American Anthropologist* 100 (3), 680–689.

Hill, J.H. (2005) Intertextuality as source and evidence for indirect indexical meanings. *Journal of Linguistic Anthropology* 15 (1), 113–124.

Hill, J.H. (2008) *The Everyday Language of White Racism.* Oxford: Blackwell.

Hornblower, S. and Spawforth, A. (1996) *The Oxford Classical Dictionary* (3rd edn). Oxford: Oxford University Press.

HUD (2012) Advertisement, accessed August 1, 2012. Online at: http://www.youtube.com/watch?v=HAZMIC_OwTw.

Jacobson, R. (1988) Intersentential codeswitching: An educationally justifiable strategy. In D.J. Bixler-Márquez and J. Ornstein-Galicia (eds) *Chicano Speech in the Bilingual Classroom* (pp. 121–131). New York: Peter Lang.

Jaffe, A. (2000) Comic performance and the articulation of hybrid identity. *Pragmatics* 10, 39–59.

Jenkins, D. (2009) The cost of linguistic loyalty. *Spanish in Context* 6 (1), 7–25.

Jensen, L., Cohen, J., Toribio, A.J., DeJong, G. and Rodríguez, L. (2006) Ethnic identities, language and economic outcomes among Dominicans in a new destination. *Social Science Quarterly* 87, 1088–1099.

Jørgensen, J.N. (2003) Languaging among fifth graders: Code-switching in conversation 501 of the Køge project. In J.N. Jørgensen (ed.) *Bilingualism and Social Change: Turkish Speakers in North Western Europe* (pp. 126–148). Clevedon: Multilingual Matters.

Jørgensen, J.N. (2008) Poly-lingual languaging around and among children and adolescents. *International Journal of Multilingualism* 5 (3), 161–176.

Konopka, K. and Pierrehumbert, J. (2008) Vowels in contact: Mexican heritage English in Chicago. *Texas Linguistic Forum* 52, 94–103.

Koontz-Garboden, A. (2004) Language contact and Spanish aspectual expression: A formal analysis. *Lingua* 114, 1291–1330.

Kroskrity, P. (1998) Arizona Tewa Kiva speech as a manifestation of a dominant language ideology. In B.B.Schieffelen, K.A. Woolard and P.V. Kroskrity (eds) *Language Ideologies: Practice and Theory* (pp. 103–122). Oxford: Oxford University Press.

Kroskrity, P. (2000) Identity. *Journal of Linguistic Anthropology* 9 (1–2), 111–114.

Kroskrity, P. (2004) Language ideologies. In A. Duranti (ed.) *A Companion to Linguistic Anthropology* (pp. 496–517). Oxford: Blackwell Publishing.

Lambert, W.E. (2003) A social psychology of bilingualism. In C. Bratt-Paulston and G.R. Tucker (eds) *Sociolinguistics: The Essential Readings* (pp. 305–321). Oxford: Blackwell Publishing.

Lambert, W.E., Frankle, H. and Tucker, G.R. (1966) Judging personality through speech: A French-Canadian example. *Journal of Communication* 16 (4), 305–321.

Lareau, A. (1987) Social class differences in family-school relationships: The importance of cultural capital. *Sociology of Education* 60 (2), 73–85.

Lareau, A. (2000) *Home Advantage: Social Class and Parental Intervention in Elementary Education*. Lanham, MD: Rowman and Littlefield Publishers.

Leeman, J. and Martínez, G. (2007) From identity to commodity: Ideologies of Spanish in heritage language textbooks. *Critical Inquiry in Language Studies* 4 (1), 35–65.

Lewis, L.A. (2000) Blacks, black Indians, Afromexicans: The dynamics of race, nation, and identity in a Mexican Moreno community (Guerrero). *American Ethnologist* 27 (4), 898–926.

Li Wei (2011) Moment analysis and translanguaging space: Discursive construction of identities by multilingual Chinese youth in Britain. *Journal of Pragmatics* 4, 122–135.

Li Wei and Lee, S. (2002) Bilingual development and social networks of British-born Chinese children. *International Journal of the Sociology of Language* 153, 9–25.

Lichter, S.R. and Amundson, D.R. (1997) Distorted reality: Hispanic characters in TV entertainment. In C.E. Rodríguez (ed.) *Latin Looks: Images of Latinas and Latinos in the U.S. Media* (pp. 57–72). Boulder, CO: Westview Press.

Lindholm-Leary, K. (2001) *Dual Language Education*. Clevedon: Multilingual Matters.

Linnes, K. (1998) Middle-class AAVE versus middle-class bilingualism: Contrasting speech communities. *American Speech* 73 (4), 339–367.

Linton, A. (2003) Is Spanish here to stay? Contexts for bilingualism among U.S.-born Hispanics, 1990–2000. *Working Paper No. 81, University of California-San Diego*. Online at: http://escholarship.org/uc/item/4rfoc6k7.

Linton, A. (2004) Learning in two languages: Spanish-English immersion in U.S. public schools. *International Journal of Sociology and Social Policy* 24 (7/8), 46–75.

Lippi-Green, R. (1997) *English with an Accent: Language Ideology and Discrimination in the United States*. London: Routledge.

Lipski, J. (1993) Creoloid phenomena in the Spanish of transitional bilinguals. In A. Roca and J. Lipski (eds) *Spanish in the United States: Linguistic Contact and Diversity* (pp. 155–182). Berlín: Mouton de Gruyter.

Lipski, J. (2002) Rethinking the place of Spanish. *Publications of the Modern Language Association* 117, 1247–1251.

Lipski, J. (2004) La lengua española en los Estados Unidos: Avanza a la vez que retrocede. *Revista Española de Lingüística* 33, 231–260.

Lipski, J.M. (2007a) Spanish, English or Spanglish? Truth and consequences of U.S. Latino bilingualism. In N. Eschávez-Solono and K.C. Dworkin y Méndez (eds) *Spanish and Empire* (pp. 197–218). Nashville: Vanderbilt University Press.

Lipski, J.M. (2007b) The evolving interface of U. S. Spanish: Language mixing as hybrid vigor. Unpublished manuscript.

López, M.A. (2009) Un microcosmos hispano: La ciudad de chicago. In *Enciclopedia del español en Estados Unidos* (pp. 161–176). Madrid: Instituto Cervantes & Editorial Santillana.

Lopez Morales, H. (2000) El español de la Florida: Los cubanos de Miami. In *El español en el Mundo. Anuario del Instituto Cervantes* (pp. 13–63). Madrid and Barcelona, Spain: Instituto Cervantes, Circulo de Lectores.

Lutz, A. (2006) Spanish maintenance among English-speaking Latino youth: The role of individual and social characteristics. *Social Forces* 84 (3), 1417–1433.

Lynch, A. (2000a) Spanish-speaking Miami in sociolinguistic perspective: Bilingualism, recontact, and language maintenance among Cuban-origin population. In A. Roca (ed.) *Research on Spanish in the United States* (pp. 271–283). Somerville: Cascadilla Press.

Lynch, A. (2000b) The subjunctive in Miami Cuban Spanish: Bilingualism, contact, and language variability. PhD Dissertation, University of Minnesota.

Lynch, A. (2009) A sociolingusitic analysis of final /s/ in Miami Cuban Spanish. *Language Sciences* 31 (6) 766–790.

Makoni, S. and Pennycook, A. (2007) Disinventing and reconstituting languages. In S. Makoni and A. Pennycook (eds) *Disinventing and Reconsituting Languages* (pp. 1–41). Clevedon: Multilingual Matters.

Mar-Molino, C. (2000) Spanish as minority language. In C. Mar-Molino, *The Politics of Language in the Spanish-speaking World: From Colonialization to Globalization* (pp. 166–181). New York: Routledge.

Martínez, G. (2006) *Mexican Americans and Language*. Tucson: University of Arizona Press.

Mastro, D.E. and Behm-Moravitz, E. (2005) Latino representation on primetime television. *Journalism & Mass Communication Quarterly* 82 (1), 110–130.

McCullough, R.E. and Jenkins, D.L. (2005) Out with the old, in with the new?: Recent trends in Spanish language use in Colorado. *Southwest Journal of Linguistics* 24, 91–110.

Meador, E. (2005) The making of marginality: Schooling for Mexican immigrant girls in the rural southwest. *Anthropology and Education Quarterly* 36 (2), 149–164.

Mendoza-Denton, N. (2002) Language and identity. In J. Chambers, P. Trudgill and N. Schilling-Estes (eds) *The Handbook of Language Variation and Change* (pp. 475–499). Oxford: Blackwell.

Mendoza-Denton, N. (2008) *Homegirls: Language and Cultural Practices Among Latina Youth Gangs.* Oxford: Blackwell Publishers.

Metcalf, A. (1979) *Chicano English.* Washington, DC: Center for Applied Linguistics.

Millard, A.V., Chapa, J. and McConnell, E.D. (2004) Ten myths about Latinos. In A. Millard and J. Chapa (eds) *Apple Pie and Enchiladas: Latino Newcomers in the Rural Midwest* (pp. 22–25). Austin: University of Texas Press.

Milroy, L. (2002) Social networks. In J.K. Chambers, P. Trudgill and N. Schilling-Estes (eds) *The Handbook of Language Variation and Change* (pp. 549–572). Oxford: Blackwell Publishers.

Milroy, L. and Wei, L. (1995) A social network approach to code-switching: The example of a bilingual community in Britain. In L. Milroy and P. Muysken (eds) *One Speaker, Two Languages. Cross-Disciplinary Perspectives on Code-Switching* (pp. 136–157). Cambridge: Cambridge University Press.

Mirón, L.F. and Inda, J.X. (2004) Constructing cultural citizenship: Latino immigrant students and learning English. *Latino Studies* 2, 237–245.

Monsivais, G.I. (2004) *Hispanic Immigrant Identity: Political Allegiance vs. Cultural Preference.* New York: LFB Scholarly Publishing LLC.

Montero-Sieburth, M. and LaCelle-Peterson, M. (1991) Immigration and schooling: An ethnohistorical account of policy and family perspectives in an urban community. *Anthropology & Education Quarterly* 22 (4), 300–325.

Montoya, M.C. (2011) Expression of possession in Spanish in contact with English: A sociolinguistic study across two generations in the greater New York metropolitan area. Phd thesis, University at Albany, State University of New York.

Montrul, S. (2004) Subject and object expression in Spanish heritage speakers: A case of morphosyntactic convergence. *Bilingualism: Language and Cognition* 7 (2), 125–142.

Montrul, S. (2007) Interpreting mood distinctions in Spanish as a heritage language. In K. Potowski and R. Cameron (eds) *Spanish in Contact: Policy, Social and Linguistic Inquiries* (pp. 23–40). Philadelphia: John Benjamins.

Morales, E. (2002) *Living in Spanglish: The Search for Latino Identity in America.* New York: St. Martin's Press.

Moreman, S.T. (2008) Hybrid performativity, south and north of the border: Entre la teoría y la materialidad de hibridación. In A.N. Valdivia (ed.) *Latina/o Communication Studies Today* (pp. 91–111). New York: Peter Lang.

Moring, T., Husband, C., Lojander-Visap, C., Vincze, L., Fomina, J. and Mänty, N.N. (2011) Media use and ethnolinguistic vitality in bilingual communities. *Journal of Multilingual and Multicultural Development* 32 (2), 169–186.

Mughan, A. (2007) 'Immigrants, assimilation, and cultural threat: A political exploration'. Online at: http://mershoncenter.osu.edu/expertise/ideas/immigrants.htm.

My Biggest Complaint (n.d.) 'Press one for English', accessed August 1, 2012. Online at: http://mybiggestcomplaint.com/press-one-for-english/.

Myers-Scotton, C. (1993) *Social Motivations for Codeswitching: Evidence from Africa*. Oxford: Clarendon Press.

Myers-Scotton, C. (2006) *Multiple Voices: An Introduction to Bilingualism*. Oxford: Blackwell Publishing.

Nafte, M. (2000) *Flesh and Bone: An Introduction to Forensic Anthropology*. Durham, NC: Carolina Academic Press.

Nava, E.H. (2007) Word order in bilingual Spanish: Convergence and intonation strategy. In J. Homquist, A. Lorenzino and L. Sayahi (eds) *Selected Proceedings of the Third Workshop on Spanish Sociolinguistics* (pp. 129–139). Somerville, MA: Cascadilla Proceedings Project.

New York Times (2010) Editorial – The candidate from Xenophobia. April 29, 2010, p. A30.

Nichols, P. (2000) Spanish literacy and the academic success of Latino high school students. *Foreign Language Annals* 33 (5), 498–511.

Nichols, P. and Colon, M. (2000) Spanish literacy and the academic success of Latino high school students: Codeswitching as a classroom resource. *Foreign Language Annals* 33 (5), 498–511.

Novas, H. (2008) *Everything You Need to Know About Latino History*. New York: Plume.

Oboler, S. (1998) Hispanics: That's what they call us. In R. Delgado and J. Stafancic (eds) *The Latino/a Condition* (pp. 3–5). New York: New York University Press.

Ogbu, J.U. and Simons, H.D. (1998) Voluntary and involuntary minorities: A cultural-ecological theory of school performance with some implications for education. *Anthropology & Education Quarterly* 29 (2), 155–188.

Omi, M. and Winant, H. (1994) *Racial Formation in the United States: From the 1960s to the 1990s*. New York: Routledge.

Ornstein-Galicia, J. (ed.) (1984) *Form and Function in Chicano English*. Rowley, MA: Newbury House Publishers.

Orozco, R. (2007) The impact of linguistic constraints on the expression of futurity in the Spanish of New York Colombians. In K. Potowski and R. Cameron (eds) *Spanish in Contact: Policy, Social and Linguistic Inquiries* (pp. 311–328). Philadelphia: John Benjamins.

Otheguy, R. (1993) A reconsideration of the notion of loan translation in the analysis of U.S. Spanish. In A. Roca and J.M. Lipski (eds) *Spanish in the United States: Linguistic Contact and Diversity* (pp. 21–45). Berlin: Mouton de Gruyter.

Otheguy, R. (2009) El llamado espanglish. In *Enciclopedia del español en Estados Unidos* (pp. 222–247). Madrid: Instituto Cervantes & Editorial Santillana.

Otheguy, R. and Stern, N. (2010) On so-called Spanglish. *International Journal of Bilingualism* 15 (1), 85–100.

Otheguy, R., Zentella, A.C. and Livert, D. (2007) Language and dialect contact in Spanish in New York: Toward the formation of a speech community. *Language* 83 (4), 770–802.

Otsuji, E. and Pennycook, A. (2010) Metrolingualism: Fixity, fluidity and language in flux. *International Journal of Multilingualism* 7 (3), 240–254.

Palmer, D. (2007) A dual immersion strand program in California: Carrying out the promise of dual language education in an English-dominant context. *The International Journal of Bilingual Education and Bilingualism* 10 (6), 752–768.

Patthey-Chavez, G.G. (1993) High school as an arena for cultural conflict and acculturation for Latino Angelinos. *Anthropology & Educational Quarterly* 24 (1), 33–60.

Pease-Alvarez, L. and Winsler, A. (1994) Cuando el maestro no habla Espanol: Children's bilingual language practices in the classroom. *TESOL Quarterly* 28 (3), 507–535.

Penfield, J. and Ornstein-Galicia, J.L. (1985) *Chicano English: An Ethnic Contact Dialect.* Amsterdam: John Benjamins Publishing Company.

Petroski,W. and Duara, N. (2008) Judge puts English only on voter forms. *The Des Moines Register,* April 4.

Petrucci, P.R. (2008) Portraying language diversity through a monolingual lens: On the unbalanced representation of Spanish and English in a corpus of American films. *Sociolinguistic Studies* 2 (3), 405–425.

Phinney J.S., Cantu, C.L. and Kurtz, D.A. (1997) Ethnic and American identity as predictors of self-esteem among African American, Latino, and White adolescents. *Journal of Youth and Adolescence* 26 (2), 165–185.

Pomerantz, A. (2002) Language ideologies and the production of identities: Spanish as a resource for participation in a multilingual marketplace. *Multilingua* 2, 275–302.

Popp. R.K. (2006) Mass media and the linguistic marketplace: Media, language, and distinction. *Journal of Communication Inquiry* 30 (1), 5–20.

Porcel, J. (2006) Research notes: The paradox of Spanish among Miami Cubans. *Journal of Sociolinguistics* 10 (1), 93–110.

Portes, A. and Schauffler, R. (1994) Language and the second generation: Bilingualism yesterday and today. *International Migration Review* 28 (4), 640–661.

Potatoe.com (n.d.) 'Mexicans are stupid', accessed August 1, 2012. Online at: http://www.potatoe.com/looselips/display_topic.php?topic_id=33269.

Potowski, K. (2004) Spanish language shift in Chicago. *Southwest Journal of Linguistics* 23 (1), 87–116.

Potowski, K. (2007) *Language and Identity in a Dual Immersion School.* Bristol: Multilingual Matters.

Potowski, K. (2008a) 'I was raised talking like my mom': The influence of mothers in the development of MexiRicans' phonological and lexical features. In M. Niño-Murcia and J. Rothman (eds) *Bilingualism and Identity: Spanish at the Crossroads with Other Languages* (pp. 201–220). Philadelphia: John Benjamins.

Potowski, K. (2008b) MexiRicans: Interethnic language and identity. *Journal of Language, Identity and Education* 7 (2), 137–160.

Potowski, K. (2009) Los hispanos de etnicidad mixta. In *Enciclopedia del Español en los Estados Unidos* (pp. 410–413). Madrid: Instituto Cervantes.

Proposition 227 (1998) English language in public schools. Online at: http://primary98.sos.ca.gov/VoterGuide/Propositions/227text.htm.

Quiroz, P.A. (2001) The silencing of Latino student 'voice': Puerto Rican and Mexican narratives in eighth grade and high school. *Anthropology & Education Quarterly* 32 (3), 326–349.

Ramírez, A. (1991) Sociolingüística del español-inglés en contacto entre adolescentes hispanos de Estados Unidos. *Hispania* 74 (4), 1057–1067.

Ramírez, J.D. (1992) Executive summary. *Bilingual Research Journal* 16, 1–62.

Ramírez, J.D., Yuen, S.D. and Ramey, D.R. (1991) *Final Report: Longitudinal Study of Structured English Immersion Strategy, Early-Exit and Late-Exit Programs for Language Minority Children.* Report submitted to the US Department of Education. San Mateo, CA: Aguirre International.

Ramirez, R.R. and de la Cruz, P. (2002) *The Hispanic Population in the United States: March 2000, Current Population Reports.* Washington, DC: U.S. Census Bureau.

Rampton, B. (1995) *Crossing: Language and Ethnicity among Adolescents.* London: Longman.

Rampton, B. (1999) Crossing. *Journal of Linguistic Anthropology* 9 (1–2), 54–56.

Raschka, C., Wei, L. and Lee, S. (2002) Bilingual development and social networks of British-born Chinese children. *International Journal of the Sociology of Language* 153, 9–25.

Resnik, M.C. (1988) Beyond the ethnic community: Spanish language roles and maintenance in Miami. *International Journal of the Sociology of Language* 69, 89–104.

Ricento, T. (2009) Problems with the 'language-as-resource' discourse. In R. Salaberry (ed.) *Language Allegiances and Bilingualism in the US* (pp. 110–131). Bristol: Multilingual Matters.

Rickford, J. (1999) *African American Vernacular English: Features, Evolution, Educational Implications.* Oxford: Blackwell Publishers.

Rodríguez, A. (2007) *Diversity.* Mountain View, CA: Floricanto Press.

Rodríguez, C.E. (1997) Visual retrospective: Latino film stars. In C.E. Rodríguez (ed.) *Latin Looks: Images of Latinas and Latinos in the U.S. Media* (pp. 80–84). Boulder, CO: Westview Press.

Roosevelt, T. (1919) Letter to Richard Hurd. Online at: http://67.19.222.106/politics/graphics/trooseveit.pdf.

Roth-Gordon, J. (2011) Discipline and disorder in the Whiteness of Mock Spanish. *Journal of Linguistic Anthropology* 21 (2), 211–229.

Rúa, M. (2001) *Colao* subjectivities: PortoMex and MexiRican perspectives on language and identity. *Centro Journal* 13 (2), 117–133.

Rubin, J. (1968) *National Bilingualism in Paraguay.* The Hague: Moulton.

Salmons, J. (2005) Community, region, and language shift in German-speaking Wisconsin. In L. Hönnighausen, M. Frey, J. Peacock and N. Steine (eds) *Regionalism in the Age of Globalism: Volume 2: Forms of Regionalism* (pp. 133–144). Madison: Center for the Study of Upper Midwestern Cultures.

Sanchez, P. (2007) Cultural authenticity and transnational Latina youth: Constructing a meta-narrative across borders. *Linguistics and Education* 18, 258–282.

Santa Ana, O. (1993) Chicano English and the nature of the Chicano language setting. *Hispanic Journal of Behavioral Sciences* 15 (1), 3–35.

Santa Ana, O. (1996) Sonority and syllable structure in Chicano English. *Language Variation and Change* 8, 63–89.

Santa Ana, O. and Bayley, R. (2004) Chicano English phonology. In B. Kortmann, K. Burridge, R. Mesthrie, E.W. Schneider and C. Upton (eds) *A Handbook of Varieties of English, Vol. 1: Phonology* (pp. 417–434). Berlin: Mouton de Gruyter.

Santiago, B. (2008) *Pardon my Spanglish*. Philadelphia: Quirk Books.

Schachner, J. (2003) *Skippyjon Jones*. New York: Puffin Books.

Schachner, J. (2005) *Skippyjon Jones in the Dog House*. New York: Puffin Books.

Schecter, S.R. and Bayley, R. (2002) *Language as Cultural Practice: Mexicanos en el Norte*. Mahwah, NJ: Lawrence Erlbaum Associates Inc.

Schmidt, R. (2002) Racialization and language policy: The case of the U.S.A. *Multilingua* 21, 141–162.

Schmidt, R. (2007) Defending English in an English-dominant world: The ideology of the 'Official English' movement in the United States. In A. Duchêne and M. Heller (eds) *Discourses of Endangerment: Ideology and Interest in the Defence of Languages* (pp. 197–215). New York: Continuuum.

Schmidt, R. (2009) English hegemony and the politics of ethno-linguistic justice in the US. In R. Salaberry (ed.) *Language Allegiances and Bilingualism in the US* (pp. 132–150). Bristol: Multilingual Matters.

Schutte, O. (2000) Negotiating Latina identities. In J.J.E. Gracia and P. de Greiff (eds) *Hispanics/ Latinos in the United States: Ethnicity, Race and Rights* (pp. 61–75). New York: Routledge.

Self, K. (2005) Talk and identity in the bilingual classroom. Paper presented at the 5th International Symposium on Bilingualism, Barcelona, March 20–23.

Sesame Street (2004) Episode 4081 treatment, accessed February 16, 2011. Online at: http://www.aptv.org/schedule/showinfo.asp?ID=120454.

Shannon, S.M. (1995) The hegemony of English: A case study of one bilingual classroom as a site of resistance. *Linguistics and Education* 7, 175–200.

Shenk, P.S. (2007) 'I'm Mexican, remember?': Constructing ethnic identities via authenticating discourse. *Journal of Sociolinguistics* 11 (2), 194–220.

Shin, H.B. and Kominski, R.A. (2010) Language use in the United States: 2007 (American Community Survey Reports), accessed April 13, 2011. Online at: http://www.census.gov/hhes/socdemo/language/data/acs/ACS-12.pdf.

Silva-Corvalán, C. (1994) *Language Contact and Change: Spanish in Los Angeles*. Oxford: Clarendon Press.

Silva-Corvalán, C. (2004) Spanish in the southwest. In E. Finegan, C.A. Ferguson, S. Brice Heath and J.R. Rickford (eds) *Language in the USA: Themes for the Twenty-First Century* (pp. 205–229). Cambridge: Cambridge University Press.

Silverstein, M. (1996) Monoglot 'Standard' in America: standardization and metaphors of linguistic hegemony. In D. Brenneis and R. Macaulay (eds) *The Matrix of Language* (pp. 284–306). Boulder, CO: Westview Press.

Smead, R.N. (2000) Phrasal calques in Chicano Spanish: Linguistic or cultural innovations? In A. Roca (ed.) *Research on Spanish in the U.S.* (pp. 162–172). Somerville, MA: Cascadilla Press.

Smedly, A. (1999) 'Race' and the construction of human identity. *American Anthropologist* 100 (3), 690–702.

Smith, L.R. (2002) The social architecture of communicative competence: A methodology for social-network research in sociolinguistics. *International Journal of the Sociology of Language* 153, 133–160.

Soliman, A. (2009) The changing role of Arabic in religious discourse: A sociolinguistic study of Egyptian Arabic. PhD dissertation.

Sowards, S.K. and Pineda, R.D. (2011) *Latinidad* in Ugly Betty: Authenticity and the paradox of representation. In M.A. Holling and B.M. Calafeel (eds) *Latina/o Discourse in Vernacular Spaces: Somos de Una Voz?* (pp. 123–144) New York: Rowman & Littlefield Publishers, Inc.

Spitulnik, D. (1999) The language of the city: Town Bemba and urban hybridity. *Journal of Linguistic Anthropology* 8, 30–59.

Stavans, I. (2000) The gravitas of Spanglish. *The Chronicle of Education,* October 13, 2000. (The Chronicle Review, B7).

Stavans, I. (2003) *Spanglish: The Making of a New American Language.* New York: Harper Collins Publishers.

Stavans, I. and Albin, V. (2007) Language and empire: A conversation with Ilan Stavans. In N. Echávez-Solano and K.C. Sworkin y Méndez (eds) *Spanish and Empire* (pp. 219–243). Nashville, TN: Vanderbilt University Press.

Stoessel, S. (2002) Investigating the role of social networks in language maintenance and shift. *International Journal of the Sociology of Language* 153, 93–131.

Suarez, D. (2002). The paradox of linguistic hegemony and the maintenance of Spanish as a heritage language in the United States. *Journal of Multilingual and Multicultural Development* 23 (6), 512–530.

Subervi-Vélez, F. (1994) Mass communication and Hispanics. In F. Padilla (ed.) *Handbook of Hispanic Cultures in the United States: Sociology* (pp. 304–350). Houston: Arte Público Press.

Swigart, L. (1994) Cultural creolisation and language use in post-colonial Africa: The case of Senegal. *Africa* 64, 175–189.

Thomas, W. and Collier, V. (1995) *Language Minority Student Achievement and Program Effectiveness. Research Summary.* Fairfax, VA: George Mason University.

Thomas, W. and Collier, V. (1997) *School Effectiveness for Language Minority Students.* Washington, DC: National Clearinghouse for Bilingual Education.

Thomas, W. and Collier, V. (2000). Accelerated schooling for all students: Research findings on education in multilingual communities. In S. Shaw (ed.) *Intercultural Education in European Classrooms* (pp. 15–36). Stoke-on-Trent: Trentham Books.

Thomas, W. and Collier, V. (2002) *A National Study of School Effectiveness for Language Minority Students' Long-Term Academic Achievement.* Final Reports, Center for Research on Education, Diversity and Excellence, UC Berkeley. Online at: http://escholarship.org/uc/item/65j213pt.

Thomason, S.G. and Kaufman, T. (1988) *Language Contact, Creolization, and Genetic Linguistics.* Berkeley, CA: University of California Press.

Topix (2011) 'Why can't mexicans speak English ????????' April 8, accessed August 1, 2012. Online at: http://www.topix.com/forum/city/los-angeles-ca/TVGSAHLS6FU9D3PQT.

Toribio, A.J. (2003) The social significance of language loyalty among Black and White Dominicans in New York. *The Bilingual Review/La Revista Bilingüe* 27 (1), 3–11.

Toribio, A.J. (2004) Convergence as an optimization strategy in bilingual speech: Evidence from code-switching. *Bilingualism: Language and Cognition* 7, 165–173.

Toribio, A.J. (2006) Linguistic displays of identity among Dominicans in national and diasporic settlements. In C. Davies and J. Brutt-Griffler (eds) *English and Ethnicity* (pp. 131–157). New York: Palgrave.

Torres, L. (2010) Puerto Ricans in the United States and language shift to English. *English Today* 26, 49–54.

Tse, L. (1995) Language brokering among Latino adolescents: Prevalence, attitudes, and school performance. *Hispanic Journal of Behavioral Sciences* 17 (2), 180–193.

Two-Way Immersion (n.d.) Directory of two-way bilingual immersion programs in the US, accessed August 1, 2012. Online at: http://www.cal.org/jsp/TWI/SchoolListings.jsp.

United States Census Bureau (2012) State and county quickfacts: Chicago (city), Illinois, accessed August 1, 2012. Online at: http://quickfacts.census.gov/qfd/states/17/1714000.html.

Urban Dictionary (2012a) accessed August 1, 2012. Online at: http://www.urbandictionary.com/define.php?term=mexican&page=5.

Urban Dictionary (2012b) accessed August 1, 2012. Online at: http://www.urbandictionary.com/define.php?term=mexican&page=7

Urciuoli, B. (1996) *Exposing Prejudice: Puerto Rican Experiences of Language, Race and Class.* Boulder, CO: Westview Press.

Urciuoli, B. (2009) Talking/not talking about race: The enregisterments of culture in higher education discourses. *Journal of Linguistic Anthropology* 19 (1), 21–39.

US English (2012a) 'Legislation'. Online at: http://www.usenglish.org/view/27.

US English (2012b) 'Official English'. Online at: http://www.us-english.org/view/302.

Valdes, G. (1988) The language situation of Mexican Americans. In S. McKay and S.C. Wong (eds) *Language Diversity: Problem or Resource?* (pp. 11–39). Cambridge and New York: Newbury House.

Valdes, G. (2001) *Learning and Not Learning English: Latino Students in American Schools.* New York, NY: Teachers College Press.

Valdés, G. (2011) Ethnolinguistic identity: The challenge of maintaining Spanish-English bilingualism in American schools. In K. Potowski and J. Rothman (eds) *Bilingual Youth: Spanish in English-Speaking Societies* (pp. 113–148).

Valenzuela, A. (1999) *Subtractive Schooling: U.S.-Mexican Youth and the Politics of Caring.* SUNY Series, The Social Context of Education. Ithaca, NY: State University of New York Press.

Vann, R.J, Bruna, K.R. and Escudero, M.P. (2006) Negotiating identities in a multilingual science class. In T. Omoniyi and G. White (eds) *The Sociolinguistics of Identity* (pp. 201–216). New York: Continuum.

Velázquez, I. (2009) Intergenerational Spanish transmission in El Paso, Texas: Parental perception of cost//benefit. *Spanish in Context* 6 (1), 69–84.

Villa, D.J. and Rivera-Mills, S.V. (2009) An integrated multi-generational model for language maintenance and shift: The case of Spanish in the southwest. *Spanish in Context* 6 (1), 26–42.

Wade, P. (2008) Race in Latin America. In D. Poole (ed.) *A Companion to Latin American Anthropology* (pp. 177–192). Oxford: Blackwell Publishing Ltd.

Wald, B. (1987) Spanish-English grammatical contact in Los Angeles: The grammar of reported speech in the East Los Angeles English contact vernacular. *Linguistics* 25 (1), 53–80.

Waterston, A. (2006) Are Latinos becoming 'white' folk? And what that still says about race in America. *Transforming Anthropology* 14 (2), 133–150.

Weinreich, U. (1967) *Language in Contact*. The Hague: Mouton.

Weisman, E.M. (2001) Bicultural identity and language attitudes: Perspectives of four Latina teachers. *Urban Education* 36, 203–225.

Weisskirch, R.S. and Alva, S.A. (2002) Language brokering and the acculturation of Latino children. *Hispanic Journal of Behavioral Sciences* 24 (3), 369–378.

Weldon, T. (2004) African American English in the middle classes: Exploring the other end of the continuum. Paper presented at NWAV 33. Ann Arbor, MI: University of Michigan.

Wiklund, I. (2002) Social networks from a sociolinguistic perspective: The relationship of the characteristics of social networks of bilingual adolescents and their language proficiency. *International Journal of the Sociology of Language* 153, 53–92.

Wilkerson, M.E. and Salmons, J. (2008) 'Good old immigrants of yesteryear' who didn't learn English: Germans in Wisconsin. *American Speech* 8 (3), 259–283.

Willig, A.C. (1985) A meta-analysis of selected studies on the effectiveness of bilingual education. *Review of Educational Research* 55 (3), 269–317.

Winford, D. (2003) *An Introduction to Contact Linguistics*. Oxford: Blackwell Publishing.

Wolfram, W. (2007) Sociolinguistic folklore in the study of African American English. *Language and Linguistics Compass* 1, 1–22.

Wolfram, W. and Thomas. E. (2002) *The Development of African American English*. Oxford: Blackwell Publishers.

Woolard, K.A. (1998) Introduction: Language ideology as a field of inquiry. In B.B. Schieffelen, K.A. Woolard and P.V. Kroskrity (eds) *Language Ideologies: Practice and Theory* (pp. 3–47). Oxford: Oxford University Press.

World English Dictionary (2009), accessed August 1, 2012. Online at: http://dictionary.reference.com/browse/ethnic.

Wortham, S., Mortimer, K. and Allard, E. (2009) Mexicans as model minorities in the new Latino diaspora. *Anthropology & Education Quarterly* 40 (4), 388–404.

Worthy, J., Rodriguez-Galindo, A., Czop Asaf, L., Martinez, L. and Cuero, K. (2003) Fifth-grade bilingual students as precursors to 'subtractive schooling'. *Bilingual Research Journal* 27 (2), 275–294.

Yahoo (2009) 'Why do we say Immigrants don't want to learn English?', accessed August 1, 2012. Online at: http://answers.yahoo.com/question/index?qid=20100319102353AAlaZCQ.

Zapata, G.C., Sánchez, L. and Toribio, J. (2005) Contact and contracting Spanish. *International Journal of Bilingualism September* 9 (3–4), 377–395.

Zelinsky, W. (2001) *The Enigma of Ethnicity: Another American Dilemma.* Iowa City: University of Iowa Press.

Zentella, A.C. (1982) Spanish and English in contact in the United States: The Puerto Rican experience. *Word* 33 (1–2), 41–57.

Zentella, A.C. (1997) *Growing Up Bilingual.* Oxford: Blackwell Publishers.

Zentella, A.C. (2003) José can you see: Latin@ responses to racist discourse. In D. Sommer (ed.) *Bilingual Games* (pp. 51– 65). New York, NY: Palgrave Macmillan.

Glossary

1.5 generation immigrants: People who immigrate as small children, before the **critical age** for language learning; see also **first generation immigrants** and **second generation immigrants**.

/æ/ raising: Change in the pronunciation of the vowel in words like 'bad' to have an /ɛ/ vowel sound, that is, sound closer to 'bed'; part of the **Northern Cities Vowel Shift**.

AAVE: African American Vernacular English, sometimes popularly referred to as 'Ebonics,' is a way of speaking associated with African American speakers and considered to be non-Standard. Varies by age, class and location of speakers.

Acquisition planning: Efforts to have certain populations learn particular languages.

Additive bilingualism: Learning to speak a second language without losing one's first language; for example, learning English but also continuing to speak, read and write Spanish.

Anglophone: Someone who speaks English as their dominant, and usually only, language.

Appalachian English: A dialect of American English spoken in Appalachia, considered non-standard.

Aspirated: Aspiration refers to the puff of air that is produced with certain consonants. Hold your hand in front of your mouth when you say the word 'cat'; most speakers of English will feel a puff of air with the production of the /k/ sound. In English, medial /k/ sounds as in 'taco' are aspirated; in Spanish, they are not.

Asymmetrical codeswitching: The use of two languages in a conversation when each person uses a different language; often found between members of different generations, e.g. the parents and/or grandparents speak Spanish, and the younger generation answers in English.

Authenticity: A 'real' or 'authentic' identity, which can be demonstrated through behaviors like language use. For some, speaking Spanish is seen as part of an authentic Latin@ identity.

Balanced bilingual: Someone who has equal proficiency in both languages they speak; an ideal that is rarely found in reality.

Bilingual discourse: The use of two languages in one conversation; can be within a word, phrase or sentence or across the turns of different speakers.

Binary race system: An ideological system under which there are only two 'racial' categories, Black and White; everyone must fit into one category or the other.

Borrowing: A word taken from one language and used in another, also called a **loanword**. The word 'patio' in English is a borrowing from Spanish.

Calque: Literal translations, often idiomatic phrases or metaphors, also known as a 'loan translation'. The English word 'skyscraper' has been calqued into many languages (e.g. Spanish 'rascacielo').

Chican@ English: A **variety** of English spoken by Mexican Americans; NOT learner English, but a native variety.

Codeswitching: Switching languages, codes, speech styles or registers in a single conversation.

Cognates: Words in one language that sound like words in another, with the same/similar meanings and a common origin. For example, English 'receive' and Spanish 'recibir'.

Colloquial: A way of speaking which is considered to be casual, not formal; the way most people speak in their interactions with friends.

Conditional: A verb form which indicates a hypothetical or possible action. In English, this is expressed with modals such as 'would'; in Spanish, there is conditional verbal morphology (e.g. *serIA* 'would be').

Conquest/colonization: The domination of a population by an outside group which comes into their territory.

Consonant cluster reduction: Dropping one or more consonants from a series of consonants in a word. For example, the pronunciation of 'post' in rapid speech without the final 't' ([pos]) involves consonant cluster reduction.

Constituted (identity): The creation of an **identity** through social practices, such as **linguistic behavior**; this means identities are never fixed, as the practices that constitute them change.

Corpus planning: The development of a **variety** of a language, usually in terms of standardization.

Covert prestige: The less-visible or hidden value of a language, such that speakers will continue to speak it because it plays a crucial role in constructing their in-group identities; contrast with **overt prestige**.

Craniofacial traits: The shape and size of cranial, facial or mandibular (i.e. jaw) features, which can be used by forensic anthropologists to provide information on the racial categorizations of human remains.

Creole origin: The theory that a language, such as **AAVE**, developed in a situation where there were many languages in contact and thus contains lexical and grammatical features of more than one language.

Critical age: In child language acquisition, the hypothesis is that language can be more easily acquired before puberty; at puberty, the brain becomes specialized in its functions, and it can no longer adapt as easily to take on new functions; this is believed to negatively influence language acquisition.

Crossing: Using a language that is usually considered to 'belong' to members of an ethnic or national group the speaker is not a part of.

Demographic factors/information: Information about people's age, racial or ethnic group categorization, and socio-economic class (along with other factors) is often collected in surveys such as the US census; these factors, along with factors such as the numbers and distribution of the members of a social group, play a role in **ethnolinguistic vitality**.

Density (of social networks): When all the people in a social network have ties to each other.

Diglossia: Use of two languages in strictly compartmentalized ways, where there is no overlap between the functions of the two languages.

Diversity: The idea that people differ in many different ways and that this should be positively valued.

Domains: Spheres of language use, i.e. school, work, church.

Donor language: The language from which an element is taken – donated – into another language.

Dual identity: The construction of two potentially conflicting identities at the same time, especially two national identities (e.g. Mexican and US American).

Dual immersion: see **Two-Way Immersion**.

Elite bilingualism: The idea that bilingualism is a social advantage; usually the attitude about learning prestigious languages by members of middle or higher socio-economic classes. Compare with **immigrant bilingualism**.

Endogamy: Marriage within the social group; contrast with **exogamy**.

English Only: A movement proposing the declaration of English as the official language of the United States, in contrast to the **English Plus movement**.

English Plus: Policy based on the belief that Americans should be able to learn both English and other languages.

Erasure: The phenomenon of ignoring or rendering invisible any practices which would contradict the **hegemonic** ideology.

Essentialism/essentialist: The view that a single identity category, e.g. 'Mexican' or 'woman', takes the same form as a pre-existing category, regardless of context.

Ethnic, Ethnic group, Ethnicity: A group that is based on descent and cultural practices; in the US, 'ethnic' is often used to refer to people or things perceived as outside of the mainstream, and 'ethnicity' is used only to refer to 'Hispanics' in the US census.

Ethnic dialect: A way of speaking which is associated with a particular **ethnic group**. **AAVE** is an ethnic dialect, as is **Chican@ English**.

Ethnifying: The creation of ethnic identity through cultural practices associated with the ethnic group.

Ethnolinguistic vitality: The degree of language maintenance, shift or revitalization a group experiences, based on **demographic factors**, **status factors** and **institutional support**.

Ethnonational ideology: An ideology that all citizens of a particular nation share the same **ethnicity**; members of other ethnic groups are not seen as **authentic** citizens of that nation.

Exogamy: Marrying outside the social group; contrast with **endogamy**.

Exoticizing: Treating members of a particular social group as if they are exotic and different simply because they are members of that group; see also **otherizing**.

First generation immigrants: The generation of a group or family that settles in a new area; i.e. the people who themselves leave their home country. Compare with **1.5 generation** and **second generation**. Also note that while this definition is the most common in the US context, this expression is sometimes used to refer to the offspring of those who immigrate (what is called here the second generation).

Grammatical gender: Marking classes of nouns as male, female and sometimes neuter. English marks gender on pronouns (e.g. 'he' and 'she') and some nouns referring to people (e.g 'hostess'); Spanish marks grammatical gender on all nouns (e.g. *la muchcha* ['the/F girl'], *la mesa* ['the/F table']).

Habitual *be:* The use of 'be' to denote a habitually recurring action found in **AAVE**.

Hegemony (Hegemonic): The dominance of one entity (especially a social group) over another. Dominance is achieved not through force but by consensus that the dominant entity is deserving of that status.

Hegemonic discourse: Socially dominant ways of thinking or talking about something or someone.

Heritage language: A term used to refer to a language that is historically associated with an **ethnic group**, regardless of whether all of the members of that group are currently fluent speakers of the language.

Heritage speakers: Used to refer to people who associate a particular language with an **ethnic group** they identify with. It does not imply that the speakers necessarily have this language as their dominant language, but does imply that older generations spoke or speak the language as their dominant code.

Heteroglossia, Heteroglossic: The notion that all ways of speaking include multiple styles, registers, dialects and languages, and that these things are not strictly bounded entities.

Hispanicization: Although this term can be used more broadly, in this volume it is used only to talk about the influence of the Spanish language – or rather, a stereotype of the Spanish language – on the English language. This is often found in **Mock Spanish**.

Human variation: The span of physical characteristics people can have. These can vary along a continuum, or progression, such as from light eye colors to darker ones.

Hybrid loanwords: Compound words which are half in the **donor language** and half in the **recipient language**.

Hybridity: The view that multiple identities can be merged into a new, single one, as in the combining of a Mexican identity and American one into a new one: Mexican American.

Iconicity (Iconic): The idea that a language comes to be not only an index of a certain group, but an icon for the group; that is, it does not merely 'point to' the social group, but is assumed to be a representation of that group, sharing characteristics with it.

Identity (Identities): In this volume and in contemporary social sciences, used to refer to a way of being which is **socially constructed**; identity is not something you 'have' but something you 'do'.

Immigration: Movement from one area to settle in another; focus on the entry into a new region.

Immigrant bilingualism: Bilingualism which results because of immigration by both the **first generation immigrants** and the subsequent generations; generally associated with poorer and less educated speakers of two languages. Compare with **elite bilingualism**.

Imperfect: A verb form which has to do with the internal time structure of an action. There is no imperfect verb marking in English; in Spanish, forms such as *vivíamos*, which can be loosely translated as 'we were living', are in the imperfect form.

Index: Pointing to something through speech, as when language choice points to social roles and the relationships between speakers; when used as a noun, a behavior which points to a particular social category.

Indian Schools: 'Mission schools' where Native American schoolchildren were educated in English and for which funds were allocated by the federal Civilization Act of 1819; the mission of these schools was primarily to assimilate Native American children into monolingual English society.

Input: The words or speech sounds we hear; input we can understand, or comprehensible input, is necessary for language learning.

Institutional support: Within the framework of **ethnolinguistic vitality**, this refers to the existence of support for a minority language within various social institutions such as schools, churches, media and government offices and services. It is believed that such support contributes to **language maintenance**.

Interdental position: The placement of the tongue between the upper and lower teeth during speech, as during the 'th' sound.

Interlocutors: A fancy, impressive-sounding word for the people you talk to; conversation partners.

Intonation: The rise and fall of pitch during speech.

Intrasentential codeswitching: Switching between languages within a single sentence.

Language as a resource: The view that languages are tools for financial, social or other success.

Language attrition: The loss of a language over the lifetime of an individual speaker.

Language choice: The use of particular languages or varieties of languages; for example, the choice to speak English or Spanish at any given time.

Language contact phenomena: All of the linguistic outcomes of two (or more) languages in contact; refers to **codeswitching** and **borrowing** as well as changes or developments in language structure.

Language ideologies: Ideas and beliefs about language form and use.

Language maintenance: The continued use of a language. This term is usually used when we discuss minority languages, such as Spanish in the US.

Language planning: Specific attempts to shape language practices, types include **acquisition planning, corpus planning, prestige planning** and **status planning**.

Language policy (Language policies): A general term used to refer to the linguistic, political and social goals which underlie **language planning**.

Language shift: The process of learning a new language and losing the first language; usually it is the minority language that is lost and the majority language which is learned.

Languaging: A term used to focus on language as a verb; the use of whatever linguistic resources the speaker possesses in social interactions. Related to **translanguaging** and **heteroglossia**.

Lingua franca: Any language that is used when a speaker does not share a native language with his/her **interlocutor**. English is a lingua franca for many immigrants to the United States who do not speak each other's languages.

Linguistic behavior: A broad term to refer to everything about how a person uses language. This includes **language choice** and other aspects of the **variety** such as pronunciation and **intonation**, but also aspects of language such as interrupting, joking, giving compliments, speaking rapidly, and so forth. Linguistic behavior is generally seen as part of the **social construction** of **identity**.

Linguistic diversity: The presence of many different ways of speaking, especially what are considered distinct languages, within a political region.

Linguistic endogamy: Marrying within one's linguistic group (i.e. someone who speaks the same language(s) as you); see **endogamy**.

Loan translation: see **calque**.

Loanshifts: Words from the recipient language which take on a different meaning because of their phonological similarity to words from the donor language; also called **semantic loans.**

Loanword: A word taken from one language and used in another, also called a **borrowing**.

Macro-level demographic categories: Categories such as 'race', social class or sex which make reference to named, pre-existent categories within a society.

Maintenance: see **language maintenance.**

Matched guise research: Research designed to get at the language attitudes of the participants, who are asked to make judgments about voices in two different languages – they are unaware that it is the same person speaking the different codes. The differences in assessment of the different 'guises' are then thought to reflect their different attitudes about the languages.

Mestiz@: A term used in Latin America to refer to people of Native American and European ancestry.

Metrolingual, metrolingualism: the use of languages which challenges their status as indices of particular ethnic, national, or other social groups, but as a fluid process. Drawing on the parallel to 'metrosexual', which denotes gender identity construction which challenges hegemonic norms for men, metrolinguals challenge the hegemonic understandings of connections between language and particular identity categories.

Minority language: All languages which are not the language spoken by the dominant majority; in the US, this means all languages other than English.

Mock Spanish: The treatment of Spanish as linguistically inferior to English and 'easy' through construction of Spanish-sounding words, as by adding an –o to words, or by using token Spanish lexical items. It is an attempt to sound like one is speaking Spanish, without having to put forth the effort to learn Spanish. It can carry an ideology that Spanish speakers are lazy or uneducated. A common example is the use of 'no problemo'.

Monoglossic language ideology: A way of thinking that values only the dominant language and ignores the presence and value of multilingualism in a society.

Monolithic: Formed out of a uniform group; in this context, used to mean that members of a social group are perceived as being all the same.

Monophthongization: The pronunciation of a vowel without the following glide, as when the vowel in 'pie' is pronounced as an 'ah' sound ([a]) without a following glide; the diphthong in this word in standard American English would be [ai].

Morphology: The study of the meaning-producing units of a language, such as morphemes or words.

Multiple negation: The use of multiple negative forms in an utterance; also called negative concord. 'I ain't got no money' includes multiple negation; **standard** English typically does not have multiple negation (*cf.* 'I don't have any money').

Multiplexity/multiplex networks: When each tie in a social network represents several different types of relationship, for example, your sister-in-law is also your neighbor and colleague.

'Native' speaker: A person who speaks a language as their dominant language, in a way that is considered to reflect acquisition of that language in natural surroundings in early childhood. It is used here in quotation marks to reflect that this is a subjective and relative category, not an absolute.

Naturalized: The assumption that a phenomenon, like gender differences, are based on fact or truth, rather than cultural constructions, and that these differences or categories have unavoidable social characteristics that can be taken for granted as 'common sense'. The belief that women (and not men) have instincts for parenting is an example of a naturalized assumption.

New World: An expression used to refer to the Americas; reveals a very Euro-centric perspective, as this area was only 'new' to the Europeans; people lived in these regions before European explorers arrived.

Non-essentialist: See essentialist.

Non-'native' speaker: Someone who is not considered to speak a language as a 'native', usually implying that they have an accent or make errors in that language. The quotation marks are used to indicate that this is a subjective and relative category, not an absolute.

Non-standard: Varieties of a language that are not the **standard** (e.g. Chican@ English or African American Vernacular English); while linguistically just as valid as any **standard language**, these varieties are often socially stigmatized.

Normalizing: Treatment of a person, thing or idea as if she/he/it is unexceptional.

Normative: An attitude that a certain way of being or acting is the default or **unmarked** way of being or acting, and that everything else is exceptional.

Normative monolingualism: An ideology in which (1) monolingualism is presented as the ideal state for social and political entities, such as nation states, and (2) multiple languages spoken by an individual must be kept strictly separate.

Northern Cities Vowel Shift: A phenomenon discussed by linguists who argue that the **vowel systems** in certain northern US cities are changing.

Otherizing: To treat someone in such a way as to emphasize their difference from you and, usually, the mainstream. This is often based on their membership in a particular social category. See **exoticizing**, contrast with **normalizing**.

Overt prestige: The value of a language, such that it may get institutional support or more ready acceptance by the mainstream population; contrast with **covert prestige**.

Phenotypes (Phenotypic): Visible physical characteristics, such as eye, hair or skin color. These traits can be used in the social construction of 'race' or other categorizations of people.

Phonological integration: The adaption of a loanword to fit into the sound system of the borrowing language.

Phrasal future tense marking: The use of a phrase, instead of verbal **morphology**, to indicate the future. English has only phrasal future tense marking, e.g. 'I WILL eat' or 'I AM GOING TO eat.' Spanish, in contrast, has future tense morphology, e.g. 'comeré' as well as phrasal future constructions (e.g. 'voy a comer').

Pluralism: A belief or attitude that there are multiple ways of doing and being, and that there is value in the differences.

Pragmatic: Aspects of language use that have to do with meaning in context.

Prestige planning: Efforts to create a higher social standing for a particular linguistic variety.

Preterit: The simple past tense; a verb form that indicates completed action. In Spanish, this is in contrast with the **imperfect**.

Pro-drop: A feature of a language which renders it unnecessary to use pronouns, because the verb carries information about the person and number of the subject. Spanish is a pro-drop language; English is not.

Production and reproduction of social inequality: The creation and perpetuation of social norms resulting in inequalities though linguistic and social practices.

Quantitative: Used to describe an analysis or research methodology which uses mathematical or statistical documentation of how often certain phenomena, like grammatical features, occur.

Quotative: A word or words indicating that what follows is quoted speech. The classic quotative in English is 'said'; in colloquial English, 'to be like' is often used as a quotative, as in 'He's like, "no way, dude".'

'Race': A socially constructed category which makes reference to **phenotypical features** to put people in groups and create generalizations about members of the group.

Recipient language: The language which incorporates – receives – an element from another language.

Recursiveness: The repetition of a certain type of relationship (between social groups or languages) repeating on different levels in society.

Regularization: The changing of an irregular form to a regular one, as when an irregular past tense verb is regularized (i.e. *struck* becomes *striked*).

Resumptive pronouns: A pronoun that refers back to a noun or pronoun in the main clause of the sentence. This is common in colloquial speech, e.g. 'My sister, SHE is the best.'

Second generation immigrants: The children of **first generation immigrants**; not the people who actually immigrated, but their offspring.

Semantic loans: Words from the recipient language which take on a different meaning because of their phonological similarity to words from the donor language; also called **loanshifts**.

Social construct: Something which is created within human culture. It is argued that 'race' is a social construct because although physical differences between groups of people exist, **human variation** does not neatly fit into biologically determined categories.

Social Network Theory: a sociological theory which, when applied to language, focuses on the social contacts of speakers as the main influence in how they speak.

Socially constructed: The attribution of meanings and values to particular physical, cultural, linguistic, ethnic or other traits based on social and cultural relationships; these are not inherent meanings and values, and are not necessarily based on fact, though they may be **naturalized** understandings of those traits.

Socio-pragmatic meaning: The social meaning of a word or way of speaking which **index**es membership in a particular social group. For instance, the socio-pragmatic meaning of speaking **Chican@ English** may be that the speaker is Mexican American.

Sound changes: Changes in vowel or consonant usage over time.

Spanglish: A term used to refer to the mixture of Spanish and English spoken by some Latin@s in the US.

Standard: A **variety** that has **overt prestige** in a given region; generally this is the variety which is taught in school, used for national broadcasts and literature, and associated with the middle and upper classes of society.

Status factors: Within the framework of **ethnolinguistic vitality**, these factors have to do with how the minority group and its language is valued by outsiders and within its own ranks. High status contributes to **language maintenance**.

Status planning: Efforts to change the functions a language fulfills in a particular society, and the rights of those who use it.

Subjunctive: Verb forms which mark tentativeness, vagueness and uncertainty. In English, the only vestige of a subjunctive is found in constructions such as 'If she WERE going. . .' **Standard** Spanish has subjunctive forms for all verbs, e.g. 'Si vaya. . .'.

Subtractive acculturation: Learning a new culture, including new ways of speaking, and giving up, or being forced to give up, old ways of being and acting. See **subtractive bilingualism** and **additive bilingualism**.

Subtractive bilingualism: Learning a new language and giving up, or being forced to give up, one's first language.

Syntax: The grammatical patterns of a language (e.g. word order). The syntax of English puts adjectives before nouns; the syntax of Spanish puts adjectives after nouns (in most cases, anyway).

Translanguaging: The use of multiple languages, dialects, registers and styles in speech.

Two-way immersion programs: Programs which offer bilingual education for both minority language and majority language students; together they learn both languages.

Unaspirated: See **aspirated**.

Unmarked: Expected or default case; in this volume, it is used to refer to **language choice** as well as the usual form of a particular grammatical construction.

Variation: Changes in an individual's speech across utterances, or across speakers.

Variety, varieties: The form of a particular language a speaker uses, such as American English or AAVE.

Vowel reduction: A decrease in number, distinctiveness or length of vowels.

Vowel systems: How the vowels in a language pattern together; this includes what sounds exist in a particular language and which distinctions are meaningful in a particular language. For example, in English there are different vowels in 'beat' and 'bit', but in Spanish the latter is not in the vowel system.

Xenophobia: Literally, fear of foreigners; usually used to refer to fear or hatred of people who are different from whatever culture the phobic person is accustomed to. Usually we think of members of the majority culture in a country as having xenophobia of members of minority groups or from different nations.

Zero copula: Deletion of conjugations of 'to be', as by speakers of **AAVE** or **Chican@ English**.

Index